Dora Renna

Language Variation and Multimodality in Audiovisual Translation
A New Framework of Analysis

Dora Renna

LANGUAGE VARIATION AND MULTIMODALITY IN AUDIOVISUAL TRANSLATION

A New Framework of Analysis

Bibliografische Information der Deutschen Nationalbibliothek
Die Deutsche Nationalbibliothek verzeichnet diese Publikation in der Deutschen Nationalbibliografie; detaillierte bibliografische Daten sind im Internet über http://dnb.d-nb.de abrufbar.

Bibliographic information published by the Deutsche Nationalbibliothek
Die Deutsche Nationalbibliothek lists this publication in the Deutsche Nationalbibliografie; detailed bibliographic data are available in the Internet at http://dnb.d-nb.de.

Cover graphic: © Walter Brattelli

ISBN-13: 978-3-8382-1594-5
© *ibidem*-Verlag, Stuttgart 2021
Alle Rechte vorbehalten

Das Werk einschließlich aller seiner Teile ist urheberrechtlich geschützt. Jede Verwertung außerhalb der engen Grenzen des Urheberrechtsgesetzes ist ohne Zustimmung des Verlages unzulässig und strafbar. Dies gilt insbesondere für Vervielfältigungen, Übersetzungen, Mikroverfilmungen und elektronische Speicherformen sowie die Einspeicherung und Verarbeitung in elektronischen Systemen.

All rights reserved. No part of this publication may be reproduced, stored in or introduced into a retrieval system, or transmitted, in any form, or by any means (electronic, mechanical, photocopying, recording or otherwise) without the prior written permission of the publisher. Any person who does any unauthorized act in relation to this publication may be liable to criminal prosecution and civil claims for damages.

Printed in the EU

LANGUAGE VARIATION AND MULTIMODALITY IN AUDIOVISUAL TRANSLATION
A NEW FRAMEWORK OF ANALYSIS

Dora Renna

List of Tables and Figures 7
Introduction 11
Chapter 1 — Accepting challenges in audiovisual translation 19
   1.1 Overcoming prescriptive approaches in AVT 19
   1.2 Expanding the scope with corpora 27
   1.3 Recognising language variation and its role in AVT 35
   1.4 Incorporating multimodality in AVT studies 44

Chapter 2 — A framework for corpus-based, multimodal analysis of language variation in source and target films 55
   2.1 Inside the source text I: language, power and variation. 55
   2.2 Inside the source text II: defining Chicano English 66
   2.3 Defining the corpus: time frame, data availability, relevance and coherence 83
   2.4 The framework and its application 95

Chapter 3 — Broadened horizons: framework application and results 121
   3.1 Language variation in source and target films: the textual dimension 122
   3.2 Language and multimodality: the diegetic dimension. 170
   3.3 An invitation to contextualization: the sociocultural dimension and some considerations on the overall results 186

Conclusion 201
References 207

List of Figures and Tables

Figures

Figure 1 Classification of the linguistic varieties............................. 98
Figure 2 Scheme as arranged in the tables of analysis for source and target text respectively. 103
Figure 3 Example of tagged line... 103
Figure 4 The same line (Gato from *Colors*) in the dubbed version.. 104
Figure 5 Model of intermodal relations, drawn from Ramos Pinto and Mubaraki (2020). 117
Figure 6 Intermodal relations in the scheme............................... 117
Figure 7 Tagged line uttered by Gato (*Colors*) with the intermodal relations in the scheme. 118
Figure 8 Gato's tagged line with intermodal relations in the target version.. 119
Figure 9 Angel's textual scatter plot. 128
Figure 10 Chuco's textual scatter plot... 131
Figure 11 Frog's textual scatter plot.. 136
Figure 12 Gato's textual scatter plot... 137
Figure 13 Santana's textual scatter plot. 146
Figure 14 JD's textual scatter plot... 148
Figure 15 Mundo's textual scatter plot. 150
Figure 16 Puppet's textual scatter plot. 152
Figure 17 Lil' Puppet's textual scatter plot. 153
Figure 18 Miklo's textual scatter plot... 163
Figure 19 Paco's textual scatter plot... 165
Figure 20 Cruz's textual scatter plot. 166
Figure 21 Montana's textual scatter plot. 168
Figure 22 Popeye's textual scatter plot. 169
Figure 23 Intermodal relations ST Angel. 171
Figure 24 Intermodal relations TT Angel. 171
Figure 25 Intermodal relations ST Chuco................................... 171
Figure 26 Intermodal relations TT Chuco. 171
Figure 27 Angel's ST and TT alternation of intermodal confirmation and contradiction in the film. 172
Figure 28 Chuco's ST and TT alternation of intermodal confirmation and contradiction in the film. 173
Figure 29 Intermodal relations ST Frog. 174

Figure 30 Intermodal relations TT Frog.. 174
Figure 31 Intermodal relations ST Gato... 174
Figure 32 Intermodal relations TT Gato. 174
Figure 33 Frog's ST and TT alternation of intermodal
   confirmation and contradiction in the film. 175
Figure 34 Gato's ST and TT alternation of intermodal
   confirmation and contradiction in the film. 175
Figure 35 Intermodal relations ST Santana. 176
Figure 36 Intermodal relations TT Santana... 176
Figure 37 Intermodal relations ST JD... 176
Figure 38 Intermodal relations TT JD 176
Figure 39 Intermodal relations ST Mundo. 177
Figure 40 Intermodal relations TT Mundo... 177
Figure 41 Intermodal relations ST Puppet. 177
Figure 42 Intermodal relations TT Puppet... 177
Figure 43 Intermodal relations ST Lil' Puppet...................................... 178
Figure 44 Intermodal relations TT Lil' Puppet. 178
Figure 45 Santana's ST and TT alternation of intermodal
   confirmation and contradiction in the film. 178
Figure 46 JD's ST and TT alternation of intermodal
   confirmation and contradiction in the film. 179
Figure 47 Mundo's ST and TT alternation of intermodal
   confirmation and contradiction in the film. 180
Figure 48 Puppet's ST and TT alternation of intermodal
   confirmation and contradiction in the film. 180
Figure 49 Lil' Puppet's ST and TT alternation of intermodal
   confirmation and contradiction in the film. 180
Figure 50 Intermodal relations ST Miklo... 181
Figure 51 Intermodal relations TT Miklo. 181
Figure 52 Miklo's ST and TT alternation of intermodal
   confirmation and contradiction in the film. 181
Figure 53 Intermodal relations ST Cruz. 182
Figure 54 Intermodal relations TT Cruz... 182
Figure 55 Cruz's ST and TT alternation of intermodal
   confirmation and contradiction in the film. 182
Figure 56 Intermodal relations ST Paco... 183
Figure 57 Intermodal relations TT Paco. 183
Figure 58 Paco's ST and TT alternation of intermodal
   confirmation and contradiction in the film. 184
Figure 59 Intermodal relations ST Popeye. 184

Figure 60 Intermodal relations TT Popeye. 184
Figure 61 Popeye's ST and TT alternation of intermodal
 confirmation and contradiction in the film. 184
Figure 62 Intermodal relations ST Montana. 186
Figure 63 Intermodal relations TT Montana. 186
Figure 64 Montana's ST and TT alternation of intermodal
 confirmation and contradiction in the film. 186

Tables

Table 1 Angel's ST and TT distribution in *Stand and Deliver*
 (1988) 123
Table 2 Chuco's ST and TT distribution in *Stand and Deliver*
 (1988) 124
Table 3 Angel's ST and TT realization in *Stand and Deliver*
 (1988) 125
Table 4 Chuco's ST and TT realization in *Stand and Deliver*
 (1988) 126
Table 5 Frog's ST and TT distribution in *Colors* (1988) 133
Table 6 Gato's ST and TT distribution in *Colors* (1988) 133
Table 7 Frog's ST and TT realization in *Colors* (1988) 134
Table 8 Gato's ST and TT realization in *Colors* (1988) 134
Table 9 Santana's ST and TT distribution in *American Me*
 (1992) 139
Table 10 JD's ST and TT distribution in *American Me* (1992) 140
Table 11 Mundo's ST and TT distribution in *American Me*
 (1992) 140
Table 12 Puppet's ST and TT distribution in *American Me*
 (1992) 141
Table 13 Lil' Puppet's ST and TT distribution in *American Me*
 (1992) 141
Table 14 Santana's ST and TT realization in *American Me*
 (1992) 142
Table 15 JD's ST and TT realization in *American Me* (1992) 143
Table 16 Mundo's ST and TT realization in *American Me* (1992). 143
Table 17 Lil' Puppet's ST and TT realization in *American Me*
 (1992) 144
Table 18 Puppet's ST and TT realization in *American Me* (1992). 145
Table 19 Miklo's ST and TT distribution in *Blood In Blood Out*
 (1993) 155
Table 20 Paco's ST and TT distribution in *Blood In Blood Out*
 (1993) 156

Table 21 Cruz's ST and TT distribution in *Blood In Blood Out* (1993) 157
Table 22 Montana's ST and TT distribution in *Blood In Blood Out* (1993) 158
Table 23 Popeye's ST and TT distribution in *Blood In Blood Out* (1993) 158
Table 24 Miklo's ST and TT realization in *Blood In Blood Out* (1993) 160
Table 25 Paco's ST and TT realization in *Blood In Blood Out* (1993) 160
Table 26 Cruz's ST and TT realization in *Blood In Blood Out* (1993) 161
Table 27 Montana's ST and TT realization in *Blood In Blood Out* (1993) 161
Table 28 Popeye's ST and TT realization in *Blood In Blood Out* (1993) 162

Introduction

This book embraces the interdisciplinary nature of translation studies (Munday 2008, 1), as it originates from the intersections of different branches of this discipline with other issues coming from various fields of investigation, to offer an innovative contribution to an urgent debate in audiovisual translation (AVT). Research in this field has long struggled to find an effective approach to deal with the complexity of the audiovisual products, whose presence is growing at an impressive rate, in a constant flow of intertwined texts and images eagerly consumed by the audience. These products, translated globally, represent the increasing interconnection of small social and linguistic realities across the planet.

During my BA and MA in Media Studies and my postgraduate degree in Linguistic and Cultural Mediation, I have always been interested in the way linguistic variation contributes to the construction of fictional "rationalizations of cultural difference," or *ethnotypes* (van Doorslaer *et al.* 2016, 3), which become a strong political tool for both oppression and resistance. Indeed, when I started dealing with AVT, I immediately turned to linguistic variation, a long-standing challenge for all translators, but with its specificities in the field of multimodal products. In particular, since I grew up in Italy in the 1990s, my attention was drawn to dubbing, which replaces the speech of the characters while leaving images and music as they are in the source version. I wanted to discover how dubbing tackles the aporia of translating linguistic variation. As a novice, at the beginning of my PhD, I tried to follow the methodology I had often seen in other books, papers and conferences. It consisted of a textual analysis of the two versions, with a thorough explanation of how certain words and sentences were translated, of the missing, replaced or kept cultural references, and at times a final judgement on whether the translation could be considered accurate or acceptable (Toury 1995), sometimes on whether it was a good or bad translation. My very first attempt at AVT studies closely resembled this structure, but my background in media studies and linguistic and cultural mediation suggested to me something was lacking—I could not figure out what. That was when my application for the CETRA Summer School at KU Leuven was accepted, and the days spent at CETRA with brilliant colleagues and amazing professors completely changed my perspective. In particular, three facts I was presented with redirected (and significantly improved) my studies on linguistic variation in AVT: 1) freeing my work from the need to establish whether the translation was good would have helped me understand it without judgement; 2) one film was not enough to understand a phenomenon; and 3) understanding AVT means to see its polysemiotic nature (Chiaro 2008). These realizations meant three more challenges to accept to achieve my aims. Indeed, AVT is often caught between extensive quantitative but only textual corpus analyses and qualitative analyses of the film as a whole, but on rather small case studies (Gambier 2006; Ramos Pinto & Mubaraki 2020). More specifically, the approach of this study is informed by other work in linguistic variation, translation studies and AVT (Assis Rosa 2011; van Doorslaer *et al.* 2016; Fought 2003; Laviosa 2002; Lippi-Green 1998; Macedo *et al.* 2003), but also other fields, such as film studies and multimodality, for example, Pastra (2008) and Ramírez Berg (2002), and especially inspired by studies that have already pioneered the methodology here implemented (Ramos Pinto & Mubaraki 2020; Ramos Pinto 2009, 2017).

To sum up, the approach adopted in this book might be worth starting from its cover, which was specifically designed to represent it. Four elements emerge from the white background. Three arches, similar in shape but different in texture and shade, intersect and partly overlap, creating colour and texture alterations. These arches are partly framed within an opaque rectangle with a blurring effect. Inside the frame, the arches are still visible, but less clearly separated. The way an audiovisual product (be it the source or the target version) is conceived here perfectly resonates with the image. The blurring rectangle is the screen, which symbolizes the act of reproducing characters and their stories. The arches are fragments that are partly within the screen, but also outside of it: they represent the three levels of analysis identified in this study, the three dimensions that compose the audiovisual product: textual, diegetic and sociocultural (Ramos Pinto & Mubaraki 2020). The extension of the dimensions outside the screen has multiple meanings: on the one hand, it represents their existence outside the screen, as parts of the reality that is reproduced through the screen, albeit in a less clear-cut way. On the other hand, their presence outside the screen also symbolizes my attempt to stretch the three of them back into reality — not just the textual one.

The textual dimension is the analysis of the linguistic element of the film, the one that is subject to the translators' and adapters' intervention. It is not just the language in itself that undergoes analysis, as the focus is understanding "the extralinguistic meanings conventionally associated with those same varieties, meanings which are then imported to the film's fictional world" (Ramos Pinto & Mubaraki 2020, 10). The research aims not to say whether the variety analysed is accurate compared to its real-world counterpart, but rather to see how its fictional transposition contributes to the construction of the ethnotypes, intended as fictional "rationalizations of cultural difference" (van Doorslaer *et al.* 2011, 3). The keyword is *prestige*, that is to say, "the character's sociocultural outline in addition to his/her position within the sociocultural fictional context" (Ramos Pinto 2017: n.p.).

The diegetic dimension has proved to be the most difficult to tackle in a research context, given the focus of corpus-based translation studies on textual aspects (Díaz-Cintas 2008; Gambier 2006). Pioneers in this dimension (Ramos Pinto 2017; Ramos Pinto & Mubaraki 2020) have turned to multimodality to seek an answer, successfully drawing from it (Iedema 2003; Pastra 2008) to replace non-quantifiable image description with the establishment of multimodal relationships that, through accurate analysis, could better fit in a corpus. While multimodality acknowledges and embraces the complexity and the unity in the perception of an audiovisual product as a whole (Bateman *et al.* 2017, 33), the quandary lies in the very concept of analysis — by its nature, to analyse means to set apart. Here cinema studies on ethnotypes provide a set of references in the selection of the modes to be isolated and analysed (Ramírez Berg 2002) to make sure no crucial element is left out.

The sociocultural dimension is only sketched in this product-based, quantitative study, more in the form of an invitation to expand the debate to more fields (e.g. psychology and economics), as it consists of the effort to contextualize a product and to understand the observed translational choices in terms of ideology, the status of translator and translation in the target context, legibility and intelligibility for the target audience, differences between source and target cultures, audience profiling and expected product function (Antonini 2008; Calvanese 2011; Pavesi & Perego 2006; Ramos Pinto 2017).

This threefold framework has the aim to analyse the character design and redesign in source and target text in a corpus of films, considering both textual and non-textual aspects at the same time. Through this framework, it will be possible to answer several questions that constitute the smaller objectives of the research:

- Which language variety was used for each character in the source and the target text (ST and TT)?
- Which strategies might have been behind the change?
- What were the most common features for conveying a certain type of language? Did they change from ST to TT?
- How did these varieties build intermodal relationships with the non-textual elements of the film?
- Did the relationships change from ST to TT, and to what extent?

Since a corpus fitting the needs of this research did not exist, I had to build my own corpus, selecting and transcribing films featuring the Chicano gangster stereotype in American film.

Another point that may be useful to introduce is the choice of the selected case study. As a teenager, I was a passionate fan of action movies and dramas, especially those relating to gangsters and thug life. However, I did not realize the stereotyping potential of these audiovisual products, which are not supposed to be cultural, until later, thanks to media studies, translation studies and critical linguistics. Going back to those movies with a different knowledge made me aware of how deeply they had affected my imagery. Indeed, movies made to entertain the audience might let a cultural message trespass conscious defences and sink deeply into their mind. It must not be forgotten that the power of media in forging human perception of reality goes beyond our consciousness. Cinema is a powerful means to shape and reinforce collective memory (Fluck 2003, 224) that transcends experience, as proved by the tendency to feel more afraid of crime when exposed to great amounts of crime-related audiovisual products than when experiencing actual crime in everyday life (Van den Bulck 2004, 247). While several minorities are featured in gangster movies, the choice of Chicanos for this work depends on the following reasons. First, my Spanish competence allows me to understand code switches and recognise phonetic and suprasegmental similarities. I was also familiar with Chicano literature and visual arts through my studies, which allowed me to better understand historical and cultural references in the films. Another factor, external to my personal background, is the growing Mexican-American community. Moreover, while it is very unlikely to imagine that there would be Anglo Americans who have never met a Mexican American in their whole life, Italy does not really have a developed community of Mexican origin. In fact, Italy has a far more recent history of multicultural contact and immigration, to the extent that second-generation immigrants are yet to be considered a substantial part of the Italian labour market (Reyneri 2011, 99-100). Second-generation citizens of foreign origin have only recently become the subject of political debate, with the discussion around *ius soli* and *ius sanguinis*.[1] Mexican immigration in Italy is rather limited and mainly concerns women; 67.3% of the 3,620 Mexicans registered in Italy in 2008 (Calvanese 2011, 34). Therefore, it is possible to assume that the media are an important source of (more or less distorted) information concerning Mexicans and Chicanos for numerous Italians.

---

[1] The attribution of citizenship in Italy generally follows the *ius sanguinis*. This means that the conditio sine qua non to be considered Italian is to have at least one Italian relative, regardless of the birthplace. On the one hand, this choice keeps a door open for those who have migrated from Italy; on the other, it can be seen as discriminating against the offspring of those who migrate to Italy, who have to go through muddled and costly procedures to obtain citizenship. The debate on the topic started in the late 1990s and periodically re-emerges (Camilli 2017).

The structure of this book is meant to take the reader into the proposed framework, from its background to a detailed exploration of its methodology, which also requires a description of the main features of the case study, to a thorough report of the findings. The first chapter briefly describes the theoretical foundations of the framework, with specific attention to its interdisciplinary approach. The disciplines that have contributed to the implementation of the framework are explored separately, and their relevance is explained. In the first subsection, Descriptive Translation Studies are considered, since through this approach the study of translation is liberated from the prescriptiveness that implies quality assessment. Subsection two calls corpus-based translation studies into question, with reference to the definition of a corpus for analysing translation. Language variation and its role in fiction are at the core of subsection three, with specific attention to their key role for authors and translators. Despite the central role of multimodality in audiovisual products, it has only recently sparked the interest of scholars, and the need for a multimodal approach is stressed in the last subsection. In particular, the main authors that inspired this book are presented here.

Against such a background, the second chapter presents the main linguistic and multimodal features of the case study while delving into the structure of the methodology, so that it can be used as a reference and as a starting point for further research in the field. In this book, methodology and results are equally important, as the debate is open, and every contribution is crucial to moving forward in research. The first two subsections introduce the case study from a linguistic point of view, exploring key concepts of linguistic variation and Chicano-English respectively. Such introduction is key to the understanding of the analysed characters, who are then presented in the third subsection, featuring a description of the Chicano gangster ethnotype and its function. More technical information about the corpus selection is provided in the fourth subsection, containing the practical considerations that informed the corpus selection. The last subsection is the heftiest, as it details the framework functioning, drawing examples from the corpus to clarify how the analysis was conducted.

The last chapter shows the results provided by the framework and offers an interpretation of the quantitative analysis of the multimodal corpus. The framework envisions three dimensions of analysis, which are analysed individually and then intertwined. The textual dimension yields important results concerning the way the films in the corpus were translated and the way language variation was linked to the prestige and social positioning of the characters in both source and target versions. Subsequently, the language results are embedded in their multimodal context thanks to a network of relationships with the other modes of the film in both the source and target version, in order to see whether and to what extent these relationships have changed through translation. The last subsection invites the contextualization of the results in a broader sociocultural dimension, to understand the reasons and the implications of translational choices.

Overall, the framework presented here, informed by the latest international trends in audiovisual translation and multimodality, works towards the complex task of operatively including multimodality in a rigorous corpus analysis of source and target versions. The aims are to advocate for and demonstrate the importance of bridging the gap between multimodality and corpus-based translation studies, and to stress the importance of the study of language variation and character design in audiovisual translation. In four years of research, dissemination and teaching,[2] such aspects have emerged as especially compelling in a world of fading boundaries between screen and reality.

---

[2] Throughout the journey that brought this book to life, I have been teaching, tutoring and guest lecturing on undergraduate, graduate and postgraduate courses at various Italian Universities (University of Bari, University of Bergamo, University of Mantua, University of Modena and Reggio Emilia and Ca' Foscari University of Venice and University of Verona), which helped me test my findings with future professionals of various fields.

Chapter 1
Accepting challenges in audiovisual translation

What is probably the most fascinating and stimulating aspect of Translation Studies (TS) is also one of the hardest difficulties to tackle; it is a complex, composite field, which tenaciously resists all attempts at simplification and reduction:

> Translation studies is the academic discipline related to the study of the theory and phenomena of translation. By its nature it is multilingual and also interdisciplinary, encompassing any language combinations, various branches of linguistics, comparative literature, communication studies, philosophy and a range of types of cultural studies including postcolonialism and postmodernism as well as sociology and historiography (Munday 2008, 1).

To these, it is possible to add the subjects related to technology, in terms of tools, methods and products (Munday 2008, 179). That is why approaching TS means accepting a range of challenges, which can lead one into uncharted territories or to cross paths with disciplines that may seem at first glance to be far removed. In the case of audiovisual translation (AVT), the interdisciplinarity is perhaps even more apparent, as taking into account the polysemiotic nature of the audiovisual product requires going beyond words (Chiaro 2008, 142-143). This chapter aims to explore the interdisciplinary challenges faced in the implementation of the framework here presented.

1.1 Overcoming prescriptive approaches in AVT

Descriptive Translation Studies (DTS) emerged as an answer to the need for TS to let go of what translation *should* be, to see clearly what translation *is*. As stated by Holmes (1988, 71-72), DTS is "the branch of the discipline which constantly maintains the closest contact with the empirical phenomena under study," and it can be divided into three main branches. The first is product-oriented DTS, concerned with existing translations. The focus can be on individual translations as well as on "larger corpuses of translations, for instance those made within a specific period, language, and/or text or discourse type [...] diachronic as well as (approximately) synchronic" (Holmes 1988, 72). On the other hand, function-oriented DTS focuses on the contextual elements surrounding the text, since it "is not interested in the description of translations in themselves, but in the description of their function in the recipient sociocultural situation" (Holmes 1988, 72), somehow overlapping with sociological analyses. Finally, process-oriented DTS aims to understand "what exactly takes place in the 'little black box' of the translator's 'mind'" (Holmes 1988, 72). This kind of research naturally involves an interest in psychology.

A direct consequence of the structure of Holmes' model is that "the development of the entire discipline is dependent on the harmonious and dynamic interaction of all three elements, which enjoy equal status" (Laviosa 2002, 10). In this sense, Gideon Toury's work brings DTS forward, as he aimed to "elevate DTS to the state of the scientific branch [...] at the heart of the discipline, [with] a distinctive internal organisation" (Laviosa 2002, 11).

Toury envisions a link between function, product and process, as "the (prospective) systemic position & function of a translation determines its appropriate surface realization (textual-linguistic make-up)," which in turn "governs the strategies whereby a target text (or part thereof) is derived from its original, and hence the relationships which hold them together" (1995, 13).[3] Toury draws his definition of function as "the 'value' assigned to an item belonging to a certain system by virtue of the network of relations it enters into" (Toury 1995, 12) from dynamic functionalism (Even-Zohar 1979 and 1990). Function is at the core of translation, as "translators may be said to operate first and foremost in the interest of the culture into which they are translating" (Toury 1995, 12).

---

[3] The author also acknowledges the possibility that the chain can go in the opposite direction, with the strategies determining the features of the product and giving it a "position in the recipient system" (Toury 1995, 14).

The centrality of function is key to understanding two crucial points of Toury's DTS. Firstly, translations are "cultural facts [...] determined first and foremost by considerations originating in the culture which hosts them" (Toury 1995, 26). Consequently, being "facts of target cultures" (Toury 1995, 29), they should be seen as texts in their own right, "which can easily function as a proper source text despite its derivative nature" (Toury 1995, 75). A text, or a body of texts, is then chosen by the DTS scholar according to criteria that are usually "external, provisional, and firmly based on the target language system" (Laviosa 2002, 12). The texts thus selected will undergo a three-phase analysis, which moves either along a discovery or a justification axis.

When working on a discovery procedure axis, the scholar uses an inductive process. The first phase will consist in situating "the text within the target culture system, looking at its significance or acceptability" (Munday 2008, 111), and attempting to formulate tentative hypotheses. The second step consists in identifying the source text (ST) as an "appropriate source text," and establishing pairs of "solution + problem" relationships which would allow the scholar to determine the relationships linking a target text (TT) to the source. However, this pairing cannot escape its own partiality and indirectness (Toury 1995, 80), and "[t]he results are flexible and non-prescriptive, if also less than rigorously systematic, means of comparing ST and TT" (Munday 2008, 111).

The third phase is the typical outcome of a (successful) inductive process, as it consists in formulating generalizations about the norms governing equivalence between the texts. This allows the reconstruction of the process of translation itself, bearing in mind that a DTS scholar has a specific mission, which is not to formulate personal evaluations concerning the attainment of equivalence:

> Equivalence [...] encompasses the actual relationships that characterise an acceptable translation in any given target culture. This means that in a descriptive study the researcher will always assume that equivalence exists. What s/he will uncover is the concrete way in which it is realised, in terms of the balance between invariance and transformation. This type of functional-relational and culturally-determined equivalence in turn constitutes a stepping stone for discovering the concept of translation which informs the target text examined. (Laviosa 2002, 14).

A DTS scholar is required to let go of any corrective attitude, to abandon what Toury (1995, 80) called the "negative kind of reasoning" — an attitude that results in a judgement of the relative success of a translation. On the contrary, DTS require the scholar to abandon any prejudice, to understand how a certain way of realising equivalence is embedded in the specific culture that generated the target text.

Contrary to the inductive discovery is the deductive justification that, in Toury's scheme, is not "offered only when the discovery procedures have already been exhausted," but "from the very start," when "explanatory hypotheses will be formulated, which will then reflect backwards and affect subsequent discovery procedures" (Toury 1995, 37-38). Moreover, since the final aim is to provide valid generalizations, it is clear that "one assumed translation, or even one pair of texts, would not constitute a proper corpus for study" (Toury 1995, 38). To find out more about a specific translator, text-type or text-linguistic phenomenon, it will be necessary to extend the corpus to include all those texts matching the chosen criteria and go through the three-phase analysis for all of the texts, which may eventually bring the study closer to higher levels of generalization, thus explaining translation according to the selected criteria.

As stated by Toury, to fully understand a translation, the DTS scholar should be able to identify the sociocultural constraints under which a translator works. These constraints might vary according to potency or along a temporal axis. The latter refers to the fact that a certain constraint may undergo "processes of rise and decline" (Toury 1995, 54) over time. Potency refers to the actual reach of a constraint, which is usually placed along a continuum between "absolute rules" and "pure idiosyncrasies" (Toury 1995, 54). Between the two "lies a vast middle-ground occupied by intersubjective factors" that constitute the norms. These are defined as "the translation of general values or ideas shared by a community — as to what is right or wrong, adequate or inadequate — into performance instructions appropriate for and applicable to particular situations" (Toury 1995, 55).

Despite being a fact of the target culture, it is necessary to remember that a translation "inevitably involves at least two languages and two cultural traditions" that are "always different and therefore often incompatible" (Toury 1995, 56). Such tension would have to be solved by the individual without any reference, and without being able to determine the way their choice will be perceived by the target culture, were it not for the "regulative capacity of norms" (Toury 1995, 56).

At different stages of the translation process, different norms come into play (Munday 2008, 112; Toury 1995). First, the initial norm is the basic choice that a translator is called to make. If the translator decides to abide by the norms of the target culture, their final product will be acceptable for the target audience—their work will be target-oriented, but this will imply significant shifts from the source text. On the other hand, choosing to privilege the norms of the source culture will produce an adequate translation that is source-oriented, but will come into contradiction with target culture norms, "especially those lying beyond the mere linguistic ones" (Toury 1995, 56). Thus, the initial norm implies a choice between acceptability and adequacy. This choice, however, cannot be said to be a neat dichotomy. Rather, it is a continuum, as even the most source-oriented translation will entail some degree of shifting from the source. This shift, according to Toury, is the "true universal of translation" (1995, 57). He also specifies that—although what he calls the initial norm would logically precede the others—micro-level decisions can be made by the translator at any point in the translating process. Such micro-level choices do not need necessarily to consistently comply with the initial orientation towards adequacy or acceptability.

Secondly, preliminary norms concern two different but often connected aspects. The first aspect is the existence and content of a definite translation policy, consisting of "those factors that govern the choice of text-types, or even of individual texts, to be imported through translation into a particular culture/language at a particular point of time" (Toury 1995, 58).[4] The second aspect is the directness of translation, which is to say "the threshold of tolerance for translating from languages other than the ultimate source language" (Toury 1995, 58).

Finally, operational norms concern "the decision made during the act of translation itself" (Toury 1995, 58). These include matricial norms, which "relate to the completeness of the TT. Phenomena include omission or relocation of passages, textual segmentation, and the addition of passages or footnotes" (Munday 2008, 112). They also contain textual-linguistic norms, governing the actual linguistic material selected for the target text, both in general and concerning a specific text type.

Toury notes that the norms concerning the language of translating may or may not reflect those governing non-translational language. Where they do not, the translation might position itself at a considerable distance from the target language:

> Operational norms as such may be described as serving as a model [...]. Every model supplying performance instructions may be said to act as a *restricting* factor: it opens up certain options while closing others. Consequently, [...] the translation can hardly be said to have been made into the target language as a whole. Rather, it is made into a model language, which is at best some part of the former and at worst an artificial, and as such non-existent variety (Toury 1995, 60).

This passage is relevant to audiovisual translation (AVT), and in particular dubbing, in a country like Italy. Indeed, this is the most often heard criticism of what has been called *dubbese* (in Italian *doppiaggese*) — its detachment from natural spoken language. *Dubbese* is "the Italian spoken in all those films, series, cartoons, sitcoms, and any other imported foreign product, which are translated for the big and the small screen [...] it is quite common on Italian TV to hear a member of a US street gang and his/her lawyer speak in the same way" (Antonini 2008, 136). This language, often seen as unrealistic and overly standardized (Chaume 2004), is the result of a specific context of translation for audiovisual products in Italy. As

---

4   Munday (2008, 112) specifies that this aspect is not effectively looked into in Toury's case studies.

will be later specified, those in charge of film transposition into the target culture do not see themselves as translators and are not trained as such—indeed, the main rule governing their work is the speakability and performability of the text for the dubbing actors (Pavesi & Perego 2006). From a purely linguistic point of view, the language of dubbing seems to be deeply affected by its need for acceptability, its policy and consequent operational norms. However, as will later be explained, the factors at stake in film translation make the whole discourse more complex and necessitate a broader discussion. In fact, it is important to remember that norms, subject to change over time and moving along a continuum of potency, are inherently subject to sociocultural specificity and instability (Toury 1995, 62).

As discussed above, DTS emerged from the need to go beyond prescriptivism, to see what translating and translation imply. That is the reason why what Toury defines as "laws" of translation are not guidelines for a "good" translation, but an attempt to generalize empirical findings in order to infer probabilistic, tentative laws of translation that might eventually prove to be universally true. The first is the law of growing standardization: "in translation, textual relations obtaining in the original are often modified, sometimes to the point of being totally ignored, in favour of [more] habitual options offered by a target repertoire" (Toury 1995, 268). This implies dismissing the source language patterns in favour of others that are more common in the target language. As Munday points out (2008, 114), this often means a "tendency towards a general standardization and loss of variation in style in the TT or at least an accommodation to target culture models," which is especially true when "as commonly occurs, translation assumes a weak and peripheral position in the target system." As already observed by this author in her pilot studies (Renna 2018), this was often the case with films in Chicano English.

On the other hand, according to the law of interference: "in translation, phenomena pertaining to the make-up of the source text tend to be transferred to the target text" (Toury 1995, 274). This law can be observed when translators "copy" features of the source text in the target text, either because there is an expression akin to it in the target language or because there is not—which would create a non-normal use of the language (Munday 2008, 114). In this case, too, acceptance of a translation behaviour is, according to Toury, strictly related to power relations between cultures: a "minor" target culture will tolerate interference from a source culture that is deemed to be "prestigious" (Toury 1995, 278).

These norms are not observable in themselves, and therefore need to be retrieved through "norm-governed instances of behaviour" (Toury 1995, 65). One precious source of information in this respect consists in textual resources, "primary products of norm-regulated behaviour" that constitute "immediate representations" of the norm that guided the translator (Toury 1995, 65). Another source of information comes from extratextual sources, which are statements coming from those involved in the translation activity (e.g., translators, critics, editors, publishers etc). The information drawn from this kind of source is taken by Toury with more suspicion because, being a by-product, it is partial and biased, and there might be a significant gap between what these sources maintain and the textual result in the translation.

Some aspects of Toury's model have certainly been challenged, and its limits have been pointed out. For example, Chesterman (1997, 64) and Hermans (1999, 77) have criticized the ambiguity of terms such as "adequate" and "acceptable" because they could also be used with an evaluative acceptation—in this sense, the terms source-oriented and target-oriented are probably safer to use. Also, Hermans (1999, 97) questions Toury's use of the term equivalence, as it is a "tainted concept" in need of "problematizing." When used "without problematizing," Hermans writes, it "destroys the possibility of critical interrogation." Munday (2008) also notes some unfilled gaps, especially linked to the weight of ideology in cultural processes and practices:

> Toury's early stance risked overlooking, for example, some of the complex ideological and political factors such as the status of the ST in its own culture, the source culture's possible promotion of translation of its own literature and the effect that translation might exert back on the system of the source culture. (Munday 2008, 115).

Munday's first point is particularly important here, as the language translated in the case study presented in this book occupies a peripheral position in its own culture, and the ideological repercussions of this positioning require specific attention. This aspect was developed further by Toury himself (2004) when he concentrated his attention on the sociocultural aspects underlying linguistic choices. Other scholars, such as Pym defend Toury's laws because, by virtue of their "probabilistic formulations," they allow for apparently contradictory tendencies: "If social conditions A apply, then we might expect more standardization. If social conditions B are in evidence, expect interference. And there is no necessary contradiction involved." (2008, 321).

The findings coming from DTS often applied to literary translation, have already been productively applied to fields like audiovisual translation (Karamitroglou 2000). Furthermore, while the theoretical debate remains open and new case studies contribute with textual and extratextual sources of information, the point of mentioning DTS here is to take it as the point of view that allows describing translation without attempting to criticize translators for not delivering a good product, but rather with the aim to understand the source text and target text for what they are.

The next challenge is tightly linked to the one just presented, as it stems from Toury's intention to reach greater accuracy in generalization by expanding the corpus as extended corpora are the distinctive feature of corpus linguistics.

1.2 Expanding the scope with corpora

As discussed in the previous paragraph, the outcome envisioned by Toury for DTS was to be able to draw more solid generalizations from a broad collection of texts. Analysing great amounts of text is one of the specific features of corpus linguistics. Thus, it might not be wrong to affirm that, if TS aims to accept the challenge of understanding broader phenomena through quantitative (or partially quantitative) analysis, it might fruitfully turn to corpus linguistics and use some of its methodologies for its own purposes.

Before moving on to the graft between the two disciplines, it is useful to have a brief outline of corpora and corpus linguistics. According to Sinclair (1996, 4), "a corpus is a collection of pieces of language that are selected and ordered according to explicit linguistic criteria in order to be used as a sample of the language." Johansson (1998, 3) provides a more general concept by defining it as "a body of texts put together in a principled way and prepared for computer processing." This last part is particularly relevant to the present developments of corpus linguistics: in fact, while early studies on corpora were carried out before the widespread of information technology (McEnery et al. 2006, 3), corpus linguistics as it is today developed thanks to software processing in the 1980s and 1990s. According to Laviosa (2002, 6), it "can be defined as a branch of general linguistics that involves the analysis of large machine-readable corpora of running text, using a variety of software tools designed specifically for textual analysis." The guiding principles of corpus linguistics (Laviosa 2002, 8; Stubbs 1993, 2; 1996, 23) include the affirmation of the central role of descriptive linguistics in informing theories of language; the empirical methods of research (preferred to intuition and introspection); the conception of language as a social phenomenon reflecting and reproducing culture; the recognition of the heterogeneity and variation of language; the mission of discovering the rules of language in use, rather than prescribing the right use of language; the conception of linguistics as social science and applied science.

It is possible to recognise some common ground between these features of corpus linguistics and the aforementioned DTS. Indeed, Laviosa (2002, 16-17) identifies similarities and differences between the two disciplines, in order to show in which ways and to what extent corpus linguistics applies to DTS. First, the disciplines share an empirical approach rather than a speculative one. The selection of the material to be analysed depends on specific criteria, set according to a certain research question. Second, both corpus linguistics and DTS rely on results deriving from a broader corpus, rather than individual texts or cases. Finally, in terms of results, both disciplines deliver their findings thanks to systematic research, and express their results in terms of probable rules of behaviour — which remain open to further investigation of broader corpora, and do not represent absolute prescriptions.

On the other hand, differences between the two disciplines should not be overlooked. According to Laviosa (2002, 16), corpus linguistics has "no clear boundaries between theory, data, description and methodology," while, as already discussed in the previous paragraph, "for Toury these elements do interact but are four distinct notions." Another difference concerns methodology, as DTS accepts a variety of methods, provided that they are "empirical, descriptive and conceived from within the discipline of Translation Studies," while for corpus linguistics the "object of study is created by the methodology itself" (Laviosa 2002, 16-17). Besides, the research in corpus linguistics does not admit psychological insights in the language user nor extratextual evidence, as it is inextricably bound to text, whereas these are accepted in DTS research. Last but not least, Toury's final aim was to elaborate "a general theory on the basis of the accumulation of facts and partial theories" (Laviosa 2002, 17), while corpus linguistics accepts partial theories and findings, as these reflect the variable and unstable nature of language.

The first to notice the potential of synergy between corpus linguistics and translation studies was probably Mona Baker, inspired by the work of Sinclair on corpus linguistics (1992). Sinclair briefly mentions translation practice as one of the possible fields benefiting from the development of large corpora. Building on his vision, Baker ties the success of translation studies in drawing credible generalizations from empirical research to the welcoming of techniques and methodologies borrowed from corpus linguistics:

> [T]ranslation studies have reached a stage in its development as a discipline when it is both ready for and needs the techniques and methodology of corpus linguistics in order to make a major leap from prescriptive to descriptive statements, from methodologising to proper theorising, and from individual and fragmented pieces of research to powerful generalizations. Once this is achieved, the distinction between the theoretical and applied branches of the discipline will become clearer and more convincing. (Baker 1993, 248).

More specifically, Baker is concerned with identifying the so-called *universals of translation*, which are "linguistic features that typically occur in translation rather than original texts and are independent of the influence of the specific language pairs involved in the process of translation" (Laviosa 2002, 18). Toury's laws, as laid out above, point the way to finding recurrent translator behaviours that may constitute the universals of translation. Among these, Baker (1993, 243-245) includes explicitation, when translators add information in the target version; disambiguation and simplification (Vanderauwera 1985, 97-98); preference for conventional grammaticality, which refers to a tendency to polish non-conventional or ungrammatical utterances; limitation of repetitions; exaggeration of features of the target language, making them more recurrent than they are in the natural target language; specific distribution of lexical items in relation to both source texts and original target language texts.

However, what is of more relevance to this research (and possibly to audiovisual translation studies more broadly) is a corpus-based research potential in terms of redefining equivalence. This becomes possible thanks to the "decline of what we might call the semantic view of the relationship between source and target texts," whose worst implication for Translation Studies was "the idea that meaning, or messages, exist as such and can, indeed should, be transferred from source to target texts in much the same way as one might transfer wine from one glass to another" (Baker 1993, 236). The most important implication in such a turn in the concept of equivalence is that meaning stems from a specific context that is both situational and linguistic, and equivalence should be found in usage rather than in semantic meaning (Baker 1993, 236-237; Firth 1968, 91; Haas 1968, 104; Laviosa 2002, 19).

In order to be able to talk about usage, however, it is fundamental to have greater amounts of data at hand, which proves once more the crucial role of corpora in descriptive translation studies. As noted by Laviosa (2002, 19), the work of Even-Zohar (1979) and Toury (1995) contributed to seeing translations as original texts, having their creativity and a specific role within the context of the target culture. This encourages a shift from individual case studies, which compare a source text and its translation to larger bodies of translated texts, either with or without comparison with source texts.

Italian dubbing offers a representative example of the role of translated texts in the target culture. In fact, the *dubbese* contributed (and contributes) to shaping the language of native Italian speakers. As mentioned earlier, *dubbese* is a rather artificial language that was born to adapt target audiovisual texts to technical needs such as lip-sync, but also as a consequence of limited time and resources available for the editing of the dubbing script. These specific features of dubbing have been the origin of several calques that, on the one hand, have become typical of translated audiovisual material (to the point of making it immediately recognisable), but on the other hand have entered the way Italian speakers use their language, both in conversation and in more formal contexts (Paolinelli & Di Fortunato 2005, 20).[5] Criticism concerning such a phenomenon is definitely not the aim of this book, which focuses on the way audiovisual translation *actually* is, rather than on the way it *should* be: indeed, the heavy impact of the language of dubbing on Italian native speakers is undeniable evidence of its potential positioning in the target society. Moreover, this proven impact may serve as further justification for a descriptive study of translation, able to give an account of certain phenomena without a reproaching attitude on the side of the investigator.

Such observation confirms Baker's words (1996, 176): "a translation, like any kind of text production, develops in response to the pressures of its immediate context and draws on a distinct repertoire of textual patterns." This means that the perceived positioning (or the social status) of the text and the translators themselves may have a significant effect on translation choices—notoriously proven to be the case in audiovisual translation. In fact, studies on the contextual aspects of audiovisual translation in Italy have demonstrated how this sector works in a counter-intuitive way, as quality is not the main focus of its agents (Antonini & Chiaro 2009, 99). External factors, such as market requirements, exert considerable

---

[5] The phenomenon is so embedded in the Italian language that it has merited the attention of the most popular Italian Encyclopedia, the *Enciclopedia Treccani*, which shows how lexical and even morpho-syntactic calques from English have been imported via *dubbese*: http://www.treccani.it/magazine/lingua_italiana/speciali/fiction/motta.html. Accessed April 29, 2021.

pressure on those in charge of film adaptation and may push the linguistic aspects of translation to a peripheral role. Such considerations open two perspectives: one is that of ethnolinguistic analysis of audiovisual translation agents and recipients, and the other is a descriptive approach to texts, which is the motive behind the present research.

After accepting a corpus-based approach to translation studies for all the above reasons, the following step concerns the way corpora should be used in translation and, consequently, to design a corpus that may fit the aims of a TS research. Halverson (1998) poses the concept of representativeness at the core of corpus definition, as it links object, theory and data. Echoing Biber (1993, 243), she stresses again the crucial role of theory before corpus-building and adds that the very first aim should be "consideration of the purpose for which the corpus is to be used" (Halverson 1998, 4). The precise delimitation of the scope of a corpus is crucial and must be clear in the mind of the researcher as well as openly declared, since "corpus-based findings cannot be generalised beyond the specific target population that a given corpus represents" (Laviosa 2002, 27).

Terminology in corpus categorization might turn out to present some issues. Laviosa's typology (2008, 33-38) was chosen here as a starting point for the corpus definition — thus, her categorization will be presented in this chapter. First of all, Laviosa (2002, 34) outlines a typology "organised along four hierarchical levels," where "[t]he first level consists of six sets of contrastive parameters that relate to the most general features of a text corpus," and the following ones concern "increasingly more specific groups of parameters."

The first level defines the corpus type by and large, according to general criteria. The first criterion is the type of texts chosen, which can be full texts, samples, a mix of full texts and samples or a monitor — full texts that are kept updated over time. The second criterion in the first level is the time frame of the corpus: it can be either synchronic when it is a snapshot of text(s) coming from a relatively limited period, or diachronic, which means that it includes texts produced during a longer period. Another important criterion concerns the specificity of the corpus: it can be general if it represents everyday language without further specification, or terminological when it includes "texts originating within specialised subject fields" (Laviosa 2002, 35). The fourth and fifth criteria for corpus definition concern the languages involved, as a corpus, can be monolingual, bilingual or multilingual, and the specific language(s) considered will contribute to specifying the corpus typology. The last specification in the first level consists in establishing if the corpus is written, spoken, or contains a mix of both. According to Laviosa (2002, 35), "[a] written corpus is made up entirely of written texts, that is written to be read while a spoken corpus consists of recorded spoken texts including those that are written to be spoken."

On the second level, Laviosa poses further specifications that depend on the ones chosen in the previous level, more specifically depending on whether the corpus is monolingual, bilingual or multilingual. A monolingual corpus can either be single, when consisting of a set of texts in a given language, or comparable, when made up of two single monolingual corpora, one of which is translational and the other non-translational. The texts can be selected according to the genre, topic, characteristics of their authors, length etc.

A bilingual corpus can be parallel when consisting of "one or more texts in language A and its/their translation in language B" (Laviosa 2002, 36). Alternatively, a bilingual corpus can be comparable — which is to say composed of two original texts in language A and language B respectively — their comparability being supported by genre, topic, period, communicative function and other relevant criteria for the research at hand.

Similarly, a multilingual corpus is parallel when consisting of "one or more texts in different languages and its/their translation(s) in different languages" (Laviosa 2002, 36). A comparable multilingual corpus will include original texts in more than two languages, whose comparability depends on specific criteria chosen by the investigator.

On the third level, a single corpus can be translational or non-translational. In the first case, it will consist of texts that are "known to have been translated into a given language" (Laviosa 2002, 37).

In the second case, the corpus will include original text in a chosen language. A bilingual parallel corpus can be mono-directional or bi-directional. A bilingual parallel mono-directional corpus "consists of one or more texts in language A and its/their translation(s) in language B" (Laviosa 2002, 37). In the second case, not only the pair A to B will be included in the corpus, but also translations in the opposite direction—language B translated into language A. A multilingual parallel corpus can be mono-source-language, bi-source-language or multi-source-language. In each case, multiple language translations will accompany the source text(s). Finally, a fourth level includes other specifications for translational corpora, which can themselves be mono-source-language, bi-source-language or multi-source-language.

Since their appearance, corpus-based translation studies have gained a central position in TS, as they offer the possibility of 1) testing hypotheses with a specifically implemented empirical research model; and 2) transforming hypotheses into tentative, probabilistic laws. Regardless of whether these tend to broader generalization or the description of a specific translation phenomenon, the advantages of rigorous corpus-based research have a significant reach in all fields of translation studies.

Corpus-based studies certainly require rigour, as well as a great deal of attention and patience, since "[w]hile the methods of analysis are empowering to the point of pure euphoria, the collection of data can be challenging to the point of deep despair" (Laviosa 2002, 119). However, incorporating (at least part of) corpus linguistics into translation studies can make the difference between relevant but limited research and arduous but comprehensive corpus-based research.

So far, the challenges mentioned in this chapter are the ones that have long since become common to numerous TS researchers and scholars. The next two challenges are certainly more specifically linked to this work and are in some cases only recently being dealt with consistently in TS.

1.3 Recognising language variation and its role in AVT

While a corpus is certainly defined by the language chosen for its texts, languages themselves cannot really fall into univocal definitions. Indeed, a feature of corpus linguistics that is crucial for its application to this research is its recognition of variation within languages. It might be worth remembering here that, according to David Crystal (2004), though corpus linguistics is standard language, it is also a variety of language that has at some point in time attained major social prestige within a community of speakers. Lippi-Green (1997) explains the nature of language variation:

> Spoken language varies for every speaker in terms of speech sounds, sound patterns, word and sentence structure, intonation, and meaning, from utterance to utterance. [...] There are three sources of variation in language: first, language-internal pressures, arising in part from the mechanics of production and perception; second, language-external influences on language, as a social behavior subject to normative and other formative social pressures; and third, variation arising from language as a creative vehicle of free expression. These forces can and do function in tandem [...] (Lippi-Green 1997, 25).

Language variation goes beyond mere linguistics, as it has profound connections with social, cultural and political aspects of society. This multifaceted reality is not only found in actual texts (written or spoken) produced by speakers in natural environments, but also in fiction. The use of dialect in fiction is not a recent phenomenon: Brodovich (1997, 26) mentions "the classic Greek comedy *Lysistrata*" by Aristophanes as an ancient example. In regards to the English-speaking world, English literature has been pervaded by language variation from its very beginning (Blake 1981; Page 1988). The first representations of dialect date back to the dawn of English literature, as one can already be found in Chaucer (Chapman 1994, 38), and an early and influential author like Shakespeare offered abundant material for research into the non-standard language for example Blake (2004). Initial instances mainly consisted of comedic insertions, until Walter Scott, who is said to have given a crucial diegetic function to the use of language variation. According to

Chapman (1994, 39), the way Scott used fictional language variation demonstrated how "dialect could not only place a character regionally but could also show register and relationships within that region." Chapman (1994) also maintains that speech in fiction can represent diversity in numerous ways — for example, opposing standard and non-standard (where the latter also includes slang and non-native speech), dialect and register, social class and even gender.

Yet specific research on this phenomenon is fairly recent. One example is Lodge, among the first to investigate the topic from a non-fictional perspective and to coin the locution "language in fiction" (1966). He noticed how, while poetry critics agreed on the profound fusion of form and content, prose critics did not generally pay much attention to the language itself. Ignoring the language as a means of communication in fiction is certainly fallacious, since everything a novelist does, "he does in and through language" (Lodge 1966, 3).

Indeed, such early use of dialect and its potential in terms of fiction suggests that awareness of linguistic variation is an integral part of the competence of a proficient language speaker, who can deduce an important amount of information by just how someone speaks, before even hearing what they say, as well as associate speech features to several other apparently unrelated features.

In fact, the reasons for and functions of fictional reproduction of language variation are manifold:

> [T]he creative use of linguistic varieties in literary dialogue helps to inform the reader about which character is speaking and under which circumstances. It becomes a textual resource that helps the reader to define the sociocultural profile of the character, as well as his/her position in the sociocultural fictional context. Knowing the social stereotypes and assumptions readers may share with the rest of the society they are a part of, the author uses fictional varieties with the expectation that this will encourage certain reactions and assumptions which will aid characterization. It leads to the stratification of the participants in the dialogue, since the speakers tend to associate higher prestige with a standard variety, and, consequently, to undervalue other varieties culturally associated with peripheral geographic spaces and with a lower sociocultural status. (Ramos Pinto 2009, 291).

Ramos Pinto's words clearly reveal that representing linguistic variation in fiction is not a simple matter of aesthetics, as it is an integral part of the plot on both the side of the author and of the audience. If a text is a product with a specific place and role within its culture, then it might not be wrong to infer that author and audience share—or are supposed to share—certain baggage of knowledge. This can be exploited by an author, who can expect that using a certain variety within a language will trigger specific reactions and assumptions in the minds of the audience. In particular, the most relevant set of information that can be transmitted through language variation concerns the sociocultural positioning of the character within the diegetic context as well as within society. The main factor in sociocultural positioning is prestige (Ramos Pinto 2017). In other words, the communicative meaning (Hatim & Mason 1990) of a certain linguistic variety consists of the fact that the latter conveys specific information related to prestige. The audience tends to expect the most prestigious social group to speak a language that closely approximates the standard, while the lower the character in the social scale, the further her/his language will stand out from the expected standard. The fictional varieties move "along an axis extending from maximum to minimum prestige (or even stigma, i.e. negative evaluation of a linguistic form), based on the speakers' evaluative attitudes towards language use" (Assis Rosa 2015, 3).

It is nonetheless important to note that fiction does not have to faithfully reproduce linguistic reality in all of its aspects, since "the literary recreation of accents and dialects has no pretensions of being accurate," which means that "the degree of linguistic mimicry depends on the author's aesthetic, narrative, thematic, stylistic or functional objectives" (Ramos Pinto 2009, 291-292). This gap between the actual use of language and its fictional counterpart is what fostered the definition of fictional language study as "fictolinguistics" (Ferguson 1998). Fictional language variation is a tool at hand for the author to use for her/his diegetic purposes.

Nevertheless, an author does not make completely deliberate use of this tool, as it still needs to convey its message to a broad and potentially indefinite audience. In order to fulfil its diegetic function, a fictional variety has to be identifiable as such, and understandable through the use of what Assis Rosa (2012, 77) calls "linguistic sensitivity" or "knowledge of sociolinguistic stereotypes." While it is not probably right to take for granted that all proficient speakers have a specific and conscious competence in terms of language variation, it would not be wrong to infer that anyone can make assumptions based on a language variety, although often drenched in stereotypes. Indeed, common stereotypes are often what an author relies on when choosing a variety: "authors generally take advantage of linguistic stereotypes easily recognized by the average reader, making sure that certain assumptions and images will be triggered" (Ramos Pinto 2009, 290).

According to Assis Rosa's scheme of language variation (2012, 77), an audience may identify "linguistic variables" that concern two aspects. The first is phonetic and phonological features, often generically grouped as "accent" (who has not heard lines such as "what a lovely accent!" or "I could tell by your accent" or "he has no accent" or "British people have a pure accent" comfortably uttered by non-linguists?) The second is that the audience is also able to recognise morphological, syntactic, semantic and lexical items, frequently grouped under the label of dialect.

These variables intersect with contextual variables such as time, geographical space, social space, individual speaker, and communicative situation, to obtain more specific information on what type of variation defines a character (or group of characters). If the language variation has to do with time, the variation can be synchronic or diachronic, and the linguistic variety will show an evolution in the development of a language. If the language variation concerns space, the variation will be regional, and a geographically located dialect or accent will emerge. If the linguistic and contextual variables suggest a social variation, the result will be a social dialect, for example, slang or technical jargon. If the features are exquisitely individual, an idiolect will emerge as the specific feature of a character (Page 1988, 97-121). Finally, when linguistic variables intersect with a certain communicative situation, the variation will be functional and expressed through a register adopted by the character(s).

Each person might agree to such statements and link them to fictional varieties used in their language. However, if fictional dialects are "culture-specific" (Brodovich 1997, 26), what happens with translation, through which a culturally embedded text should become intelligible to a different culture? That is when the third challenge comes into play: translating fictional language variation to make the character recognisable — often seen as an impossible task for translators (Fedorov 1985, 145), although unavoidable, given the diegetic and meta-narrative power of fictional language variation (Assis Rosa 2012, 77).

Translating language varieties creates a deep tension between (as Toury puts it) adequacy and acceptability in translation, especially because languages vary and so does the organization of the speakers in social, geographic and cultural terms. Moreover, different countries may have different conventions when it comes to representing linguistic variation in fiction (Brodovich 1997), which may not work in other contexts. Thus, translators must consider the target audience and find a mediation that allows them to keep the message while making sure it is intelligible and acceptable:

> [T]he recreation of linguistic varieties results from the mediation, not only of the purposes to be fulfilled by the translation in the target culture, but also from what has been established by that system's literary tradition or factors such as legibility, intelligibility and the medium in which the translation will come to light. (Ramos Pinto 2009, 292)

Literary tradition has a strong influence in determining what a translator is allowed to do with varieties. Ramos Pinto (2009, 293) collects the possible strategies a translator may opt for, according to factors that are both related to the text itself and the broader context of the target culture. She identifies the first turning point in the choice between preserving or non-preserving linguistic variation (thus normalising the text), but she also warns that — even though normalisation itself is listed among the universals of translation (Baker 1993) — it is rare for a complete normalisation of the whole text to take place. It is instead more likely for normalisation to affect secondary characters. A further normalising factor concerns the importance of the variation itself within the plot, as a consequence of "the relationship between the hierarchy established among plot elements and the recognition of linguistic variation as a peripheral element" (Ramos Pinto 2009, 293). Eliminating variation may also represent a political statement, in case the translator decides to opt for translating a whole text into a non-standard variety: this way, a translation can "change the relation of linguistic forces, at the institutional and symbolic levels, by making it possible for the vernacular language to take the place of the referential language" (Brisset 1996, 345).

The number of possible options dramatically increases when the translator decides to preserve (at least partially preserve) the variation of the source text. The second choice s/he is called to make concerns time and space coordinates. The translator can either preserve both, change both — thus changing time of narration and place of setting — or keep only one of the two — thus having either a same-place/different-time combination or a same-time/different-place combination. When making such a choice, it is important to ponder all the elements at stake. If changing time and place might allow the translator "to avoid the problem of recreating a language from decades ago, about which he or she may not possess enough information," it is also true that "because of the modifications it imposes on the text, the non-preservation of one of the coordinates may cause critics to classify the translator's work as an adaptation" (Ramos Pinto 2009, 294).

If the translator decides to keep the space-related coordinates, s/he can either do so by using "familiar features recognized as non-standard in the target culture or to make use of features not familiar to the target culture receiver" (Ramos Pinto 2009, 294). If recognisable features are opted for, the possible declinations in the text move along an axis from more to less normalised. One possibility is to add explicit indications of the variation, which would compensate for the elimination of the non-standard element. Alternatively, the translator might leave only those features that explain power relationships among characters e.g. forms of address and honorific forms, (Ramos Pinto 2009). Another option is to upgrade the standard part of the text to a more formal language so that the variation tends upwards rather than downwards (Yu 2017). Other options are: using oral features, to communicate a diversion from the standard without resorting to non-standard features that may be perceived as wrong; using a mix of various non-standard varieties, to convey the polarization without making a specific reference to a group in the target culture; using a specific non-standard variety, bearing in mind that its social meaning for the target audience can be rather specific.

The translator, however, might also opt for features that are not already known by the audience. This happens, for example, when the clash between setting and linguistic variety jeopardises the whole credibility of the text (Brodovich 1997), or when the choice of a specific target language variety might cause discontent because of the social meaning of the variety in the original text.[6] Another reason for using unfamiliar features is that the source text itself presents unfamiliar (i.e. made up) features—Ramos Pinto (2009, 295) takes the slang created by the characters of Anthony Burgess' *A Clockwork Orange* as an example.

The translator might choose to directly import the features as they are in the source text—as will later be shown, this has often been the case with the Italian dubbing of Chicano gangsters' code-mixing in American movies. Other options are to use the lexical features of the source text while adapting their spelling to the target language norms or to develop a virtual dialect. Ramos Pinto (2009) stresses that there are no better or worse strategies—rather, a certain solution might turn out to work well in a certain situation—and also reminds us that most often translators will use a mix of strategies to achieve the best results.

---

[6] To better explain this last point, the recounting of a direct experience with students might be useful. During a workshop (held in English) at the University of Verona in 2016, I asked a group of Foreign Languages postgraduate students what dialect they would use to translate African American English into Italian. A student proposed a southern dialect because, in her view as a northern Italian person, dialects from the south are "less understandable." When I reported the answer to southern Italian Media Studies postgraduate students at the University of Bari during a guest lecture in 2017, they immediately replied they felt offended and underlined that, to them, northern dialects are just as incomprehensible.

The translator also has to take into consideration the social and political implications of certain linguistic choices, as an ideology is a crucial factor in determining the type and strength of stereotypes in society. In particular, negative prejudices are often attached to orality, typical of those peripheral varieties in social and geographic terms. Indeed, according to Bandia (2011, 108), orality is "an important factor in the aesthetic representation of otherness, the assertion of marginalized identities through a variety of art forms," especially because the strong oral tradition of numerous colonized cultures is often presented as a sign of illiteracy. The recognition of such a role of orality in culture triggered the interest and concern of TS:

> [p]reoccupation with issues of ideology, identity and power relations led to a growing interest in the translation and representation of minority cultures. [...] suffered the negative stereotyping associated with non-literate cultures. [...] their languages are often marginalized in the global cultural space. (Bandia 2011, 109)

Chicanos and Chicano English will prove here to be a relevant example of the way otherness is subject to stereotyping in the dominant US culture, and the use of Chicano English in American cinema tends to confirm—and reinforce—those prejudicial attitudes. In fact, when ideological content linked to power relations is involved, the translator will have to handle an even more delicate task, representation of the other in a new context, tightrope walking on a taut line between centre and periphery, dominant and minority cultures. As mentioned before, the representation of language variation does not have to be accurate. Nevertheless, it has enormous power, since "[a] sense of nationality and ethnicity, with its attendant stereotyping, still informs our daily lives" (van Doorslaer *et al.* 2016, 1). In this sense, the main issue for both author and translator is not identity itself, but how identity is represented in fiction, with all the possible aspects of selection and manipulation.

The study of image (or imagology) has its origin in comparative literature (Leerssen 2007), but its potential in terms of Translation Studies should not be underestimated, as it provides a series of key concepts and guidelines (van Doorslaer *et al.* 2016; Leerssen

2007). First, rather than actual cultural differences, the central issue for authors and translators alike is the construction of ethnotypes, which are fictional (and stereotyped) "rationalizations of cultural difference" (van Doorslaer *et al.* 2016, 3). The role of fictional characterization in building ethnotypes stems from "the (neo-) Aristotelian nature of the idea of 'character' as an instance of [...] 'motivation:' i.e. the narrative predication of behaviour and acts to actorial figures, linking 'what people do' to 'how people are'" (van Doorslaer *et al.* 2016, 3). Another crucial point is that the lack of consciousness in ethnotype-evoking strengthens the ethnotype itself, as the reasons behind it are not questioned. The role of this research is to retrieve the origin of those images and their evolution, to demonstrate that "ethnotypes are ingrained discursive tropes rather than empirical observations" (van Doorslaer *et al.* 2016, 3). The discursive nature of ethnotypes is also proved by their variability in both moral and psychological terms; new ethnotypes "emerge from the need to contradict earlier ones" (van Doorslaer *et al.* 2016, 4). To demonstrate the ideological constructedness of a stereotype, analysis can be deployed in three directions: textual (analysing the discourse built within the text), contextual (looking at its relationship with the real world) and intertextual (following the fictional use of a common place across texts).

The need to study ethnotypes has multiple reasons. Primarily, these representations have existed for an incredibly long time, which demonstrates their importance. Furthermore, since they are an actual challenge for translation practitioners, scholars should not turn a blind eye to them. Finally, their presence poses a series of ideological questions that, if ignored, might go unnoticed by professionals and audiences alike, contributing to the creation of cultural barriers.

There is one last challenge to accept, however, which adds an extra level of complexity to the points explored so far. The nature of the challenge is vaguely anticipated by the term 'imagology' itself. A stereotype can be delivered through linguistic means, but a way to make it even more powerful is to intertwine it with a visual representation.

1.4 Incorporating multimodality in AVT studies

John Bateman notes a jarring contradiction in the way the relationship between text and image is natural in everyday life and communication, but thorny in theoretical studies:

> In many respects, and in many contexts, combining text and images is seen as the most straightforward, the most natural thing in the world. People have been putting textual information and images together for thousands of years [...] "texts" and "images" are generally addressed by very different groups of disciplines and those disciplines often take different views both on just what they are describing and how descriptions should be pursued. (Bateman 2014, 5)

Another crucial aim of this work consists in methodologically retrieving the union between (acted) text and image, in order to acknowledge multimodality, defined by Bateman (2014, 6) as "the investigation of diverse modes of expression and their combination," and by Pérez-González (2014, 185) as "the combination of speaking, writing, visualization and music." Moreover, "[t]he terms *mode* and *modality* designate each type of acoustic and optic meaning-making resources or signs involved in the creation of such composite texts" (Pérez-González 2014, 186) — movies being a suitable example. In fact, movies are audiovisual texts, and audiovisual texts "involve the simultaneous deployment of several sign repertoires (including but not limited to speech or the written language of subtitles, film editing, image, music, colour or perspective)," perceived by the audience simultaneously through "the synchronized use of multiple media" (Pérez-González 2014, 186-187). The concept of multimodality was first introduced by the work of Kress & van Leeuwen (1990) and van Leeuwen & Jewitt (2000).

The combination of different modes of expression results in something more than mere addition since, as explained by Jay Lemke, the presence of more modes multiplies the meaning conveyed (for example, by a film):

> When the resources of multiple semiotic systems are codeployed: 1) each semiotic can contribute componentially to each [...] functional aspect of meaning (e.g. lexical name and figural image to a presentational construct); 2) each can internally cross-modulate meanings across functional aspects

(e.g. alternating point-of-view shots helping to construct a visual-organizational sequence); and 3) functionally specialised meaning resources in one semiotic combine with those for a different function in another semiotic to modulate any aspect of the meaning of the joint construct (e.g. the visual juxtaposition of verbal captions can allow their thematic meanings to interact with the different sizes of two graphs to determine their relative importance. (Lemke 1998, 92)

The complexity of a multimodal text lies in the complementarity and mutual support of its modes, to the point that it is impossible to do without any of them. Indeed, people with sight or hearing impairment (to whom complete access to the multimodal product is precluded) need specific aid in order to be able to fully understand (and enjoy) an audiovisual product (Díaz-Cintas *et al.* 2010).

Nevertheless, the fact of carrying out such a composite task remains largely unacknowledged, since "[w]hen 'reading' a multimodal text, average recipients will normally become only dimly aware of the fact that they are processing information encoded in different modes," to the point that these become "a single unified *gestalt* in perception." Kress *et al.* (2001) and Stöckl (2004) also proved that multimodality does not only concern audiovisual products, as it is also intertwined with the way human communication works—especially for what concerns teaching and learning—and they propose a multimodal approach to communication.

The fact that this process of paramount importance works so smoothly without a conscious effort depends on a human neurological predisposition; in contrast, the role of the researcher is "to meticulously dissect an apparently homogeneous and holistic impression" (Stöckl 2004, 16) to shed some light on the way it works.

If the multimodality of an audiovisual product is so important for its full comprehension, if multimodality is part of the human brain, and if the role of the translator is to deliver a product that can have a function in the target culture—how can TS tackle this issue?

Until not long ago, multimodality was not really a central theme in TS, as its existence was acknowledged but not investigated. In 2002, Frederic Chaume wrote:

Few authors have made a profound study on the peculiarities of the construction of audiovisual texts, of the semiotic interaction that is produced in the simultaneous emissions of text and image, and the repercussions that this has in the process of translation. (Chaume 2002, 3)

Chaume's description points towards multimodality and underlines that not many authors have investigated it. A few years later, a similar idea was expressed by Yves Gambier (2006), who underlined the paradox of studying screen translation without including the non-textual in the corpora. While it would be wrong to imagine this is due to laziness in research, the reason should probably be found in the tools that have so far been available to researchers — bearing in mind that tools like media, languages and technology work as extensions of the human mind and culture (McLuhan 1964). Indeed, while audiovisual communication is inextricably bound to image, which is probably its most important component, research has increasingly concentrated on the verbal element (Díaz-Cintas 2008).

On the side of AVT professionals, the divide between text and image may depend on the fact that the "industry's surveillance of professional audiovisual translation continues to impose the excision of language from other forms of meaning-making (forcing translators to restrict their involvement to the mediation of language)" (Pérez-González 2014, 185). However, with more recent developments in terms of digital technologies, this situation has gradually started to change, which has pushed AVT activities towards a more multimodal and audience-participatory direction (Pérez-González 2014).

Nevertheless, most research on the topic is limited to the textual dimension. According to Ramos Pinto and Mubaraki (2020), the focus on the written mode is especially apparent in corpus-based research (which is today particularly appreciated by TS scholars). Corpora techniques (and technologies) have been focusing on textual analysis. This creates a rift between what the audiovisual product is and the way it is analysed. The authors note that audiovisual translation studies tend to focus either exclusively on text in order to analyse large corpora, or use qualitative (and smaller) case studies to look at a broader range of aspects of the audiovisual product. Some researchers have noticed this space in AVT Studies, and have worked to build multimodal corpora, which is anything but easy since the problem is not just to have the audiovisual material stored there, but also to make it analysable and processable (Allwood 2008).

One example is the *Forlì Corpus of Screen Translation* (*Forlixt 1*), which contains the source and dubbed versions of thirty Italian and German (and a few French) films, and includes both audiovisual material and transcripts (Valentini 2008).

Another corpus is TRACCE (Jiménez Hurtado & Soler Gallego 2013; Jiménez & Seibel 2012), which contains hundreds of movies and audio descriptions. It includes three levels of semantic tagging: "Narrative" (intended as *mise-en-scène*), "Image", and "Grammar"; and, for each of them, a conceptual map of possible ramifications (Jiménez & Seibel 2012, 413-415). The software used was *Taggetti*, specially created for tagging audiovisual products translated through audio-description (developed by Gizer.net and the University of Deusto, Spain), along with its evolution, *Taggetti 2*.

One last example is the *Pavia Corpus of Film Dialogue* (PCFD), a parallel corpus of twenty-four British and American films with their dubbed Italian versions – as well as a small number of movies in Italian as a comparable source. The corpus consists of "orthographic transcriptions of the film lines as they were uttered on screen, segmented and, in the case of the parallel corpus, aligned on a turn-by-turn basis" (Freddi 2013, 495).

While the efforts made in these corpora are certainly remarkable, Ramos Pinto and Mubaraki (2020) emphasise that the amount of resources and labour required in the analysis of the data imposes relative limits to the work of individual researchers, who will be discouraged from attempting such a daring project.

In this sense, inspirational suggestions concerning the study of multimodality have been made by authors who work with multimodal language and translation. In his recounting of the development of multimodality studies, Iedema (2003) points to four key research directions:

1. [Multimodality] is concerned to include in its analyses of representations and give proper recognition to semiotics other than language;
2. [Multimodality] focuses on the relationships between these different semiotics, and on the "division of labour" between them in particular representations;
3. [Multimodality] aims to understand and describe in "phylogenetic" terms the displacement of some semiotics by others (e.g. the displacement of the linguistic by the visual);
4. [Multimodality] links the potential of the different semiotics deployed to how they affect (enable and constrain) interaction and formation of subjectivity. (Iedema 2003, 48)

The second point is crucial. While having text and video recordings is certainly a great step forward in recognising multimodality, storing the two things in parallel might not necessarily reveal much about the connection between the two. It is better to ask the core question: how do textual and non-textual modes combine in order to create something more than a simple sum of the two? This is not a simple question since, as previously mentioned, the modes are perceived simultaneously.

Although her background is not Translation Studies, Pastra (2008) worked towards the implementation of a system capable of making the relationship between modes more visible. She argues that, although "everyday interaction is predominantly multimodal," there is still a "poor understanding of multimodal human behaviour" (Pastra 2008, 299). She attempts to describe "semantic interrelationships between images, language and body movements [...] from a message-formation perspective rather than a communicative goal one" (Pastra 2008, 299), intending to achieve descriptive power and computational applicability in her system. Descriptive power refers to the fact that "the framework should be general enough to describe the interaction between any media pair," while computational applicability means that the framework "should guide the computational modelling of multimedia dialectics as evidenced in multimodal human behaviour" (Pastra 2008, 300). For this purpose, the COSMOROE (CrOSs-Media inteRactiOn rElations) framework was implemented—corpus-based, descriptive, focused on interactions between modes. The relations are built by analogy with figures of speech (e.g. metonymy) and an "attempt to capture the semantic aspects of the message formation process itself" (Pastra 2008, 306). The COSMOROE contains vignettes, crime-scene photographs and travel documentaries — the latter providing the richest data to analyse. Pastra also hypothesises the use of COSMOROE for audiovisual fiction but admits that the interactions in these products may drift apart from the relations established in everyday interactions (better mirrored by travel documentaries). Pastra's framework presents a complex diagram of relations and subrelations.

The main relations are 1) equivalence, present when "the information expressed by the different media is semantically equivalent" (Pastra 2008, 307); 2) complementarity, when "the information expressed in one medium is (an essential or not) complement of the information expressed in another medium (Pastra 2008, 308); 3) independence, when each medium conveys an independent message, regardless of whether the messages are reciprocally coherent or not. These main relations are further divided among subrelations. For example, the equivalence relations change based on whether they are literal or figurative, while the complementary relations are divided into subtypes based on whether the complementarity itself is essential or non-essential to message comprehension. Independence can be a) contradiction, when the messages passing through the modes are opposite to one another b) symbiosis, when "one medium provides some information and the other shows something that is thematically related, but does not refer or complement that information in any way" (Pastra 2008, 313); c) meta-information, if one mode carries "extra information independent from pieces of information expressed by the other media, but [...] inherently related to them" (Pastra 2008, 314).

In order to retrieve this kind of information, the COSMOROE framework relies on multiple annotation systems that, as stated by the author, are demanding "in terms of cognitive effort and time" (Pastra 2008, 319) and might still present cases in which the relation is not necessarily intuitive for the annotators. Nonetheless, COSMOROE is a precious contribution, as it moves a step further in the attempt to answer the question: "what kind of semantic associations take place when humans combine pieces of information from different media in multimodal communication?" (Pastra 2008, 321).

Pastra's work inspired the multimodal analysis carried out by Dicerto (2014; 2018), who built a corpus of multimodal source texts (e.g. adverts, comic strips, web pages, graphs — no videos were included), thus expanding interest in this model in the field of translation. Dicerto edits Pastra's model to make it suitable for her research purposes. Primarily "relations of contradiction are not treated as a sub-type of relations of independence, but as a category of its own whose sub-types coincide with the ones shown by the relation of equivalence" (Dicerto 2014, 79). Moreover, Dicerto attempts to combine Pastra's model with the framework developed by Martinec & Salway (2005), to add "a category identifying a visual-verbal relation in which a textual element is crucial for the recipient to be able to select one of two (or more) meanings associated with a polysemic word/image as the intended interpretation within that context" (Dicerto 2018, 84). In the context of communication studies, Martinec and Salway had developed a system aimed at analysing intermodal relationships based on "the relative status of images and text, and how they relate to one another in terms of logico-semantics" (Martinec & Salway 2005, 337). In particular, they identified the relationships between text and image in terms of the dichotomy between equal and unequal, to understand whether the modes were independent, complementary, or one was subordinate to the other (Martinec & Salway 2005, 349). The merging of these two models implies adding logico-semantic relationships to the (edited) COSMOROE scheme.

The purpose of Dicerto, however, is limited to static multimodal texts and is not entirely descriptive, as she suggests that her model be used by translation trainees aiming to understand the relation between modes in the source text and similarly reproduce them in the target text. Undoubtedly, Dicerto acknowledges the fact that two main obstacles might jeopardise resemblance between source and target text: namely 1) the inability (due to the translator) or the impossibility (due to linguistic or external restrictions) "to reproduce the logical form" (Dicerto 2014, 82) and the relative intermodal relations; 2) differences between source and target culture's "contextual and/or encyclopaedic knowledge to which the textual resources appeal in order to suggest explicatures and implicatures meant to lead the recipient towards a certain interpretation" (Dicerto 2018, 85).

A step closer towards intermodal relations, larger corpora and descriptiveness of source and target text is made by the contributions of Ramos Pinto (2017) and Ramos Pinto and Mubaraki (2020). Despite their focus on subtitling, these works seem particularly relevant to this research. As such, they will be used as a reference in the description of the analysis carried out here. In fact, they retrieve the issue of translating non-standard language and assume a descriptive and corpus-related perspective.

The model implemented in Ramos Pinto (2017) and Ramos Pinto & Mubaraki (2020) has multiple functions. First, it serves to identify the linguistic varieties and the way those were expressed through speech in both source and target text. The subsequent step consists of retrieving the communicative function of the varieties and their relations with other modes. Consequently, it allows the inference of the strategies adopted (based on the product) and the understanding of their impact on the other modes. Finally, hypothesising possible external factors impacting the translation process helps avoid simplistic judgement on the success of a strategy (in line with the purposes of DTS). The model has proven its effectiveness on a large corpus (Ramos Pinto & Mubaraki 2020).[7]

The analysis works on textual, diegetic and sociocultural dimensions. For that concerning the textual dimension, by looking at the target text, Ramos Pinto (2017) identifies two sets of possible strategies: on the one hand, *neutralization strategies*, which can either tend towards discourse standardization or discourse dialectization (Ramos Pinto 2017, 22) (also see paragraph 1.3); on the other hand, *preservation strategies* are possible as well. Among these, the most

---

[7] This article presents an innovative AVT multimodal framework and was a crucial inspiration for this research: I was able to have access to it in advance during my visit to the University of Leeds in 2018, where the authors Sara Ramos Pinto and Aishah Mubaraki worked on AVT and multimodality within the centre for Translation Studies (CTS).

recurrent is probably centralization, "for the cases in which the TT presents a lower frequency of non-standard features (or the choice of more prestigious features/variety in relation to the ST) and can thus be placed closer to the centre of prestige" (Ramos Pinto 2017, 23). Maintenance and decentralization are also possible, "respectively [for] cases in which the TT presents a similar or higher frequency of non-standard features in relation to the ST" (Ramos Pinto 2017, 23).

The research into the diegetic dimension has the purpose of finding out the way "non-standard varieties' of communicative meaning and diegetic functions are constructed in an audiovisual context" (Ramos Pinto 2017, 23). In particular, the author envisions three main modes participating in meaning-making: the *spoken mode*, the *mise-en-scene mode* and the *subtitles mode*. These contribute to the construction of meaning in both source and target text. Within the spoken mode, the objective should be to look at how the non-standard variety was created, namely through accent (see paragraph 1.3) and/or vocabulary/morphosyntax. The *mise-en-scene* mode might be subdivided into costume and make-up, figure behaviour and setting.

In this sense, it is crucial to note that selecting the 'portions' for the analysis presents several issues: as mentioned earlier, in a multimodal product all the modes are processed simultaneously, and separating them is a counter-intuitive effort. In addition, separating also means deliberately selecting from a product that exists by virtue of its entirety. That is why, in suggesting a selection of subcategories for each mode, Ramos Pinto (2017, 24) suggests that "after considering the elements more directly participating in the construction of the character's profile," adding more categories might be considered.

Once the modes and their subcategories are outlined, the subsequent step is to distinguish whether these reciprocally establish relations of contradiction or confirmation. Contradiction is two modes expressing opposed meanings (Pastra 2008; Ramos Pinto 2017). If the non-standard variety is used in contradiction with the other modes, the function of language is to create a distance between the character who is speaking and those around them (which can have various purposes depending on the broader plot). A relation of confirmation is established when the meanings expressed by each mode comply with the character's profile. If this happens,

> "the presence of the non-standard variety leads to the identification of the characters as part of a regional/social group [...] introducing authenticity and [...] establishing interpersonal relationships of solidarity (with characters who are part of the same group) or power (with characters who are not part of the same group." (Ramos Pinto 2017, 24)

The relation of confirmation is further subdivided in Ramos Pinto & Mubaraki (2020), who adds the relation of complementarity, retrieving Pastra's (2008) category. After looking at the ST, the construction of meaning in the TT also needs thorough analysis, bearing in mind that the TT also contains the subtitles mode, which needs to be added to the equation and divided between vocabulary/morpho-syntax and graphic features. Indeed, changes in the intermodal relationships within the TT help to understand whether the ST relationships have been kept, modified, or cancelled. In turn, intersecting strategies and TT relations might shed light on the "possible impact of the strategy and procedures adopted in preserving or altering the intermodal relations established and, consequently, the diegetic functions they support" (Ramos Pinto 2017, 26).

Lastly, the function of the sociocultural dimension is to "contextualize the identified strategies within the broader cultural context" (Ramos Pinto 2017, 29). This kind of evaluation will prevent the researcher from formulating uninformed judgements concerning the quality of the product or the success of the strategies. For this purpose, a list of key factors is compiled (but left open for more). The ideological context has a pivotal role, as it determines whether the translator's creativity is encouraged or repressed. Another element to consider is the differences between source and target cultures—the more distant these are, the more difficult it will be to reproduce the same linguistic varieties and intermodal relations. The status granted to AVT and its agents are also fundamental: is the translator supposed to be creative or will deviation be interpreted as a mistake? In this sense, the translator's working conditions cannot be ruled out: little recognition, tight deadlines and low pay might influence the way a translation is handled. The expected audience of an AV product also influences the translator's choices, as a product that is meant to be sold has to respond to its clients' needs and expectations. Analogously, the target product's function within its culture (see paragraph 1.1) will trigger certain expectations related to innovative solutions — in particular, translations accepted by the target culture as innovative tend to display a greater number of non-standard features (Ramos Pinto 2010).

Accepting the challenge of multimodality in audiovisual translation is to move in territory only partly charted so far. Although it is increasingly being explored and acknowledged, it does not have fixed paths yet — which makes the challenge more arduous but definitely worth the endeavours.

Chapter 2
A framework for corpus-based, multimodal analysis of language variation in source and target films

2.1 Inside the source text I: language, power and variation.

To problematize the relationships between language(s) and power means to problematize the monolithic equation 'one land, one people, one language,' which requires some degree of prescriptivism, with "a normative enterprise, dictating what constitutes correct language use" (Wasow 2001, 295). The notion of correctness in a language is inextricably linked to a comparison between what language is and what it should be, therefore to the positing of a standard. However, concerning English, what has been considered the standard is a variety that was deliberately attributed a major social prestige within a community of speakers (Crystal 2004). This implies that its prestige is neither natural nor innate: it is bound to a specific time and to a specific group of people. Nevertheless, the speakers of that variety are considered the gatekeepers of correct language, and all others should adhere to that standard to approximate correctness (Milroy 2002, 22). This conviction is the joining link between standard and standardization, which is more closely related to sectors like education, government, and administration (Mesthrie 2000, 21). Standardization implies choosing a historically and geographically specific variety and de-historicising and de-localising it, to transform it into an abstract universal. Once its situatedness is removed, it can be taken as the most desirable linguistic attainment, which prompts the misleading assumption that any language could exist "in a vacuum" (Macedo *et al.* 2003; 2016, 31). Despite its extremely limited spread (Crystal 2012, 505-518), standard English is still considered the ideal achievement for native and non-native speakers alike. It is, however, no more than a myth, a "magical and powerful" construct, able to "motivate social behaviors and actions which would be otherwise contrary to logic or reason" (Lippi-Green 1997, 41).

It is not easy to replace the concept of a standard, especially since it is supported by authoritative bodies and figures, and that is where the role of ideology intertwines with language-related attitudes and behaviours. Norman Fairclough has laid out a specifically linguistic viewpoint on power and ideology, stemming from the assumption that "the exercise of power, in modern society, is increasingly achieved through ideology, and more particularly through the ideological workings of language" (Fairclough 1989, 2).

Fairclough retrieves Foucault's orders of discourse, defining them as "clustering sets or networks" of "underlying conventions" (Fairclough 1989, 28) that direct a discourse. Orders of discourse organise the validity of discourses hierarchically in different settings (Fairclough 1989, 29-30). However, as stated by Foucault himself, power is omnipresent, as it "is produced at every instant, at every point, or moreover in every relation between one point and another. Power is everywhere: not that it engulfs everything, but that it comes from everywhere" (Foucault 1991, 122). Thus, forms of resistance must be taken into consideration, too: not only social and political but also linguistic ones. An example of these is what Halliday calls "anti-societies" and "anti-languages." An anti-society is created and lives as a conscious act of resistance, as it "is set up within another society as a conscious alternative to it. It is a mode of resistance, resistance which may take the form either of passive symbiosis or of active hostility and even destruction" (Halliday 1978, 164). Anti-languages are the mode of linguistic expression of such societies — one typical example being the languages of the underworld. These have specific features such as re-lexicalization and over-lexicalization. What makes anti-languages worth analysing for linguists is that "the phenomenon of the antilanguage throws light on the difficult concept of social dialect, by providing an opposite pole, the second of two idealized extremes to which we can relate the facts as we actually find them" (Halliday 1978, 178). By positioning itself as the antipodal opposite of mainstream language, an anti-language reveals the existence of a far more complex spectrum of languages in society, which challenges the monolithic idea of a national language and a nation as a place where a specific language—and only that language—is spoken. Halliday envisions two idealized societies positioned at the antipodes of a spectrum: on the one hand, a monolithic society where only one language is spoken (idealized thesis), on the other hand, a polarized society where only a main language and an anti-language—completely different from each other—are spoken (idealized antithesis). Reality is usually somewhere on the continuum between these two extremes:

> A nonstandard dialect that is consciously used for strategic purposes, defensively to maintain a particular social reality or offensively for resistance and protest, lies further in the direction of an antilanguage; this is what we know as a "ghetto language." (Halliday 1978, 178-179).

In Halliday's view, those commonly referred to as "non-standard" dialects are less dichotomized versions of the more extreme anti-languages and, as such, have a certain distance from the ideal unifying language represented by the standard.

Moving towards the antithesis, the relationship between the two languages becomes more conflictual, where dominant vs. ghetto language is a sharper social and linguistic division compared to standard vs. non-standard language. A number of examples have been provided for the language along the anti-line: the language of the underworld is an extreme form of anti-language. African-American vernacular English is an example of non-standard language, less extreme than the underworld language: "consciously used for strategic purposes, defensively to maintain a particular social reality or offensively for resistance and protest [it] was born and developed as a ghetto-language" (Halliday 1978, 179; Kochman 1972). Most vernacular subvarieties of Chicano English, the ones generally associated with gangs, are placed towards the anti-language end of the continuum, and their prominence derives from the mediated representations of their speakers (Fought 2003, 6-7).

Halliday's depiction of language and society from a perspective that takes variation and conflict into account is an ideal starting point for exploring the theme of language variation while taking the issue of power imbalance into account. It must be remembered that language variation is an unescapable reality, one of the "linguistic facts of life" affirmed by Rosina Lippi-Green (1997, 25-29). In her words:

> Spoken language varies for every speaker in terms of speech sounds, sound patterns, word and sentence structure, intonation, and meaning, from utterance to utterance. [...] There are three sources of variation in language: first, language-internal pressures, arising in part from the mechanics of production and perception; second, language-external influences on language, as a social behavior subject to normative and other formative social pressures; and third, variation arising from language as a creative vehicle of free expression. These forces can and do function in tandem [...] (Lippi-Green 1997, 25).

The study of language variation across different social classes was first introduced by William Labov (1966; 1972; 1997) with an analysis of the way pronunciation varied among New Yorkers working in department stores of three price ranges, from the most expensive to the cheapest. He assumed that this would imply a different social class of customers and an attempt to meet certain linguistic expectations on the side of the personnel (Labov 1997, 170). Labov's work[8] is restricted by all the limits of a very first attempt in this direction (Mesthrie 2000, 97), but was a fundamental contribution to sociolinguistics, as it set forth a series of pivotal variables in a range of language-related research topics, from education to media representation.

Furthermore, an inverse reading of Labov's findings is that it is possible to infer the social positioning of a person by the way s/he speaks. In this sense, it is worth noting that Labov (1972) also underlined the role of mediated representation of language. His analysis revealed the existence of three types of variables showing social variation: indicators, markers and stereotypes. Indicators are subtle features, quite hard to notice for non-trained speakers, which do not trigger specific reactions in the listeners, while markers are the most prominent signals of a specific social position — most

---

[8] His results were further confirmed from across the ocean by Peter Trudgill's research into social variation in a much smaller and closed environment, the city of Norwich (1974). He considered aspects of grammar, as well as pronunciation.

listeners can gather social information from them, even when the speaker displays them unconsciously. Stereotypes are conscious characterizations of a certain group most widely acknowledged by outsiders, who often learn them from a caricatured media portrayal. Therefore, stereotypes tend to be most hastily judged and stigmatized.

While language variation has multiple causes and forms, for the purpose of this research two types of dialect are especially relevant. The first one is sociolect or social dialect, a variety "determined by social environments or associated with a particular social group" (Durrell 2004, 201). This definition has something in common with the essence of Chicano English, as Chicanos may be seen as a specific social group. Although the terms "sociolect" and "social dialect" can be used to identify a distinctive dialect emerging from any social feature that does not depend (or exclusively depend) on geographical position, it is "most often used in connection with variation linked to social class" (Durrell 2004, 201). In the English-speaking world, social class may determine a substantial sociolectal variation, which can be an index of a broader situation of social injustice and inequality. Higher classes will speak a variety that approximates the standard, as previously discussed, thus attaining a perceived prestige that lower-class varieties do not have. However, especially in more recent times, the division in social classes might not always apply, proving too rigid when compared to contemporary society. That is why a valid alternative to social class is the concept of a "social network," intended not in the sense of social media but as social organization and relationships: "[s]ocial class is fundamentally a concept designed to elucidate large-scale social, political, and economic structures and processes, whereas social network relates to the community and interpersonal level of social organization" (Milroy & Milroy 1992, 2).

The second type of dialect worth considering shows the inherent level of complexity within a society. It was first noted by Labov during his aforementioned analysis of New Yorkers, in particular when he noted the fact that Puerto Ricans seemed to have "patterns of consonant cluster simplification which are different from those of both black and white New Yorkers" (Labov 1972, 118). What

Labov found is now called an ethnolect. Clyne defines ethnolects as "varieties of a language that mark speakers as members of ethnic groups who originally used another language" (2000, 86). But what does ethnicity mean? Is it possible to take such a concept for granted?

As underlined by Fought (2006), providing an exhaustive definition of ethnicity is not an easy task, even when starting from the currently accepted idea that ethnicity is a social construction. Up to the present day, it has been impossible "to arrive at a set of quantifiable morphological and physiological features whereby we can unequivocally compartmentalize all human beings into a small array of discrete races" (Zelinsky 2001, 8). This proves that there is no such thing as a biological division among human beings; nor is there any biological justification for racism. However, this does not suddenly wipe away centuries of racial clashes and discrimination influencing the way ethnicity is perceived in the public imagery. In the words of the American National Research Council:

> The concepts of race and ethnicity are social realities because they are deeply rooted in the consciousness of individuals and groups, and because they are firmly fixed in our society's institutional life. Further, these concepts are sustained by several mechanisms that frame the categories of race and ethnicity in terms of kinship and descent, group intermarriage and reproduction, distinctive geographical location and residence, specification in law and policies, discrimination and prejudice, and self-identification. (Smelser *et al.* 2001).

There have been several attempts to define ethnicity, ethnic groups and race, some of which are worth mentioning here. One is Cohen's, according to whom ethnicity is "a set of descent-based cultural identifiers used to assign persons to groupings that expand and contract in inverse relation to the scale of inclusiveness and exclusiveness of the membership" (Cohen 1978, 387). Such a definition is not too distant from Barth's list of the features that identify an ethnic group:

1. Is largely biologically self-perpetuating
2. Shares fundamental cultural values, realized in overt unity in cultural forms
3. Makes up a field of communication and interaction

4. Has membership which identifies itself, and is identified by others, as constituting a category distinguishable from other categories of the same order. (Barth 1969, 10-11).

In her efforts to define the concepts of ethnicity, ethnic group, and race, Fought explains that it is fundamental to look at *"both self-identification and the perceptions and attitudes of others"* (author's italics), (2006, 6). Although it is vital for individuals to recognise themselves as belonging to a certain group, it is also true that no one can "be completely free of the views and attitudes of others in the society" (Fought 2006, 6), which most often happen to depend on phenotypes.

With these landmarks in mind, it is possible to go back to the definition of ethnolect and critically understand the way ethnicity, race and language intersect. Language has enormous power in marking one's belonging and influencing the way an individual is perceived. This means that the participation of language within the broader framework of identity is not secondary.

Identity is in fact a very complex matter where, apart from ethnicity and race, other features, such as social class/profession, gender, sexual orientation and territorial belonging, all play roles in different ways at different times. Language speaks for itself but also accounts for the self-expression and the presentation of many other aspects of identity, as stated by Le Page and Tabouret-Keller when proposing linguistic behaviours as "acts of identity" (1985, 14). Since language is such a pivotal part but also an invaluable instrument for identity construction (Lippi-Green 1997, 30), it should not be surprising that several linguistic resources developed to enable humans to both express and identify those identities. Fought (2006, 21-23) gathered some of the most relevant, which are hereby summarized:

- A *heritage language* is the result of a life-long commitment to the preservation of one's origin — learning it and keeping it alive by using it. The heritage language immediately identifies the speaker as a member of a certain group.
- *Code-switching.* While many will forget how to speak their heritage language or will grow up without learning it, it is

possible at all levels of competence to display belonging by using a few words. This allows showing attachment to heritage but also an embracement of a more complex identity (code-switching will be explained in better detail in the following pages).
- Specific linguistic features are "a key element in the indexing and reproduction of ethnic identity, just as they are for other aspects of identity, such as gender or social class" (Fought 2006, 22). They can be anything from phonology to lexico-grammar.
- Suprasegmental features. However close to standard a speaker is in their phonology and grammar, suprasegmental traits — such as a more syllable- or stress-timed intonation — often actually reveal ethnic belonging.
- Discourse features, intended as pragmatic aspects of communication (e.g. turn-taking) can also be linked to specific ethnic groups.
- Using a borrowed variety, which is not part of the speaker's heritage, but serves them to construct items such as masculinity (Chun 2001), or belonging to a peer group (Franceschi 2014).

From the ideological point of view, however, using the term ethnolect entails some issues. First, identifying non-whiteness with ethnicity might implicitly mean accepting the idea that white dialects are not ethnic, which is an ethnocentric view. This is especially dangerous in places like the United States, where discriminatory practices often pass through language differences:

> "The designation "ethnolect" can be part of a more insidious practice. In the dominant discourse of American dialectology, the white Anglo variety is considered a regional dialect, while African American and Latino varieties are considered ethnic dialects [...] the dichotomy between regional and ethnic varieties and the lack of attention to regional varieties of African American and Latino speech underscores a deterritorializing discourse of subordinated racial groups" (Eckert 2008, 27).

In this sense, another implication of talking about ethnic dialects might be to (more or less consciously) consider regional dialects of white English, while neglecting regional differences in what are considered as ethnic varieties. Moreover, while in nations like the United States ethnic heritage might significantly influence speech, it might not be as relevant in other areas of the world (Le Page; Reaser 2004; Tabouret-Keller 1985; Walker & Meyerhoff 2006). It is also essential to bear in mind that an ethnic group cannot be considered a monolithic and uniform group with immutable features, whose members (each and all of them) constantly feel the same about their identity. Indeed, an ethnic community as a whole has fading boundaries: it changes and evolves through time; it has members who perceive their affiliation in different ways; and the same person might modify his/her perception of belonging (and consequently their linguistic behaviour) according to context (Fought 2006, 16-17, 20; Schiffrin 1994, 197; Zelinsky 2001, 44;). Nevertheless, it must not be forgotten that the perception of ethnicity has a great impact on the way people depict themselves and others, since "race as something collectively perceived, as a social construct, far outweighs its dubious validity as a biological hypothesis" (Zelinsky 2001, 9). That is why, instead of completely dismissing the concept of ethnicity when considering language, it may be worth making an effort to problematize it as part of a more complex identity, made of several layers that do not necessarily act at the same time or live peacefully with each other. Indeed, identity is a repertoire that one can draw from in different ways, according to factors such as context, communicative strategies or interlocutors:

> Speakers may heighten or diminish linguistic displays that index various aspects of their identities according to the context of an utterance and the specific goals they are trying to achieve [...] "repertoire of identity," in which any of a multiplicity of identities may be fronted at a particular moment. [...] speakers may index a polyphonous, multilayered identity by using linguistic variables with indexical associations to more than one social category. (Barrett 1999, 318).

The process of selection is extremely dynamic, not necessarily (or completely) conscious, and it can be symptomatic of power imbalance when generated by more or less interiorized social pressure. Identity, and all the linguistic fragments that contribute to the construction and self-construction of each person and community, cannot be fixed — but they do exist in their social deployment. This is evident in the way any individual is judged and classified according to categories such as gender, ethnicity, nationality, religion or social class. In the realm of interpersonal relationships, perception can be heavier than reality.

All this must be taken into account, and should be carefully considered when approaching the study of a specific linguistic group, and Chicanos are no exception. In fact, Chicano English is a variety that depends on factors such as social class and ethnicity. However, it was also generated as an ultimate consequence of language contact. Language variation and contact can overlap when a language varies in a bilingual or multilingual community, where code-switching and code-mixing can easily happen. Traditionally, code-mixing was defined as the alternation of languages within a sentence, while code-switching is the alternation of languages between sentences (Winford 2003, 105). However, it is not always easy to draw a line between the two, and that is why some scholars tend to avoid the dichotomy or to opt for one all-encompassing definition, for example, see Matras 2009, 109.

Through a series of studies and experimentations on the topic (Giles 1973; Giles *et al.* 1991; Giles & Powesland 1975; Soliz & Giles 1987), Giles showed that a bilingual speaker might change the way they speak according to their interlocutor, and called this process speech (or later communication) accommodation. Accommodation might trigger two procedures: one is convergence, the attempt to modify one's speech to make it similar to the interlocutor's; the other is divergence, which consists in differentiating one's speech from the interlocutor's. Both are usually aimed at specific communicative and social effects, respectively to reduce or to emphasise the social distance between the participants in a communicative event. However, accommodation does not happen in a deterministic way and is not necessarily perceived according to the general principle that convergence equals positive, and divergence equals negative.

Other research in the field of language choice concentrated on the habitual use of two (or more) available languages. While a multilingual speaker can potentially resort to any language at any time, the research found that a speaker will tend to attribute to each language a different use, which is considered proper for the specific interlocutor, occasion and topic (Fishman 1972). Thus, "proper" is what meets "widespread sociocultural norms and expectations" (Fishman 1972, 441). That is how each language in a bilingual or multilingual community becomes proper to a specific domain. A domain is "defined [...] in terms of institutional contexts and their congruent behavioral co-occurrences [...] major clusters of interaction [...] multilingual settings and [...] interlocutors" (Fishman 1972, 441). Each domain consists of these elements, whose combination is recurrent in a specific society. Family, education, workplace, peer interaction, public and political communication are all valid domain examples.

The theory of domains, however, should not obscure the fact that code-switching may also depend on a personal choice bound to specific aims of the speaker, which is to say that code-switching can indeed work as a communicative strategy. For example, an interaction can switch when the participants find out they belong to the same ethnolinguistic group, to create a social bond based on the shared background, to then switch back to a more general/formal variety as soon as an "external" participant joins the conversation (Myers-Scotton 1993, 88). This happens in the analysed film *Blood In Blood Out* (1993) when the white Chicano Miklo reveals his origin to another Chicano by speaking Spanish, and a Spanish-only conversation follows (*Blood In Blood Out* 1993, 31.44-32.12).

A switch can also take place within a communicative event based on the general meaning attributed to a specific language. For example, if in a bilingual community a language is associated with authoritativeness, a switch to it can be used as a way to end an argument (Gal 1979, 113). The switch can also be an unmarked choice when the aim of using more languages at the same time lies precisely in their co-existence as a sign of dual identity (Myers-Scotton 1993, 118-119). Sometimes, however, code-switching can purposely go against expectations, with the specific purpose of inviting the interlocutors to go beyond the social protocol and express their true selves (Myers-Scotton 1993, 131).

Gumperz (1982) attempted to summarize all of the possible functions of code-switching in conversation, intended both as switch and mix (see the previous distinction). The first function is that of reported speech (Gumperz 1982, 75-76), which can convey a message with a higher level of authenticity — although the speaker can also decide to translate the utterance for reasons of clarity (Gumperz 1982, 82). A second function identified by Gumperz (1982, 77) is addressee specification when the mixed utterance is aimed at involving a speaker of the mixed language or at excluding someone who will not understand it. Gumperz also talks about interjection (1982) when the switch is used as a sentence-fille, which is especially recurrent in Chicano gangster films (Renna 2017, 2018, 2019). Reiteration is the fourth function and consists in repeating the same message in more languages to make sure it is understood by all of the interlocutors. Message qualification serves to qualify constructions "such as sentence and verb complements or predicates following a copula" (Gumperz 1982, 79). The sixth function is that of marking personalization versus objectivization. In this case, one language represents something closer to the speaker (and the hearer) while the others probably convey a minor involvement. Thus, the switch can mark the difference between "talk about action and talk as action, the degree of speaker involvement in, or distance from, a message, whether a statement reflects personal opinion or knowledge, whether it refers to specific instances or has the authority of generally known fact" (Gumperz 1982, 80).

2.2 Inside the source text II: defining Chicano English

English has not always been the language spoken in the area now known as the United States as the territory was affected by the settler colonization phenomenon, which swept away most of the native language and their speakers (Saraceni 2015). For that matter, English is by no means the official language in the federal constitution, while it has been declared so in several states.[9] However

---

[9] The US Constitution, despite some attempts in the opposite direction, does not establish an official language at a federal level, see http://constitutionus.com/, accessed April 29, 2021, while 32 states decided to select English as their official

recently it might have arrived, it is now considered an acceptable standard to be taught and learned.

The current US demographic configuration is the result of subsequent (and still ongoing) waves of migration (Acuña 2011). From a linguistic point of view, this implies a multi-layered linguistic landscape that, according to the US Census Bureau, can boast "at least 350 languages spoken in US homes."[10] Out of a total population above 5 years of age, counting about two hundred and ninety-one million people, slightly more than sixty million speak another language.[11] Such a condition naturally makes language contact among different communities likely. It might be worth spending a few words on the specification: "at least three hundred and fifty languages spoken in US homes." The word home might seem irrelevant but is important to understand the issue of language(s) in the country. Homes are where other languages can be spoken, as they are usually cut off from any other context. On an institutional level, Macedo *et al.* underline that "even without a rigid policy, the United States has managed to achieve such a high level of monolingualism." According to their analysis, despite the public celebration of diversity, the US has implemented "a covert assimilationist policy," enforced through "periodic assaults on languages other than English" operated by public institutions and bodies such as "media, educational institutions, and government agencies" (Macedo *et al.* 2003, 23).

In particular, people of Mexican origin have lived in the United States since the aftermath of the Mexican American war of 1848, which led to the US acquisition of today's Arizona, California, Colorado, Nevada, New Mexico and Texas (Penfield & Ornstein-Galicia 1985, 1).[12] The languages of the two groups have come into

---

(or one of the official) language: https://www.wnd.com/2018/01/32-states-make-english-official-language/. Accessed April 29, 2021.

[10] The data were released in 2015 by the US Census Bureau. https://www.census.gov/newsroom/press-releases/2015/cb15-185.html. Accessed April 29, 2021.

[11] The spreadsheets with detailed information are available on the US Census Bureau website: https://www.census.gov/data/tables/2013/demo/2009-2013-lang-tables.html. Accessed April 29, 2021.

[12] The history of Chicanos in the US may provide useful insights on their language and current condition. Treating it here, however, would lead the argumentation

variable degrees of contact throughout the US, especially in the areas that used to belong to Mexico and along the borderlands now separating the two states. What is now called Chicano English is the result of this contact:

> Chicano English [...] is a contact dialect, one that emerged from the setting [...] in which two languages, English and Spanish, were present. [People of Mexican origin] spoke a non-native variety which included phonological, syntactic and semantic patterns from their first language, in this case Spanish. But the children of these immigrants generally grew up using both Spanish and English (possibly in different settings or with different people). As the community began to stabilize, so did a new dialect of English. (Fought 2003, 14).

Chicano English (henceforth CE) was originally born as an interlanguage, but it does not seem to be an intermediate step in a shift from Spanish to English, in which case it would have been most likely for the former language to disappear within a few generations. Conversely, Chicano English developed and stabilized into an independent and distinctive language with its own native speakers:

> Chicano English is an ethnic dialect that children acquire as they acquire English in the barrio or other ethnic social setting during their language acquisition period. Chicano English is to be distinguished from the English of the second-language learners [...] Thus defined, Chicano English is spoken only by native English speakers. (Santa Ana 1993, 15).

Santa Ana's words mean that CE is a variety of English in its own right. In fact, with its persistence in time (Metcalf 1979; Penfield & Ornstein-Galicia 1984) it has proved to be an "autonomous social dialect with distinct characteristics passed on by mutual processes of linguistic transmission" (Godinez 1981, 45). In this sense, it seems close to the definition of the aforementioned "sociolect," which is a variety "determined by social environments or associated with a particular social group" (Durrell 2004, 201). Furthermore, given its inextricable link to a specific national group, it can also be linked to the definition of ethnolect, intended as "varieties

---

adrift. A particularly influential work, which served as a crucial reference here, is Rodolfo Acuña's *Occupied America: a History of Chicanos* (2011).

of a language that mark speakers as members of ethnic groups who originally used another language or distinctive variety" (Clyne 2000, 86). However, it is worth remembering that the ethnolect label for languages like Chicano English can be counterproductive, since ethnolects and minority dialects in general often tend to be "reified," treated "as a fixed rather than a fluid entity," whose identity is "compartmentalized, allowing one to think of an ethnolect as a discrete system indexical of ethnicity alone" (Eckert 2008, 26).

In this sense, it is important to stress once again that it is spoken by native English speakers, an aspect confuting the idea that the peculiar features of Chicano English are a consequence of an incomplete acquisition of English in people fundamentally classed as *hispanohablantes*. Chicano students have been classified as "LEP" (Limited English Proficient) because the features of Chicano English are mistaken for the interference of Spanish (Fought 2003, 4). Bilingualism among Chicanos only depends on one's personal background. From a linguistic point of view, it is impossible to distinguish a bilingual Chicano English speaker from a monolingual one, the same way it would be impossible to know if someone knows a second language by just hearing them speaking their native idiom (Fought 2003).

Based on similar assumptions, another myth about Chicano English is that it is basically the same as Spanglish, which is to say the act of code-switching between English and Spanish. Indeed, while code-switching is among the typical competencies of a Chicano English speaker, "it is a separate phenomenon from Chicano English and should not be confused with it" (Fought 2003, 5-6). Chicano English speakers, in fact, do not need to resort to Spanish, and can definitely live without code-switching. When they do use Spanish, it is mainly to achieve a specific communicative purpose. As Gumperz (1982) puts it, the function of the switch can be interjection or personalization versus objectivization. With reference to the Latino communities in the United States, Poplack (1980, 589) talks about emblematic switches, aimed at stressing one's belonging to a certain community. To activate this kind of switch, it is not necessary to be bilingual, as it generally requires a rather limited set of emblematic words.

Another myth about Chicano English, which is also an integral part of the cinematic use of this variety, is "a tendency for those outside the community to associate Chicano English, particularly when it falls at the more non-standard end of the continuum, with gang members" (Fought 2003, 6). While being a member of a gang is a reality within the Chicano communities, it is misleading and simply wrong to equate this variety with participation in criminal activities. Such a conviction derives from the recurring use of this variety to depict members of a gang in the media—neglecting all other kinds of people belonging to the Chicano community.

Chicano English is not a monolithic variety spoken in the same way across the community. For example, belonging to a gang or the desire to dissociate oneself from the local gangs can determine specific linguistic choices, but accepting any aprioristic assumption can result in the fostering of stereotypes (Fought 2003, 7).

It is worth noting that differences among CE speakers can stem from various factors. One is certainly geography, as Chicanos are spread across the whole southwest of the US, but also in other areas of the nation, and their speech can receive different inputs from the other varieties locally available. Another factor is the consistency of contact with speakers of the local Anglo/white variety of English, as well as with speakers of other minority Englishes (e.g. AAVE). In this sense, Santa Ana (1993), drawing from Baugh (1983), has distinguished among more or less vernacular sub-varieties of CE according to their markedness in comparison to the white varieties, explaining it in terms of contact between Chicanos and Anglos:

> Vernacular Chicano English (VCE) is the spoken dialect of Chicano speakers of English who have minimum contact with non-Chicanos in their daily communicative life. [...] There is no lack of second- and third-generation Chicanos who live their lives in major US cities without significant contact with non-Chicanos. The rural isolation in turn-of-the-century Texano, New Mexican Hispano, and Californio communities has been replaced by urban segregation in barrios that are overwhelmingly Chicano. (Santa Ana 1993, 25).

It is important to specify that the variety of CE that will be taken into consideration here is the one spoken in California and, more specifically, in Los Angeles—a multilingual and multicultural metropolis where the huge Latino community coexists with the white majority, other minorities (e.g. African Americans), and a great number of migrant communities (Fought 2003, 12-13). The choice is driven by the fact that several movies starring CE speakers (and all the movies included in this research) are set in Los Angeles—East Los Angeles, more precisely. What follows is a brief description of the main features of this variety that guided my analysis.

Phonology

Phonology, along with more suprasegmental features like intonation and stress patterns, is the most prominent trait of CE, differentiating it from the local variety spoken by Anglo Californians. CE has its own phonology that, although surely related to its Spanish heritage, should not be mistaken for a Spanish accent. Indeed, "[m]any elements of CE phonology do reflect the influence of Spanish, but some may come from contact with other dialects" (Fought 2003, 63).

Santa Ana (1991, 139-184) was among the first to explore vowel reduction in CE speakers, and he found a less frequent occurrence of this trait in CE speakers than in their white counterparts. The result was later confirmed by Fought (2003, 64), who reports that the most common examples in her field study are *together* realized as [tʰugɛðɚ] and *because* realized as [bikəz], where Anglo speakers are more likely to replace the first vowel with a reduced sound such as [ɨ].

Both authors (Fought 2003; Santa Ana 1991;) also noted a recurring lack of glides, in particular for the high vowels realized as [ij] and [uw] by the Anglo speakers and, although less frequently, for [ej] and [ow]. Another distinctive feature is the tense realization of [ɪ], pronounced as [i], but this particular trait in CE speakers is very limited, and the occurrences were noted by Fought (2003, 65) in the realization of the gerund morpheme *-ing*. This feature seems to be more prominent in non-native speakers of Mexican origin. As far as CE speakers are concerned, only those of more vernacular subvarieties seem to have a realization of [ɪ] that is slightly more tense in other positions (apart from the -*ing* suffix). There is also a tendency to front the low back vowel [ɑ], realising it as [a] (e.g. *talk* realized as [tʰak]). The fronting of the vowel /u/ seems to be common in young Californian CE speakers (Fought 1999, 11) and, as will later be explained in more detail, it might derive from contact with the local Anglo dialect (Fought 2003).

Regarding consonants, CE displays a feature that is typical of AAVE but is also found in several varieties of English in the world, which is the replacement of apico-dental fricatives [θ] and [ð] with the apico-dental stops [t̪] and [d̪] respectively. Indeed, an Anglo-like realization of the apico-dental fricatives is so uncommon that Jenkins (2000, 137), in her attempt to find a common grammar of English as a Lingua Franca, excluded their realization from the group of consonants deemed as necessary for mutual understanding. According to Mendoza-Denton's study of female gangsters (2008), this trait has come to be seen as a symbol of toughness in Northern California. Examples of this phenomenon are *something* realized as [səmt̪n] and *then* realized as [d̪ɛn] (Fought 2003, 68). Moreover, CE displays a tendency to consonant cluster reduction (like AAVE; Fought 2003; Thomas 2007;). The reduction can involve a final *t* or *d* in a cluster (Santa Ana 1996, 75-138) but also a whole cluster (e.g. *hardware*), realized as [hɑwɚ]). According to Santa Ana, this feature shows a certain level of resistance to the assimilation of CE into the "nonethnic regional dialect." It might be worth noting that deletion of final consonants, even when these are not part of a cluster (e.g. *met some* realized as [mɛsəm]), is extremely common in CE: it is even possible to have "four or five final consonants in a row" (Fought 2003, 69) left unpronounced, e.g. *wouldn't get lost* realized as [wʊn gjɛ las].

Suprasegmental traits
Perhaps even more than single phonetic features, what makes CE recognisable in terms of sound is its suprasegmental traits. Often considered a sign of lacking command of English (González 1984, 39), they were studied to a lesser extent by the linguists investigating the language of Chicanos. Santa Ana (1991) noted that, when it comes to rhythm, CE seems to tend towards syllable-timing — like

Spanish — while American English is stress-timed. It is oversimplifying, however, to think that a language is either stress-timed or syllable-timed: it is better to imagine those two extremes as the poles in a continuum, along which languages and dialects can be positioned.[13] In fact, the stress shifting happens more often and in a more noticeable way in non-native English speakers of Mexican origin, who tend to replicate the syllable-timing of their native language into English. CE is placed somewhere in between the two and, among the dialects of English, it is one of the most syllable-timed (Fought 2003, 72).

Just like music, CE has a distinctive rhythm, but also a specific melody. Indeed, intonation patterns carry the influence of Mexican Spanish, which differs from peninsular Spanish. Matluck (1952) was probably the first to notice and name the peculiar intonation pattern of Mexican Spanish, which he called the "circumflex" intonation pattern (Matluck 1952, 119). The finding was later confirmed with more quantitative examples by Penfield & Ornstein-Galicia (1984, 37-39). In fact, while Anglo English declaratives have a descending contour, Mexican Spanish and CE ones (even more than peninsular Spanish) tend to have a rise-and-fall pattern, or sometimes a higher end. Such an ascending intonation is associated with questions or segments of sentences in most dialects of American English, and this is probably why this trait is perceived as a signal of non-standardness, and often used in caricatured reproductions of Mexican speakers, along with other forms of altered and exaggerated speech (Fought 2003; Hill 1993). Such a musical pattern, distinguished from the one of peninsular Spanish, is a unique bequest of Nahuatl, one of the Uto-Aztecan languages spoken in the area since before the arrival of European colonizers in the Americas (Matluck 1952, 119).

---

[13] A significant contribution to the deepening of the discourse on stress patterns came from the development of the Pairwise Variability Index (PVI), which allows the quantifying of rhythm in languages, so as to place them along a continuum going from the most stress-timed to the most syllable-timed (Nolan 2009).

Morpho-syntax

Chicanos can speak a less vernacular variety of CE, in which case their morpho-syntax will tend to follow the general pattern of white American English speakers, or a more vernacular variety, which means they will display non-standard features that are either shared with other non-standard varieties or CE-specific. Since, as explained by Halliday (1978), non-standardness exists along a continuum, the more vernacular the speech pattern, the more and more often non-standard features will appear. In some instances, it is difficult to trace the origin of a marked feature, as more possibilities are equally acceptable — it is likely for such traits to have emerged as an effect of convergence of more influencing factors.

As for the features that are shared with several non-standard dialects of English, it is worth mentioning the lack of agreement of the third person singular, concerning regular and irregular verbs as well as the past of the verb *to be* (*was/were*). Fought (2003, 94-95) provides some examples from her on-field study: "Everybody knew the cowboys *was* gonna win again" or "Otherwise, she *don't* know Brenda." This feature shows a tendency to regularize what can be perceived as an irregularity of the English language.

Some AAVE features are often noticed in the most vernacular of CE speakers, which seems quite peculiar, given that Chicanos do not necessarily have close contact with African Americans in Los Angeles (Fought 2003, 95). On the contrary, the two groups often clash with each other — a contrast that, starting from rival gangs, often spreads across the two communities. An example showing the animosity between the two groups can be the Chicano use of the racial slur *mayate* (fem. *mayata*, plur. *mayates*, *mayatas*) to talk about African Americans (Acuña 1996, 152-153).[14] Nonetheless, the two varieties do have morpho syntactic traits in common, such as the use of habitual *be*, especially recurring in Chicano males' speech patterns, e.g. "The news *be* showing it" (Fought 2003, 96), which is an emblematic verbal marker of AAVE (Green 2002, 54).

---

[14] *Mayate* is a word of Nahuatl origin, and indicates the *Cotinis mutabilis* species of beetle (Polkinhorn *et al.* 2005, 41).

Other features have a more ambiguous origin, for example, the negative concord also referred to multiple negatives, e.g. "Things *ain't* gonna *never* change in LA *no* more" (Fought 2003, 97). Very common in AAVE, it also exists in other non-standard varieties and is often displayed by non-natives of Mexican origin and bilingual CE speakers in California and elsewhere in the US (Fought 2003; Frazer 1996). More than two negations are allowed in CE, and the negative can be transferred to a subordinate clause — as in AAVE, but also in Spanish and other romance languages.

Semantics and lexicons

A lexicon, more than other features, depends on many elements, rather than just being Chicano. Indeed, factors like age, gender, education or geographical positioning have a pivotal role, and that is why certain lexical choices can characterize small groups or even single individuals. Moreover, a lexicon is the most likely to change over time, and what applied at the time of the movies in this case study might not apply today.

It is easy to imagine that gangs have their own slang, and it must be remembered that, in the reality of the Chicano society, gangsters are a minority. However, gangster slang is the most likely to be heard and associated with Chicanos in the movies, including the ones that are part of this case study. A gang member is a *cholo* (fem. *chola*, plur. *cholos*, fem. plur. *cholas*), (Polinkorn *et al.* 2005, 21), while an older gang member is a *veterano* (Fought 2003, 46; Polinkhorn *et al.* 2005, 63-64). In the 1940s, gang members were also referred to as *pachucos* (fem. *pachucas*), (Polinkhorn *et al.* 2005, 46). When a new member is accepted in the gang, they can either be *jumped in* — a rite of initiation implying a beating for the newcomer — or *walked in*, when they are admitted without the beating (Fought 2003, 46). It is common practice for the gang members to *throw signs*, which is a specific hand gesture that reproduces the gang initials: doing so in another gang's territory is a sign of challenge, while it is considered as a greeting among fellow gang members (Fought 2003, 46-47).

Examples of gang-related phonetical and syntactic variation

Fought (2003) chose a phonetic and a syntactic feature of CE and explored the sociolinguistic variability of their use among her sample Californian CE speakers, in order to understand what certain features say about the speakers' identity — with particular attention to gang belonging. Indeed, a gang can be considered a community of practice, which "has its own life and develops its own trajectory" (Mendoza-Denton 2008, 211). As a consequence, behavioural and linguistic choices of those who belong to this community, who orbit around it or who define themselves against it, might be expected to overlap to some extent.

In particular, Fought considered the phonetic feature of /u/-fronting, absorbed by CE speakers from California Anglo-English speakers (Fought 1999, 11), and the morpho-syntactic negative concord that, opposed to standard American English, might have been drawn from AAVE or Spanish — in both cases, peripheral languages and groups. In this sense, the /u/-fronting can be considered a 'conservative' norm, a way to sound closer to standard speakers, while negative concord, with its clearly non-standard connotation, can be considered a way to sound 'tough' and to go against norms.

Results showed that the social opposition between gang members and non-gang members is also a linguistic one, both from a phonetic and morpho-syntactic point of view. Gang members might not have a specific awareness of the vowel fronting process in itself, but they certainly tend to keep a distance from the language of the (white) authorities. Moreover, they usually come from working-class and low-income families (Fought 2003, 52), which makes them objectively less likely to be in contact with speakers of more standardized varieties (Santa Ana 1993, 25). That is probably why they tend to diverge from the Anglo habit of fronting the /u/ sound, while displaying a broad use of negative concord, as a clear signal of non-standardness. For the same reason, non-gang members show greater adherence to standard grammar by using negative concord far less than their counterparts and /u/-fronting significantly more.

Spanish competence and degrees of bilingualism

As previously discussed, CE is not a synonym of Spanglish, and code-switching is not an integral part of its speech patterns. Spanglish itself, as a phenomenon of linguistic mix and mutual influence between English and Spanish, has its expressions in all the communities of *hispanohablantes* in the US, e.g. Cuban, Puerto Rican and others (Rothman & Rell 2005). It was also established above that CE speakers are often English monolinguals. Nevertheless, Spanish is still a part of Chicano heritage and does have a role in the lives of most CE speakers.

There seem to be factors favouring the maintenance of some degree of Spanish, which are opposed to those factors pushing for a complete shift towards English. For Chicanos, a close bond to older family members, specific efforts on the side of the parents, Mexican baby-sitters in early years, and acknowledgement of the Mexican heritage seem to be factors favouring maintenance (Fought 2003, 153-155). Personal history and affective bonds prove to be key for language maintenance (Schumann 1978).

Shifts to English, conversely, usually happen not because Spanish was not learned at all, but rather because the Spanish learned quickly at home is wiped out as soon as the child starts attending school — where, as previously shown, bilingual teaching is lacking or non-existent, most students, teachers and administrative staff speak English, and children can even be ridiculed for speaking Spanish. In fact, studies on children of pre-school age have shown that their bilingualism proves to work efficiently for both English and Spanish, and would not be damaging for either (García 1983) but the rejection of Spanish is fundamentally activated at a social level. The fall in Spanish literacy caused by faulty education had already been noticed between the 1980s and 1990s, even though many employers might see Spanish proficiency as an asset (Acuña 1996, 220).

In the analyses carried out with real speakers, there was a substantial discrepancy between an earlier study of Santa Ana (1991) and a more recent one by Fought (2003). While the former found Los Angeles gang members to be "fiercely monolingual" (Santa

Ana 1991, 174), moved by no desire to speak Spanish, the latter states that "[n]ot only were most of the gang members bilingual, but they also tended to be very positive about the Spanish language and Mexican ethnicity" (Fought 2003, 203). Such a striking difference could depend on a number of factors, from the specific sample of the researchers to the period in which the interviews were carried out. It is important to underline both perspectives and to see how they relate to the linguistic behaviour of the cinematic gangsters.

Code-switching
Communities living between two languages can display variable degrees of code-switching, and Chicanos are no exception. Switches to Spanish while speaking English were few. Never motivated by the inability to say something in English (García 2005, 28), switches are mostly emblematic statements of ethnic pride (Poplack 1980, 589) and involve minimal portions of their utterances. Indeed, emblematic switches do not require high levels of Spanish proficiency. According to Poplack, non-fluent Spanish users can code-switch, keeping grammaticality in both languages, by resorting to switches of single emblematic words or tags. There is a difference, however, between Fought's teenage speakers (who were teenagers in 2003) and her older speakers (in their forties in 2003), who were more likely to extensively switch to Spanish, not because of a lack of competence in English, but rather out of a fully aware choice to display their belonging through language (Fought 2003, 159).

Although CE speakers can be considered such without resorting to code-switching, their role in the community should not be underestimated. The speakers interviewed by Fought (2003, 208-210) seemed unaware of the fact that CE is a distinct variety of American English. Many identified Chicano language with code-switching. Most had positive attitudes about switching between English and Spanish and declared that they did it often, especially at home with their Spanish-speaking family members. It was appreciated by both monolingual and bilingual Chicanos, with few exceptions. The main reason for appreciating code-switching was its practical role in the community since constantly moving between two linguistic worlds means being able to communicate effectively with people with all levels of command of both English and Spanish.

After investigating the essence and meaning of their language variety, it is worth explaining the nature and role of Chicanos' mediated image. Stereotyping can have a neutral definition when intended as the act of creating mental categories to organise human thought. However, when it is stained by ethnocentrism and prejudice, it becomes a way to create an unbridgeable distance between the in-group "us" and the out-group "them" (Ramírez Berg 2002, 14-15). Thus defined, a negative stereotype has a set of features defining it. According to Ramírez Berg, negative stereotypes have eleven common characteristics. First, they are applied with rigid logic, which means that belonging to a certain group categorically implies a series of assumptions. Their strength also comes from the fact that they may be partially fact-based so that any real-life example contributes to their strength. However real they might seem to some, they remain simplified generalizations implying the homogeneity of the out-group: a stereotype is "the part that stands for the whole" (Ramírez Berg 2002, 16). This is linked to their partial correlation with facts as the negative examples are singled out and become the symbol of a whole group. For this reason, they do not serve to predict actual behaviours: confronted with the heterogeneous reality, those who are not willing to change their mind will simply rule out any contradictory data that may unsettle the stereotype.

From a historical point of view, they lack context and positioning: although partially based on historical or current events, they need to abstract from them in order to conceal the difference between themselves and their factual counterparts. Rather than by their resemblance to facts, they are normalised by repetition. While a director might say s/he is simply "telling a story," the regularity of recurring patterns concerning (for example) the Latino character in the role of the gangster reveals a more or less conscious mechanism. This reiteration is what makes a stereotype credible:

> A "vicious cycle" aspect to repeated stereotyping arises because expressing learned stereotypes reinforces and to that extent validates and perpetuates

them. Stereotypes are false to history, but conform to another historical tradition—namely, the history of movies and movie stereotyping. They begin, over time, to become part of the narrative form itself—anticipated, typical, and well nigh "invisible." Ironically, then, representation becomes narration. (Ramírez Berg 2002, 19)

Moreover, attitude shapes and consolidates the belief in a certain stereotype (Allport 1954). The belief reaches the discriminating group but is also interiorized by the discriminated, who may develop a sense of self-loathing from a young age (Stephan and Rosenfield 1982). Those strong beliefs are also the prelude to actions that often take the shape of racial violence, hate crimes and lynching (Acuña 2011).

While stereotypes can be reciprocal, they work better when the discriminating in-group has a socially and politically dominant position, since the dominant group usually controls media representations and public narrations (Ramírez Berg 2002, 20-21). The ideological core of any stereotype replicates the colonial system since while representing the other as inferior, evil and savage, stereotypes imply a power relationship aimed at affirming and preserving the status of the dominant group. Even inside an in-group, there usually is an internal hierarchy. Here, stereotypes address the weaker parts of the group (poor, disabled, ill etc.).

Finally, stereotypes are usually defeated by knowledge: while people may refuse contact with the other group, once contact has been established it is more likely to let go of preconceptions.

For what concerns Chicano media images, the main issue is partiality. In fact, the media portrayals of Chicanos tend to represent all of them as gangsters, as pointed out by Fought (2003, 6-7):

> [T]here is a tendency for those outside the community to associate Chicano English, particularly when it falls at the more non-standard end of the continuum, with gang members. Contributing to this effect are a number of movies with Latino casts that focus on the gang lifestyle, and which are exactly the movies where CE is most likely to be heard.

The movies portraying Chicanos are so often centred on gangs that they seem to establish an inevitable link between Mexican origin and natural "proclivity towards criminality and violence"

(Ramírez Berg 2002, 39), to the extent that gang membership and Mexicanness become one.

In this light, the ideological weight of the mediated stereotype becomes manifest. There is a substantial difference between an individual stereotype, existing as an abstract categorization, and a mediated stereotype, projected on the screen as a "public commodity" (Ramírez Berg 2002, 38). The latter is made for repetition and sharing, to fulfil its social function. A mediated stereotype becomes a sign with meaning, like any other mediated message, and as such it has different connotative layers that participate in its communicative meaning — Ramírez Berg's semiotics of stereotyping applied to Chicanos, as well as to other Latinos (2002, 39-41). A mediated stereotype contains several layers of meaning, conveyed by different kinds of data. Borrowing terms from semiotics and the aforementioned image of the *Bandido* as an example, the image on the screen is a signifier that has a denotation and a connotation (Ramírez Berg 2002, 39). While the denotation is simply that of a dark-skinned male wearing *sombrero* and *bandoleras*, the connotation goes way beyond, as it conveys information - connotative data, at several levels.

First of all, it conveys racial data, where the darker skin becomes a violation of the Anglo whiteness; national data — a Chicano is not identified as a "(North) American" (Ramírez Berg 2002, 40), and is therefore marked by otherness, which most often finds its strongest expression in the linguistic otherness; narrative data: a Chicano is most of the times a villain or an anti-hero;[15] behavioural data, which is to say the alleged inclination to antisocial and criminal attitudes; psychological data, linked to the behavioural aspect, which define the Chicano as an unstable sociopath, often addicted to alcohol or drugs; moral data: being villains or anti-heroes, the Chicanos are either immoral — recognising and despising righteous actions — or amoral — incapable of making a distinction between

---

[15] An anti-hero is the protagonist of any kind of story (novels, films etc.) "notably lacking in heroic qualities" (https://www.britannica.com/art/antihero. Accessed April 29, 2021).

right and wrong; ideological data: thus configured, their very existence is a threat to the integrity of the white American ideology.

According to Bender (2003), there may be a reason why Latinos/as (and Chicanos in particular) periodically become targets of stereotyping in the media:

> Media tend to spotlight gangs and their supposed resurgence during any economic recession. Perhaps gangs serve as a handy clarion call to arms against the Latina/o community in times of economic strife, generating public hysteria and justifying enhanced border security and local policing measures. (Bender 2003, 38).

Early historical facts were then deformed and stripped of their original context to become universal mediated stereotypes; subsequently, more recent facts, filtered through existing prejudices, modernized the external features of an old idea, just to make it more contemporary. In the early days, this process conceived the cinematic *Bandido*, with his typical traits: "the unkempt appearance, the weaponry and *bandoleras*, the funny-looking sombrero, the sneering look" (Ramírez Berg 2002, 17). This set of characteristics has come to identify the rude and sociopathic villain of many western movies set in the 1880s, while in historical reality this was the typical outfit of the rebel fighters of the Revolutionary War of Mexico between 1910 and 1920, fighting against the dictator Porfirio Díaz by the side of Pancho Villa and Emiliano Zapata (Ramírez Berg 2002). This deformed image has later merged with two incidents in Los Angeles that hit the headlines in the 1940s and marked the "eventual shift in media focus from the rural *Bandido* [...] to the urban Latina/o gang member or gangster" (Bender 2003, 3). The first was the finding of a Mexican boy killed by the Sleepy Lagoon swimming hole in 1942. His homicide was initially attributed to gang warfare and, despite the claims being discarded on appeal, that hypothesis received the most media attention. The second was the Zoot Suit riots of 1943 when numerous young Mexican Americans were attacked by "off-duty Anglo servicemen, with the aid of Anglo civilians" (Bender 2003, 35), their signature zoot suits stripped off and set on fire and their heads shaved. Although it was essentially a hate crime, the media portrayed it as a punishment against gangsters

(Bender 2003, 36). Forbidden after the riots, zoot suits have now been replaced by "gang colors and low-riders" (Bender 2003, 36) in the media imagery.

2.3 Defining the corpus: time frame, data availability, relevance and coherence

The corpus was specially built for this research. I transcribed and analysed semi-automatically the texts of both source and target versions. Alignment and tagging were carried out manually in a Microsoft Office Excel™ worksheet, while the calculations were made using the software MathCad™, which was also used to generate most of the graphs and tables. The corpus specifications are based on Laviosa's typology (2002, 33-38):

Level 1
Sample — since this research aims to learn more about character design, the analysis focuses on a selection of characters who respond to the Chicano gangster profile. Instead of indiscriminately analysing the whole text, the analysis takes each character separately, and then compares and combines the results.
Synchronic — the films selected were all released between 1988 and 1993 (the reasons are explained in the following pages).
General — although all the characters are Chicano gangsters, they are portrayed in different contexts of their everyday life (school, street, home, jail, etc.).
Bilingual, English and Italian (but...) — the corpus includes the source text film in English and its dubbed version in Italian. However, both the source and the target version contain a third language, Mexican Spanish, in the form of code-switching.
Mixed written and spoken (but...) — the corpus contains transcriptions of both the source and the target text the way they appear in the films (without the pre-production screenplay as a reference), which means it is "written to be spoken as if not written" (Taylor 1999, 248). Also, it takes multimodal relations (Ramos Pinto & Mubaraki 2020) into consideration, thus introducing a non-textual dimension in the corpus.

Level 2
Bilingual Parallel (and aligned) – the corpus is structured so that the two versions are in parallel. Given the fluid nature of speech and the absence of reference to screenplays, the unit selected for the alignment was the line, intended as the utterance, however long or short, that a character would give before being interrupted by another element. The signals of line change follow the typical screenplay structure: someone else's taking turn (either talking or using body language to answer), long interruption (usually 3 seconds or more) during which something happens informing the character of something they did not know, change of scene (intended as "[a] unit of dramatic action by the unity of time and proximity of space," Gurskis 2006: 180).

Level 3
Bilingual Parallel Mono-directional – as aforementioned, the corpus contained samples of the source text and their translations.

Level 4
Translational Mono-source-language – since Chicano gangsters are not the most common characters in Italian cinema, only American source texts were included.

Before moving on to a more detailed analysis of the corpus, it is worth introducing the movies that made it to the final selection.

Once movies featuring Chicano gangsters had been decided upon as a general object of study, it was crucial to apply filters to limit the scope of this research. On the one hand, it was necessary to reduce the number of movies, in order to carry out a more detailed analysis, able to go one step beyond the observation of linguistic phenomena and translational procedures. On the other hand, the selection of movies had to cover specific areas of interest that are relevant for the research topic. In this sense, both the plot of the movies and the time of release had an important role. In terms of character design, it was important to have examples of Chicano gangsters in different roles within the plot. Finally, real-life conditions such as availability of the movies, especially of the Italian versions, time at hand, and the fact that the work was carried out by one person alone, had to be taken into consideration.

It is worth explaining how those elements worked as filters, to show how the final selection of movies came to be.

Time frame – time frame refers to various kinds of time-related features. The first decision concerned opting for either diachronic or synchronic analysis. Each offers specific advantages and implies specific methods of research. The limited number of movies, as well as their discontinuous releases, made diachronic research feel chaotic, at least without detailed research on factors that fall out of the scope of this work.[16] The alternative was synchronic research, whose general aim is to capture a snapshot of a specific moment. In order for this snapshot to be meaningful, it is necessary to select a historical period that stands out for its peculiarities, both in terms of movie production and historical facts. The production of movies featuring Chicano gangsters concentrates on specific periods, and they happened to correspond with the turn of each decade. This certainly captures the attention and requires an explanation from history. Remembering a quote from Bender (2003, 38) – "[p]erhaps gangs serve as a handy clarion call to arms against the Latina/o community in times of economic strife" – it is possible that immigration trends may have a role.

In fact, these expansion trends overlap with the exponential increase in immigration from Mexico recorded at the turn of each decade (Zong & Batalova 2018). The following step is to choose which of these would offer more data for the analysis.

Data availability, relevance and coherence – the 1970s to the 1980s passage would be historically relevant, as it was the first time such movies appeared, replacing or just remodelling the *Bandido* from western movies. However, there are problems in considering this period from the data point of view. First, only three movies

---

[16] This kind of analysis would involve a broader range of subjects than this book already tries to comprise, as it requires a solid background of cinema history and economics, as well as specific data about box office, VHS and DVD sales, streaming rates and downloads. Although relevant and thought-provoking, this would require a range of competences and specific research that would take the work too far away from its main focus.

were found. Out of these three, the two from 1979, *Boulevard Nights* and *Walk Proud*, were not available in Italian. Moreover, the other movie, *Zoot Suit* (1981) is in my movie collection, but it is completely different from all the other movies, as it is the only one belonging to the musical genre. This puts it on another level, both in terms of fictional language and of translation procedures, so that it is not really comparable with the others (Mateo 2012, 119).

Another possibility was to consider the passage between the 1990s and the 2000s. This passage would have the advantage of being closer to the present time, with more data at hand both in terms of movie availability and contextual information. However, a quick look at the historical context reveals the first issue: the wake of the 2000s, with the twin towers attack and the war on terror, saw the rise of the Middle East terrorist stereotype as the new American Other, in the news as well as in entertainment media (Corbin 2017).[17] A further problem in considering this decade is that Chicano gangsters are not featured in main roles in any of the movies. This suggests that their existence is already assumed to be a given fact, undeserving of specific attention, probably because the previous movies had already created a recognisable profile. As a consequence, these movies offer a limited set of data for analysis.

The disadvantages of those two passages were compensated for by the advantages of the remaining 1980s to 1990s option. First, this is the decade passage offering most movies. Moreover, in these films it is possible to find Chicano gangsters in a range of roles, spanning major to minor. This option also includes movies that are especially focused on Chicano gangster identity and lifestyle, and relative uniformity of genres, moving on a continuum between drama and crime, with some hints of action. Unfortunately, among the movies shot between 1988 and 1993, *Mi Vida Loca* (1993) and

---

17 For example, IMDb lists no less than 38 titles under the category "Films about September 11 tragedy" (https://www.imdb.com/list/ls056745046/. Accessed April 29, 2021), which includes both movies and documentaries, either about or related to the twin tower attack. The same happens in the news, as reported by a research by the University of Alabama quoted in *The Guardian*, according to which "[t]error attacks by Muslims receive 357% more press attention" (Chalabi 2018).

Falling Down (1993) were not available in Italian, and had to be discarded.

I was then left with four movies, about nine hours for the source text, a value that doubles to eighteen hours when counting in the target versions, out of which I extracted the samples (2,835 lines). The chosen medium was DVD, mainly for availability reasons, given the difficulty of finding working VHSs for both the versions of the movies and the impossibility of retrieving movie theatre versions.[18] After the data gathering and analysis, the author managed to access partial VHS recordings and found out that the DVD version was most likely not redubbed.[19] The time frame choice is also consistent with the translation technique choice. Italy relied heavily on dubbing for movies as well as TV series and sitcoms (see chapter 1), thus the choice of dubbing is also consistent with the investigation into character profile. Gathering information about distant realities was more difficult than it is today: the internet, for example, became broadly available to the Italian public during the late 1990s and did not then contain the overwhelming amount of (constantly updated, not always reliable) information that is currently available online.[20]

The chosen movies are relevant from both a linguistic and a character design point of view. There follows a brief synopsis of the films and an outline of the characters chosen for the analysis and the relevance of each film to the research. It is important to describe the personalities of the characters, in order to better understand how these relate to their linguistic behaviour and multimodal relations.

---

[18] While looking into the Italian versions of the movies, I found that the distribution group of *Blood In Blood Out* (Buena Vista Home Entertainment) had been bought by a much bigger company (Disney Home Video). When contacting this company, I was told that they kept no record of the movie.

[19] Therefore, the sociocultural context considered in the analysis will be the one of the original film release.

[20] For detailed information about the internet spreading in Italy in the 1990s, see: http://www.repubblica.it/tecnologia/2016/04/29/news/30_anni_di_interne t_la_timeline-138625953/. Accessed April 29, 2021.

Stand and Deliver
Released: 1988
Genre: Drama, biography, inspirational
Director: Ramón Menéndez
Time: 99m
Italian title: *La forza della Volontà* (will power)
Summary: The story of the inspirational teacher Jaime Escalante, who challenges Chicano student dropouts in Los Angeles. The film is based on the true story of students who, — supported by their maths' teacher — fought back against discrimination and poverty by achieving amazing results in calculus — a crucial step towards a valid university degree and a good career. The film was added to the National Film Registry of the Library of Congress in 2011.[21]
Characters analysed: *Angel, supporting role* — portrayed by Lou Diamond Phillips, an actor of Filipino origin.[22] Angel is a young *cholo*, who lives alone with his ill grandmother and takes care of her. He initially does not care about school, but soon discovers that he is interested in mathematics thanks to his teacher Jaime Escalante. He has a dual nature: on the one hand, he is hot-headed and instinctive; on the other, he is good-natured and intelligent. The latter aspect emerges increasingly during the movie, although he also preserves part of his tough appearance.

Chuco, minor role — portrayed by Daniel Villarreal, a Chicano actor. Chuco is a young *cholo*, with no further background provided. He does not want to study, and his only ambition is to become a criminal. He is a bully, and he initially challenges the teacher and pushes his friend Angel to do the same. When he understands that being in class requires serious effort he drops out but

---

[21] The film registry was established by a national law of the US, the National Film Preservation Act: "Under the terms of the National Film Preservation Act, each year the Librarian of Congress names 25 films to the National Film Registry that are "culturally, historically or aesthetically" significant. "These films are selected because of their enduring significance to American culture," said Billington. "Our film heritage must be protected because these cinematic treasures document our history and culture and reflect our hopes and dreams" https://www.loc.gov/item/prn-11-240/. Accessed April 29, 2021.

[22] https://www.imdb.com/name/nm0001617/?ref_=ttfc_fc_cl_tl9. Accessed April 29, 2021.

respects Angel's choice to leave gangbanging, and in the end, helps renovate Escalante's car when he needs it to help his students.
Why it is relevant: This film is based on a true story, it was awarded inclusion in the National Film Registry, and it portrays a broad range of Chicanos: out of the whole class only two are *homeboys*, and one decides to change his life thanks to education. Thus, although the way gangsters are portrayed still recalls that stereotypical image, it offers a less negative view of the East Los Angeles reality. Furthermore, since most movies featuring Chicano gangsters have crime as a central theme, this film offers a view of this character in a different context.

Colors
Released: 1988
Genre: Action, crime, drama
Director: Dennis Hopper
Time: 116m
Italian title: *Colors — Colori di Guerra* (war colours)
Brief plot: The story of two police officers fighting crime and gang violence in East Los Angeles. One is older and tries to dissuade gangbangers by establishing a relationship with them, the other is a short-tempered rookie who gets carried away too easily. They end up in the middle of a war among African American and Latino gangs.
Characters analysed: *Frog, villain* — portrayed by Trinidad Silva, a Chicano actor (1950-1989), who also starred in *Walk Proud* (1979). He is the leader of the mixed-race '21 street' gang, which initially is the underdog in the *barrio*, but towards the end of the movie, they gain a better position avenging a drive-by shooting perpetrated by African Americans in their area. He always looks rather relaxed and makes use of drugs. He initially tries to stop his younger brother Felipe from entering the gang, but eventually is forced to let him in.

Gato, villain — portrayed by Steven Camarillo. He is a hot-headed member of the '21 street' gang, no further background is provided for him. He is a drug addict, sees gang membership as something unavoidable for people from his *barrio*, and is convinced his fellow gang members are his family.

Why it is relevant: Although released in the same year as *Stand and Deliver*, this film has a completely different approach. It looks at gangsters from an external perspective and hints at the fact that *cholos* do not really seek an alternative, as gang membership is their only creed. The protagonists are white police officers fighting against hordes of African American and Latino gangsters, who do not know any better than murdering and using drugs.

American Me
Released: 1992
Genre: biography, crime, drama
Director: Edward James Olmos
Time: 121m
Italian title: *American Me – Rabbia di Vivere* (anger of living)
Brief plot: The rise and fall of a young Chicano becoming the leader of the Mexican Mafia. Partly inspired by the story of the gang leader Rodolfo Cadena (Rafael 2007). Olmos, director and lead actor of this movie, also plays Professor Escalante in *Stand and Deliver* and the protagonist of the musical *Zoot Suit* (1981), becoming a recurring presence in this kind of film until the early 1990s. The story is centred on gang membership and shows the downward spiral that entering a gang implies: losing all those one cares about as well as one's self.
Characters analysed: *Santana Montoya, main role* – portrayed by Edward James Olmos, actor, director and producer of Mexican descent.[23] Santana is the son of a *pachuca* and the white marine that raped her on the Zoot Suit Riots night. The repressed rancour of his stepfather (who had to watch the rape while being beaten up by a group of marines), the latent pain of his mother, and their poverty, drive Santana towards gang membership. He is put in prison, where he becomes the leader of the Mexican Mafia, *La Eme*. Once out, he falls in love and sees what drug dealing does to his people. He wants to change his life, but loses control over the business and is eventually assassinated by his own gang.

---

[23] https://www.imdb.com/name/nm0001579/. Accessed April 29, 2021.

JD, villain — portrayed by William Forsythe. His character is inspired by Joe (Pegleg) Morgan, a Slavic-American who grew up in East Los Angeles and became a respected leader of the Mexican Mafia while in prison (Katz 1993). He is a white kid living in the *barrio* and Santana's best friend and fellow gang member since a young age. He, too, is convicted and becomes Santana's right-hand person. He pushes Santana into a hopeless competition against the Italian mafia, which will cost *La Eme* several lives.[24] When he notices that Santana wants to change his life, he orders his murder.

Mundo, minor role — portrayed by the Mexican American Pepe Serna.[25] He is the last to join Santana's small gang outside of jail, is convicted with them and participates in the building of *La Eme*. No background is given for his character, but he often does dirty jobs like murdering.

Puppet, minor role — portrayed by Danny De La Paz, who also starred in *Boulevard Nights* (1979).[26] The character is not given any particular background, apart from information about his family. His brother is the junior gang member Lil' Puppet, his cousins are Julie, the woman Santana falls in love with, and the young Neto, who dies because of uncut drugs. He had let his brother into the gang to protect him in prison but will be forced to kill him when Lil' Puppet commits an unforgivable mistake.

Lil' Puppet, minor role — portrayed by Daniel Villarreal further indicates the tendency to have the same actors playing the same roles.[27] He is a tattoo artist who ends up in prison for a small crime, uses drugs, and is introduced to *La Eme* by his older brother Puppet.

---

[24] The Italian American mafia has been used as the symbol of undefeatable crime organisation in another movie focused on crime organisations, even though it was made outside Hollywood: the yakuza film *Brother* by Takeshi Kitano (2000). The Japanese clans fight each other with more or less equal forces, they take over from the Mexicans in Los Angeles, but when they 'dare' challenge the Italian mafia, the protagonist's clan is completely wiped out.

[25] https://www.imdb.com/name/nm0346595/?ref_=nv_sr_1. Accessed April 29, 2021.

[26] https://vimeo.com/32768140. Accessed April 29, 2021.

[27] A notorious example of the same tendency in more recent years is Noel Guglielmi, a Mexican-American actor who often plays the *cholo*, and whose character is often named Hector. https://www.imdb.com/name/nm0346595/?ref_=nv_sr_1, last visited April 29, 2021.

When faced with the violence of gang membership, he wants to quit, and when he accidentally causes Santana's arrest, is killed by his own brother a few days after he gets married.

Why it is relevant: *American Me* and *Blood In Blood Out* have similarities in their plots. and some characters overlap. However, they have very different approaches to the same subject. *American Me* focuses on the dramatic aspects of gang membership and on the personal path of a man (Santana) who realizes he has made terrible mistakes that have caused pain to himself and others because of the grudge he inherited, — originating before he was born, and consuming his mother and father. The film portrays the encounter between young kids from the *barrio* and gang membership as an inevitability. From a screenplay point of view, *American Me* offers a range of characters — from a protagonist who is capable of introspection to a peripheral figure whose psychological profile is only sketched.

Blood in Blood Out (Bound by Honor)
Released: 1993
Genre: crime, drama
Director: Taylor Hackford
Time: 173m
Italian title: *Patto di Sangue* (blood oath)
Brief plot: The lives of three Chicanos from East Los Angeles, based on the life of the poet Jimmy Santiago Baca, screenwriter of the movie. Two stepbrothers and a cousin start off in the same gang until a series of unfortunate events and bad choices drive them onto very different paths. It is inspired by similar events as *American Me*, but the story is built in a more fictional way (e.g. the names of the existing gangs are modified).
Characters analysed: *Miklo Velka, main role* — portrayed by Damian Chapa, an actor of Irish, Mexican, Italian and Native American descent.[28] Miklo has a violent Anglo father he hates, and a Mexican mother he loves. Despite his Mexican descent, he has Anglo features (he, too, is inspired by Morgan like JD in *American Me*) that

---

[28] https://www.imdb.com/name/nm0152082/?ref_=nv_sr_1. Accessed April 29, 2021.

cause him discrimination in the Chicano community. He constantly feels the need to prove himself and wants to enter his cousins' gang, as he thinks of it as a consecration of his belonging. When he is arrested, he enters a powerful Mexican American gang (overcoming discrimination there, too). He is paroled, but the difficult conditions for former convicts push him into crime again, until his leg is shot off by his cousin, a former gangster. He eliminates and replaces the former leader of the gang, who had been his mentor in jail. He finds his sense of belonging in the gang, which he sees as his family.

Paco Aguilar, main role—portrayed by Benjamin Bratt, who has mixed ancestry[29]. At the beginning of the story, he is an impetuous and proud young man with no love for hard work. He is the leader of the street gang *Vatos Locos* and Miklo's cousin. After a series of negative events lead to his and his cousin's arrest, he decides to avoid jail by serving in the army and becomes a detective. After his little brother dies because of heroin, he decides to join the drug squad. When he finds out Miklo is involved in crime again after being paroled, he shoots his cousin while he is running away. He also fights his stepbrother, a drug addict who accidentally caused their little brother's death. He is divided between his sense of duty as an irreprehensible detective and his old bond with his former gang members, who are also part of his family. He dresses like a detective and acts according to his role, but does not lose his fiery and aggressive attitude while finding a new sense of belonging in serving law and order.

Cruz Candelaria, main role—portrayed by Jesse Borrego, a Chicano actor.[30] He is Paco's stepbrother, Miklo's cousin, and a member of *Vatos Locos*. He is a promising artist with a passion for Aztec culture and Mexican tradition, but after being attacked by a rival gang his spine is severely damaged, and he turns to heroin to ease the pain. While he is under the effect of heroin, his little brother tries his drugs and dies. His family do not talk to him for years (apart from Miklo), but eventually, they forgive him, and he finds a way

---

[29] His mother is a Peruvian Quechua: https://www.biography.com/people/benjamin-bratt-9542258. Accessed April 29, 2021.
[30] Originally from San Antonio, Texas: https://www.imdb.com/name/nm0001963/. Accessed April 29, 2021.

out of addiction. He believes that a sense of belonging comes from never forgetting the bond created by surviving the tough reality of the *barrio* together.

Montana, supporting role — portrayed by Enrique Castillo. Montana has some features in common with Santana from *American Me*. Wise and contemplative, he is the leader of the jail gang *La Onda* and Miklo's mentor. During the film, he reveals he has a daughter he has never met because he has been in prison for a very long time. He starts studying and realizes that Chicanos need to stay out of jail and live honestly, but his moderation is perceived as a betrayal by his right-hand men, Magic and Miklo. The two decide to murder him in secret, right on the day he would have met his daughter.

Popeye, villain — portrayed by Carlos Carrasco, an actor from Panama.[31] He fully embodies negative stereotypes: a drug addict with no talent, he is a coward who does not hesitate to take advantage of any opportunity to further his own interests, even if it means damaging others. He initially pretends to be Miklo's friend, but then tries to rape him, and insults his white skin (Popeye is particularly dark). Once out of jail, he steals money from his fellow gang members and mismanages the gang's business, until Miklo takes his place.

<u>Why it is relevant</u>: This film has a somewhat ambivalent approach towards gang membership. While it certainly shows its negative aspects, it also leaves room for sympathising with the gangsters, or at least for understanding their point of view. It also opens the possibility of leaving gang membership for good and changing one's life.

The film covers a long period and several topics: from the tragic escalation of violence when joining a gang, to gang violence, to the difficulties faced by former convicts in overcoming prejudice and living honestly and drug addiction. It also shows an array of characters with different roles in the plot, each of them embodying at least part of the stereotypes of Chicanos. Also, given that it lasts nearly three hours, it is the one where most time is dedicated to outlining different characters.

---

[31] https://www.imdb.com/name/nm0140033/?ref_=tt_cl_t8. Accessed April 29, 2021.

2.4 The framework and its application

The main inspiration for the framework came from the work of Ramos Pinto (2017) and Ramos Pinto & Mubaraki (2020). Although, in the case of Portuguese subtitling of British English diastratic variation, their work had a multimodal approach for analysing non-standard speech in audiovisual products. In particular, their scheme included three dimensions of investigation: textual, looking for the "meanings associated to certain varieties" (Ramos Pinto 2017, 21); diegetic, concerned with the way "the non-standard varieties' communicative meanings and diegetic functions are constructed in a fictional audiovisual context" (Ramos Pinto 2017, 23); sociocultural, whose aim is to explore the socio-cultural context, looking for the possible reasons behind the products and their translated versions.

The first two dimensions, in particular, are the focus of the product-based analysis of this work. The sociocultural dimension, on which some hypotheses will be proposed here, would need further investigation through Toury's extratextual sources, e.g. interviews with the translators, adapters and dubbing actors; reception studies.[32]

Textual dimension

The textual dimension scheme is informed by the work of Assis Rosa (2012; 2015); Brodovich (1997); Ramos Pinto & Mubaraki (2020) and Ramos Pinto (2017). Following the concept of *fictolinguistics* (Ferguson 1998), rather than "evaluating the varieties' real-world accuracy and consistency," AVT study aims to identify "the extralinguistic meanings associated with those same varieties [...] then imported in the film's fictional world" (Ramos Pinto & Mubaraki, 2020). The necessity for this kind of shift depends on the nature of the audiovisual product and even more on that of its translation. If the source text is still more or less close to its real-world

---

[32] Given the amount of work the framework implementation and corpus analysis required, it was not possible to analyse the extratextual sources at this stage. Its importance would require further research, based on the data and results gathered and analysed here.

counterpart (Fought 2002), the cultural specificity of a non-standard variety like Chicano English can hardly be rendered realistically in a different linguistic context, as was partly proved in my smaller studies (Renna 2017; Renna 2018; Renna 2018a; Renna 2019).

Carmen Fought (2002) mentions *American Me* in her study of Chicano English — she explores a broader range of genres, the film by Olmos being the only gangster movie included in her analysis. Indeed, the movie was criticized by the Latino community (Berumen 1995) for its focus on gang membership. Fought (2002) has analysed Chicano English in real life and then its representation in a small number of movies. In her opinion, *American Me* offers a partial view of Chicano English:

> The language in *American Me* is certainly affected by the gang theme. The varieties of English shown tend to be non-standard versions of CE [...] This 'tough' portrayal of Mexican-Americans as gang members is also reinforced linguistically by a much higher use of taboo language [...] The characters in this movie who are not gangsters are mostly non-native speakers. [...] this type of pattern in films tends to reinforce the stereotype that CE is spoken by gang members, as well as the idea that other Mexican-Americans just speak 'broken' learner English. (Fought 2002, 218).

This suggests that the language of the movies if they follow the pattern of *American Me* suggested by Fought (2002), will tend towards the non-standard end of the CE continuum. On the other hand, as mentioned in chapter 1, Italian *dubbese* usually tends towards language standardization.

There is also another element complicating the picture: in this corpus, not only standardness or non-standardness of the language were to be taken into consideration, but also the fact that CE is characteristic of a certain ethnocultural minority group. This group is composite: some speakers who tend towards the California Anglo English standard and others towards more vernacular forms. California Anglo English, too, can be spoken in a more prestigious sub-variety, or tend towards orality (Assis Rosa 2015) and substandardness.

Taking as a starting point Ramos Pinto & Mubaraki's scheme (2020), based on British English and Portuguese subtitling, helped define the specific categories to take into consideration. Ramos

Pinto & Mubaraki imagine a scheme where on the one hand there is standard language, whose main function is to convey high prestige, high sociocultural status and/or belonging to a central region. On the other hand, the non-standard dimension has a broader range of variation. First, it includes oral, containing features of oral speech such as contractions, which conveys a lower prestige and a colloquial and informal communicative context. Second, the nonstandard varieties can be regional, when features signalling belonging to a peripheral region determine a lower prestige. Finally, the most complex category of nonstandard is substandard, which conveys the lowest prestige. It includes substandard regional varieties, conveying low sociocultural status and belonging to a peripheral region; substandard social, conveying low sociocultural status and low educational level; substandard social specific, which conveys the same low sociocultural status and low educational level, but also specific information that allows the audience to identify the character as a member of a specific social group.

To the classification of varieties, Ramos Pinto & Mubaraki (2020) add a second level of classification based on the realization of these varieties, which allows the determination of which linguistic elements contribute to the identification of a certain variety. The features are divided among morpho-syntactic, lexical, phonetic, and orthographic (for subtitles).

In order to apply the logic of their scheme to the corpus at hand, it was necessary to make some changes in terms of integrations, substitutions, or small tweaks. The modifications stemmed from a series of factors. First, in this corpus, the variation is both social and ethnic, which doubles some categories while making others irrelevant. For example, in the source language, both CE and Anglo English have their own standard and nonstandard subvarieties (although the standard of CE is perceived as less prestigious than the Anglo standard because it belongs to a discriminated minority). Second, sometimes, in the target texts, a marker of belonging to a minority ethnic group can be added to an otherwise standard language that could also belong to a member of a dominant (white) ethnic group. Finally, sometimes the characters switch to Spanish for a whole line, instead of just using it in code-switching.

The result was the following scheme (Figure 1):

Figure 1 Classification of the linguistic varieties

This classification was devised after having watched all the movies and their dubbed versions several times, in the attempt to cover all the varieties used in both texts. It is worth noting again that the language analysed here is fictional, appositely constructed to provide the audience with sociocultural information, rather than to represent the linguistic reality of the portrayed speakers. The terminology used for the definitions does not specifically refer to Chicanos and CE and/or Italian because a successful framework thus implemented would work with other minorities (especially those involved in diasporas and/or colonialism). Within a colonial system or any society that contains minorities, there is likely to be a local version of the "English with an accent" (Lippi-Green 1997. n.p.), which denotes an ethnocultural heritage considered as Other from the dominant one.

Here, the standard category is divided between dominant ethnic groups and minority ethnic groups. In the ST of this corpus, the first case is represented by Anglo English in its most prestigious variety, denoting the highest socio-cultural status; the second case consists of the kind of CE that is expected from an educated Chicano, which approximates the dominant standard. In both cases, the category 'exotified' was included: while, in fact, code-mixing has its rules, passing from one language to another for lengthy parts of discourse can be interpreted as a sign of incomplete knowledge of a language (Gumperz 1982; Lippi-Green 1997). However, a small instance of lexical code-switching that does not involve rude language and profanities can serve as colouring, to give that particular line an exotic feeling for the audience. This can happen in both the standards and can have an "emblematic" function (Poplack 1980, 589) or serve as a way to personalize communication or create solidarity with the interlocutor (Gumperz 1982). The presence of an exotified standard is the reason why its counterpart is called neutral, as it does not have the same connotation resulting from the occasional code-switching.

What falls outside the realm of standard language generally belongs to a non-standard that, in turn, is divided into subcategories. Once again, the first subdivision is between the non-standard language spoken by the dominant ethnic group (in this case Anglos) and the one spoken by the minority (in this case Chicanos). Both the dominant and the minority substandard, following Ramos Pinto & Mubaraki (2020), are divided between oral and substandard. According to Assis Rosa (2015), some morpho-syntactic and lexical features distinguish an oral discourse from a standard one, and her distinguishing features were adopted here: exclamations (both clausal and phrasal), question tags, fillers (e.g. well, um), changes of topic, reformulations, false starts, stressing, hedging, backchannelling, forms of address, frequent deictics, low lexical density, high dependence on context and strong interpersonal component (vs. referential component). To these, the specific case or minority ethnic group oral requires adding the use of Mexican Spanish code-mixing, but only when this includes words that are not rude (and could be considered no less than oral in Mexican Spanish, too), for instance *casa, madre, vamonos* (house, mother, let us go). The phonetic traits of oral speech tend to diverge from California Anglo English more than in Standard CE, e.g. replacement of apico-dental fricatives [θ] and [ð] with the apico-dental stops [t̪] and [d̪] respectively.

The lowest subtype of non-standard language is substandard, which indicates the lowest educational level and socio-cultural prestige. In this corpus, there are two kinds of substandard: one spoken by the dominant ethnic group, the other by the minority group. In both cases, some signals of substandardness are those linguistic features that fall within the definition of incorrect grammar, usually denoting a lack of education, some examples common to both sub-standards being: 1) *grammar*: double negation, auxiliary omission or contraction, no third person -*s*, no marking of difference between present and past tense, no marking of difference between singular and plural, excess of prepositions; 2) *lexicon*: youth slang or sociolect slang; swearwords and profanities. In the case of minority substandard, additional features should be mentioned. The first is the use of vernacular AAVE items, e.g. existential BE, labelling: these are common in the non-standard speech of other marginal communities in fiction (Renna 2015). The second is the code-switching of words that are not acceptable in the mixed language (in the case of this corpus, Mexican Spanish): some examples are swearwords e.g. *cabrón* (bastard), *chingao* (from *chingado* [fucked] used as an expression of disappointment), and Spanglish words such as *huacha* (or *wacha*), which is a Hispanification of the verb *to watch*.

From the phonetic point of view, some traits tend to converge with California Anglo English in their more standard versions, while they acquire more elements in common with other non-standard dialects (e.g. AAVE) and with Spanish as they drift towards more vernacular forms, e.g. a tense realization of [ɪ] slightly in other positions apart from the *-ing* suffix, common to all CE speakers. The difference is especially evident in terms of suprasegmental traits. An example that clearly shows the difference can be found towards the end of the film *Stand and Deliver*. The class is unfairly accused of having cheated to pass the calculus exam, as they all had good marks and made similar minor mistakes—but, really, it is because their marks are 'too good' to be coming from a school in East Los Angeles. Angel, who has already become a good student but still dresses like a *cholo*, uses prosody to mock the interiorized prejudice of his Chicano examiner, as he pretends to take the blame and, in so doing, suddenly switches to much more vernacular prosody:

> Examiner: *Permiso*. I come from this neighborhood. *Yo vengo de este barrio*. I know that sometimes we're tempted to take shortcuts. Tell me the truth. What happened? *Dime la verdad*.
> Angel: Ok. We're busted. Why don't we just admit it?
> Examiner: How did you do it?
> Angel: I got the test ahead of time and passed it out to everyone else.
> Examiner: How did you get it?
> Angel: Mailman. I strangled him. His body's decomposing in my lockeeeeer.
> *all the students laugh*
> (*Stand and Deliver* 1988, 1:10:34-1:12:17)

Of course, Angel did not kill anyone, and his sudden change of prosody makes everyone realize he was mocking the examiner for his racism. The last sentence (underlined in the quotation) is pronounced quickly apart from the last word, with a growling voice and strong syllable-timed prosody and the "circumflex" intonation pattern (Fought 2003, 72; Matluck 1952, 119). Normally, Angel does have phonological traits of Chicano English, but not as vernacular: in that sentence, his prosody recalls that of characters like Popeye (*Blood In Blood Out*), who embodies the most typical gangster stereotype.

Finally, the category of Other language was needed for the sentences uttered in a language that is neither SL nor TL—in the case of this corpus, Mexican Spanish. In this category are included utterances in Spanish, utterances in Spanish with some code-mixing in English (e.g. "*High roller* o qué? Mira, papá!" Cruz in *Blood In Blood Out*, 09.09-09.13), and sentences with reiteration code-switching (Gumperz 1982), where the first sentence is uttered in Spanish.

As in Ramos Pinto & Mubaraki (2020), the textual dimension analysis is completed by a level dedicated to the linguistic realization of a variety, although a small modification was necessary: since the focus of this research is on dubbing, the orthography section was discarded, and the phonetics' section—including both phonemes and prosody traits—was repeated for both source and target text.

The categories thus obtained were included in a scheme, which was built in parallel for both source and target languages.

As already mentioned, the unit of analysis is the line. Therefore, the tagging was carried out on a line basis. Each line has attributed to it a value of one or zero, depending on whether a certain line could be considered as belonging to that variety or not. Then, value one was attributed to the categories phonetics/lexicon/morpho-syntax depending on whether one or more of these elements marked the belonging of a line to a certain linguistic variety.

Language Variation and Multimodality 103

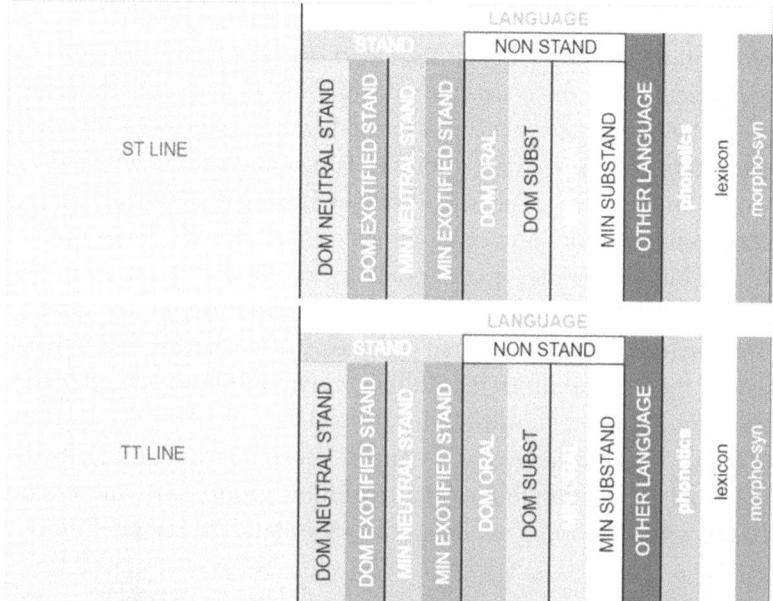

Figure 2 Scheme as arranged in the tables of analysis for source and target text respectively.

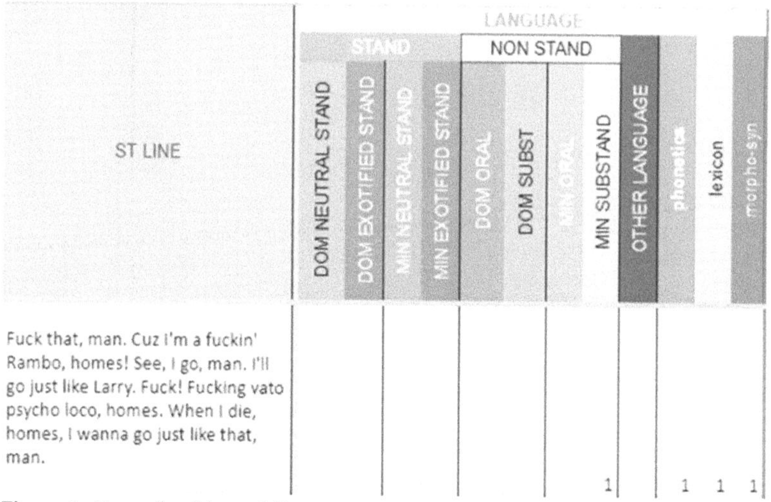

Figure 3 Example of tagged line

The value 1 corresponds to a satisfied category; the empty space is a zero. In this line (Gato from *Colors*), all the linguistic elements hint at the 'minority substandard' category. Attributing a certain category to the lines uttered by a character is more than an exercise of taxonomy: as previously discussed, each category provides information about the character's positioning in terms of ethnic and social belonging, sociocultural and educational level. In this case, the whole structure of the utterance is recursive, filled with swearwords and labelling. The use of code-switching distinguishes a Chicano gangster from any other gangster (e.g. African Americans in *Colors*, but also whites in *American Me* and *Blood In Blood Out*). The linguistic realization of a certain line provides further material to 1) understand the use of fictional varieties; 2) see whether and to what extent the realization in the dubbed version follows a similar pattern. For example, Figure 4 is the dubbed version of the line by Gato (*Colors*): here, the language is equally substandard, but it lacks the marker of belonging to the minority ethnic group, since there is no code-switching, and pronunciation is the standard Italian dubbese.

TT LINE	LANGUAGE											
	STAND				NON STAND							
	DOM NEUTRAL STAND	DOM EXOTIFIED STAND	MIN NEUTRAL STAND	MIN EXOTIFIED STAND	DOM ORAL	DOM SUBST	MIN ORAL	MIN SUBSTAND	OTHER LANGUAGE	phonetics	lexicon	morpho-syn
E chissenefrega, tanto sono un cristo di Rambo anch'io. E anch'io me ne vado, me ne vado sicuro come Larry. Cazzo, come quel gran paraculo di svitato fratelli. Quando crepo fratello, voglio farlo esattamente in quel modo.						1					1	1

Figure 4 The same line (Gato from *Colors*) in the dubbed version.

Comparing the different renderings of the source and the target text also allows another type of observation, which concerns the macrolevel strategies that may have inspired the translators in the rendering of the ST varieties. Ramos Pinto (2009; 2017) identifies two main groups of strategies. The first is neutralization strategies, including discourse standardization (using standard language only) and discourse dialectization (using non-standard variety only). The second group includes the preservation strategies: the first is centralization, "in which the TT presents a lower frequency of non-standard features (or the choice for more prestigious feature/varieties in relation to the ST) and can thus be placed closer to the centre of prestige" (Ramos Pinto 2017, 23). It closely recalls Toury's law of growing standardization (1995). Other preservation strategies are maintenance and decentralization, "to illustrate, respectively, the cases in which the TT presents a similar or higher frequency of non-standard features in relation to the ST" (Ramos Pinto 2017, 23).

The two examples above serve to illustrate the way the table was filled, but it is important to remember that an analysis of a whole character is not best carried out based on a single sentence with its translation. While in this sentence the low educational level of the character is still evident, his ethnic belonging is not. This does not, however, mean that the information cannot be retrieved from the broader linguistic and non-linguistic context. That is why the next step will be illustrating how the diegetic dimension was built in this corpus.

Diegetic dimension

The diegetic dimension is the one that analyses the relationships between the textual dimension and the broader audiovisual context. Looking into these is the key to understanding the "communicative meanings and diegetic functions" (Ramos Pinto 2017, 23) of the varieties and the way these two dimensions interact in order to deliver a message that does not rely exclusively on one of the two but stems from their relationship. The analysis of these elements requires a certain familiarity with the language of films, which is worth detailing to clarify how the non-linguistic categories were selected.

In their analysis, Ramos Pinto & Mubaraki (2020) include non-textual elements such as accent, costume and make-up, figure behaviour and setting. For this study, however, it was crucial to intersect these categories with specific research that has shed light on the Chicano gangster stereotype, carried out by Ramírez Berg (2002), using a scene from the film *Falling Down* (1993) as an example. Berg has investigated the audiovisual language of the Latino stereotype, and the observations on this corpus confirmed his analysis. In particular, he has classified all the cinematic elements that come into play when creating and establishing a mediated stereotype, what he calls the "poetics of stereotyping" (2002, 42). Among these, many can be found in the following corpus, and some examples will be reported here to show the multilayered structure of the cinematic text that, as stated by Chiaro, has a "polysemiotic nature" (2008, 143). As mentioned in Chapter 1, it is a compound of non-verbal and verbal, as well as of visual and acoustic elements that intertwine constantly. Among the non-verbal visual elements, Ramírez Berg includes scenery, lighting, costumes and make-up and body language; non-verbal acoustic elements include music, sound effects and body sounds. Verbal visual elements are anything that is written and visible to the audience, while verbal acoustic is the whole set of dialogues, and also in many cases the song lyrics.

While the cinematic analysis by Ramírez Berg contained a wide range of factors, the broader scope of this work required a simplification of his categories. First, his analysis focuses on a single scene only, allowing for a more detailed look. Secondly, he does not focus on translation. Furthermore, some categories are especially relevant when the Latino characters are the antagonists of a white Anglo protagonist. Since most of the movies in this corpus have Chicanos at the centre of the diegesis, these categories will not be included in the subsequent analysis. One example is framing. In the movies where gangsters are secondary characters (and even more in classical Hollywood movies), framing has a pivotal role in defining power relationships, since the main character occupies the "upper one-third and the central vertical third of the screen" (Bordwell 1985, 51). Ramírez Berg adds that the main character occupying this position is often a WASP male, whose personality and life path are narrated in detail, while the remaining space is "the realm of minor characters and stereotypes" (2002, 44), whose personalities and life stories remain flat, impersonal or untold.

However, given that most movies under consideration are focused on the Chicano characters, and only have white characters as secondary, I followed the choice of Ramos Pinto and Mubaraki (2020) to leave framing out, since it is not among the categories that are more closely in the meaning-making process. The categories selected for this analysis are hereby illustrated. The scheme is informed by the work of Ramírez Berg (2002), Pastra (2008), Ramos Pinto (2017) and Ramos Pinto & Mubaraki (2020), and tailored to satisfy the needs of this research.

Setting

Elements like *mise-en-scène*, set design and lighting merge to create the right atmosphere for the scene to become a clearly identifiable narrative device. The corpus of films included in this analysis displays examples of the way the environment surrounding the gangsters is built to confirm and echo their dangerous lives and violent natures. These categories, separated in Ramírez Berg (2002), are here merged under the name setting. The *mise-en-scène* concerns the way the scene is spatially staged. According to Ramírez Berg, the movies where non-whites are secondary characters (or villains) have a recurring pattern in terms of character disposition: "when a First World hero enters the Third World and confronts the native, two things are virtually guaranteed: he […] will be surrounded by a larger band of natives, and his […] immobility will contrast with their usually frenetic activity" (2002, 45). Stillness denotes intelligence and reflection, while frenetic activity reveals animal-like behaviour (Renna 2019).

Lighting is also very important, with dark and threatening nights and overly lit exterior daytime scenes. Ramírez Berg underlines that lighting is usually "based on a white skin standard" (2002, 54), which often means that the reflection on paler skins is optimal, while it is not sufficient for darker-skinned actors, who in turn need extra lighting, making them look sweatier, and thus, more agitated, frantic and wilder overall.

Other elements contributing to the visual environment surrounding the characters are the set design and art direction. The setting of the films starring Chicano gangsters is usually East Los Angeles, and amongst the distinctive elements, Ramírez Berg cites the "deserted hill, amid the graffiti-laden[33] rubble of the decaying ghetto [...] destroyed building, and [...] crumbling concrete" as the signals that characters are in an "inner-city war zone" (2002, 51). In this respect, the inner-city war zone does have some similarities with the desert of the US southwest and the Middle East, and with the jungles of Africa and South America – the "inherently hazardous" (Ramírez Berg 2002, 51) habitats of cinematic Others. To the setting outlined by Ramírez Berg, I would like to add some more, found in movies starring Chicano characters (both in this corpus and in my previous studies). For what concerns exterior scenes, other possible settings are ghetto streets characterized, in a similar manner to the aforementioned deserted hills, by decaying buildings covered in graffiti, either in the form of Mexican-themed wall art (e.g. Holy Mary of Guadalupe, Aztec pyramids), or fuzzy gang signs. Humble stores with shop signs in Spanish are an integral part of the landscape, as they help to situate East Los Angeles as a non-American area (Landry & Bourhis 1997, 25). Often green spaces are present, although they are usually untidy, to further hint at wilderness. In the corpus here analysed, three films out of four begin with a journey through the ghetto, by car in *Colors* (1988) and *Stand and Deliver* (1988), and on foot in *Blood In Blood Out* (1993). In all cases, these scenes provide a quick but effective introduction to "a whole different country" (*Blood In Blood Out* 1993, 2.16-2.18). However, it is worth noting that the road trip in *Colors* assumes a clearly Anglo-like point of view, so the camera tends to linger on depressed areas rather than folkloric angles, and is accompanied by white rock music. Conversely, the other two East Los Angeles tours are made from a more Latino-like point of view, and therefore also show more positive sides of East Los Angeles – distant, a little wild, but an also proudly Latino/a corner of Mexico in the United States (this is especially the case of the initial tour in *Blood in Blood Out*), as suggested by the Mexican folk music accompanying the scenes.

---

[33] The remarkable murals and paintings attributed to the character Cruz Candelaria in *Blood in Blood Out* were created by the self-taught Chicano artist Adan Hernandez: https://vimeo.com/73042148. Accessed April 29, 2021.

When it comes to the rest of the exterior scenes, *Colors* tends to keep a negative perspective, *Blood In Blood Out* a more ambivalent one, *Stand and Deliver* a positive one (which becomes more negative at night) and *American Me* tends to outline a neat separation between the scenes in East Los Angeles and the setting where most parts of the film take place, which will be discussed later on.

Interior scenes, too, tend to display recurring patterns, especially when it comes to houses. There are two main kinds of houses in these movies. One I would define as the *casa*, which is inhabited by the members of the *familia*. It is usually a crime-free zone, where non-gang members live a simple life, bound to the traditional Mexican values of family and religion, but usually also poor, and crowded with multiple generations. This kind of image reflects the stereotypical situation of immigrant families — living in ghetto areas, with large households sharing relatively small spaces, (Bustamante & Winton Reynolds 1992, 291; García 2002, 58). This kind of house is humbly furnished, and religious icons are often visible in the background — outside the houses, there is often a shared courtyard, where old men sit in the sun and younger children play, but only until they become young gang members.

Opposed to the *casa* there is what I would call the *pad*, which is the base of the gangsters' illegal activities, e.g. cutting drugs, having gang meetings or drug parties. This house can be furnished like the *casa*, but often looks more cluttered: here women are usually not admitted unless they are gang members or prostitutes. Thus, since the *macho* stereotype prevents a man from having a tidy house without a woman's touch, the *pad* is usually messy and dirty. Sometimes, instead of a *pad*, the gang will meet in an abandoned building or an even more improvized location — e.g. a family vault in a cemetery (*American Me*). The jarring contrast between the idyllic *casa* and the crime-ready *pad* confirms both Ramírez Berg's idea of stereotyping as vague and imprecise (2002) and the principle proposed by van Doorslaer *et al.* (2016, 3-4), according to whom different (and opposed) stereotypes overlap because they were born in response to different needs at different times.

Another setting that dominates *American Me* (1992), is persistent in *Blood In Blood Out* (1993) and makes its appearance in *Colors*

(1988), is the prison. In *American Me*, the protagonist and his crime partners are first inmates of juvenile prison, then pass on to Folsom. Except for one of the three (the white Chicano JD), that is the place where they spend most of their lives. The protagonist of *Blood In Blood Out* is jailed in San Quentin, and there he finds a new and strong gang of which he becomes a part—he and his peers spend most of their lives there, too. In *Colors*, the leader of one of the gangs ends up in jail indefinitely for not paying parking tickets, while his major crimes will only be punished at the end. The only film where prison does not appear is *Stand and Deliver* (1988), since the main *homeboy* is saved by the school, and in particular by discovering he has a talent for maths—his best friend is too lazy or not intelligent enough, so drops out.

Going back to the prison scenery, many parts of the prison appear on screen, from claustrophobic cells and narrow tier corridors to noisy and dangerous common rooms, from the sunburnt and crowded prison yards to the visiting rooms and less typical areas such as kitchens, libraries, and stockrooms. In *American Me* and *Blood In Blood Out* prison life is shown from various points of view. On the one hand is the cruelty: the heavy bullying newcomers have to undergo, sexual violence as a form of establishing dominance, racial hatred, the impossibility of trusting anyone and careless homicides. On the other hand is (a distorted vision of) manhood and solidarity: the opportunity of climbing the social ladder and leading a gang, of earning money through illegal activities e.g. gambling, contraband or drug dealing, and the possibility of finding loyalty at least in some of the fellow gang members. From a more figurative point of view, the jails are bare and austere, while at times cells are made more personal through pictures, drawings or holy icons. The yards are equipped with minimalist gym gear (especially for weightlifting) and monitored by armed guards from a distance (which does not really prevent anyone from committing crimes in the daylight during the movies).

While these locations can be considered the cinematic gangsters' habitat, the gangsters occasionally visit other settings: schools (*Stand and Deliver*), hospitals, Mexican stores or small restaurants, parole offices and police stations. In these places, the gangster character might be more or less out of place and has to decide whether to act accordingly or not.

Music

Music, either in the background or played by the characters, often contributes to the setting. Ramírez Berg (2002, 48) maintains that its characterising power depends on "decades of Hollywood's conventionalized and imperialistic portrayals of others." Often heard in this corpus is African American music from the 1970s and 1980s: the movies are set in a period ranging from the 1950s to the 1990s. The fact that black music is played so often when Chicanos are on the screen confirms the homogenization of anything that is not white. For example, the main soundtrack of *Colors* (1988) is composed by an important African American artist, Herbie Hancock.[34] Apart from in *Stand and Deliver*, African American music of various genres can be heard across the movies, going from Big Daddy Kane (*Colors*), and Garnett Mimms and the Enchanters (*American Me*) to Jimi Hendrix (*Blood In Blood Out*).

Quite recurrent is music with *mariachi* or western influences or Mexican folk music. Trumpets and *guitarras* dominate, connecting the contemporary gangster with the *Bandido* tradition (Ramírez Berg 2002, 17). The main soundtrack of *Blood In Blood Out* (1993), composed by Bill Conti, is a relevant example. In *American Me*, two songs are performed by a band whose name is *Mariachi Sol de Mexico*. *Stand and Deliver* is especially rich in songs with a strong Latino influence.

Rap is present, too, although much less than the younger audience might expect today, probably because most of these movies are set before the 1990s, and rap only became seriously popular in the late 1980s (Campbell 2012, 327). While rap music only appears at the end of both *American Me* and *Blood In Blood Out*, its presence is more constant in *Colors*, and there is no sign of it in *Stand and Deliver*.

---

[34] Herbie Hancock might not be extremely famous in Italy, but—with a long career and a long list of awards to his name—he certainly needs no introduction in the US (Wendell 2018).

Tribal, Caribbean or ritual-sounding music occasionally appears, and a good example is "K'in Sventa Ch'ul Me'tik Kwadalupe,"[35] the soundtrack of the *Dia de los Muertos*[36] celebration in *Blood In Blood Out*. Although more commercially, the main theme of *Stand and Deliver*, composed by Craig Safan, has a Caribbean sound to it—albeit blended with a sound typical to the 1980s. Finally, the films also include more conventional soundtrack melodies, e.g. music conveying a sense of danger, victory or drama. These can keep some Mexican or western-like influence or come from the Anglo mainstream. The latter is the case when it comes to the final song of *Stand and Deliver*, performed by the Californian and white band Mr. Mister.

It is worth noting that some songs are used in more than one film, confirming their function as part of the scenery, and a reflection of the characters' personalities and lives. One example is "Lowrider" by War, which can be found in three films out of the four (all but *Stand and Deliver*). This is probably due to the fact that the lowrider, the car to which the song is dedicated—a vehicle with a lowered chassis, often sporting artistic paintings on the body— has been typical of Mexican American neighbourhoods since the time of the zoot suiters (Chappel 2012), and has also become a common part of the Chicano gangster-mediated stereotype. War are also the artist behind another recurring song, "Slippin' into Darkness," which can be found in both *American Me* and *Blood In Blood Out*. The song lyrics suggest a bad habit or an addiction that gradually makes someone lose their mental sanity. Since both movies tell stories of people becoming increasingly involved in the gang members' lifestyle, the lyrics seem particularly fitting. The two aforementioned movies have other artists in common also, although via different songs. One is Santana, present in *American Me*

---

[35] Ritual music for the worship of Holy Mary of Guadalupe. In the film, only the first 40 seconds can be heard, amplifying its evocatory power. https://www.youtube.com/watch?v=oospWucgxac. Accessed April 29, 2021.

[36] *El Dia de los Muertos*, or Day of the Dead, is "on November 1 and 2, the dates of the Roman Catholic celebration of All Saints' Day and All Souls' Day. A syncretic mix of Catholic beliefs and indigenous practices of honoring the ancestors, the two days are considered as one holiday throughout Latin America" (Marchi 2006, 262).

with the notorious "Oye Como Va" and in *Blood In Blood Out* with "Jin-Go-Lo-Ba". The other is the Chicano rapper Kid Frost, chosen for the ending theme for both *American Me* and *Blood In Blood Out*, with "No Sunshine" and "La Raza" respectively. Los Lobos are common performers to *Colors* and *American Me*, with "One Time One Night" in the former and "Shotgun" in the latter.

After considering the environment in which the characters are immersed, the next step is an analysis of the components of the "poetics of stereotyping" that concern the characters themselves, and the way they appear and behave on screen, as well as their interlocutors.

Behaviour

Ramírez Berg defines "acting conventions" (2002, 53) as specifically codified behaviours of the gangsters who, most of the time, seem to portray perfectly "the facial scowl, the aggressive attitude" and "the simmering hostility" that are typical of the "tough homeboy," whose state of mind is usually "unstable, irrational, combustible" (Ramírez Berg 2002, 53-54). This is evident in each of the movies, and some examples can clarify this point. In *Stand and Deliver*, when Angel finds out his exam results are at risk, he acts unreasonably, provoking a police officer and causing an argument with his best friend; he seems to think 'if people do not believe I can be a good citizen, then I am going to act like a bully.' In *Colors*, while the main gang is talking to a former gang member who is trying to convince them to give up on crime, they switch without warning from a largely friendly attitude to an aggressive one. In *American Me*, Santana is assassinated by his gang members because he is losing the aggressive attitude that turned him into a gang leader, and a more aggressive gang member takes his place. In *Blood In Blood Out*, all the tragedies hitting the main characters are due to a series of wrong choices prompted by a mix of irrationality and machismo. Nonetheless, they tend to fall into the same pattern over and over again. This confirms the aforementioned layers of the stereotype — in particular, moral data, psychological data and ideological data.

Phenotype

According to Ramírez Berg, casting has the same function today that make-up had in the blackface era (2002, 50). The skin of the characters is part of the narrative device that classes them in specific roles before they can say or do anything. It is not necessary for the characters to be portrayed by actual Chicanos: sometimes they are, e.g. Edward James Olmos; sometimes they are not, e.g. Benjamin Bratt and Lou Diamond Phillips. In a case outside this corpus, the film *Training Day* (2001), the main gangster is played by Cliff Curtis, a New Zealander actor of Maori descent, and he is also the one displaying the most traditional links to Mexicanness, especially in his Italian dubbing (Renna 2019). In two of the movies, there is at least one white Chicano who eventually becomes the leader of the gang. The historical origin of the white Chicano gangster image is Joe 'Pegleg' Morgan (Katz 1993). The fact that in both the movies the white Chicano becomes the gang leader by betraying the Chicano who was his mentor can be interpreted in different ways. On the one hand, it can show the cruel and ruthless nature of Anglos, who take advantage of Chicanos by being even more cruel and pitiless. On the other, the fact that a white man can decide to be a Chicano gangster and reach a leading position in the gang may suggest interiorized racism, since the Chicanos need a white leader to become stronger and united; moreover, a white man can do anything he wants, even 'play the Chicano,' and he will still do it 'better' than any other non-white.

The reason why this category is named "phenotype" is the debate concerning the meaning of ethnicity. In a movie, the real origin of a character is not necessarily important for the audience, who are only looking for a certain series of phenotypical traits that may make the character look like s/he belongs to a certain ethnic group—regardless of whether these people are actually Chicanos, or Peruvians or Filipinos. This once more suggests a (colonial) continuity with the black face make-up.

Costumes and make-up

When it comes to costumes, gangster women (restricted among the films in this corpus to *Colors*) tend to wear heavy and dark make-up, as well as cheap-looking and sometimes revealing clothes. They tend to have brown to black hair (some bleached or with highlights).

The men look like a visual representation of the general gangster identikit provided by the Los Angeles Police Department on the page "How Gangs Are Identified:"

> Most gang members are proud of their gang and freely admit their membership. Many display tattoos openly and dress in a style identifying their particular gang. [...] The uniform of Hispanic gangs is standard and easily recognizable. Most gang members adopt a basic style that includes white T-shirts, thin belts, baggy pants with split cuffs, a black or blue knit cap (beanie) or a bandana tied around the forehead similar to a sweat band. [...] Gang clothing styles can be easily detected because of the specific way gang members wear their clothing. Examples are preferences for wearing baggy or "sagging" pants or having baseball caps turned at an angle. [...] some gangs like to wear plaid shirts in either blue, brown, black or red. These shirts are worn loosely and untucked. [...] Other signs that youngsters may have joined gangs include [...] specific hairstyles (such as shaving their heads bald, hair nets, rollers or braids).[37]

Examples of these features—in terms of behaviour, phenotypes, costumes and make-up—can be found in all the movies. Of course, another typical clothing option is the convict uniform—sometimes worn neatly, at others customized to have a tougher look. By make-up, it is important to note, this author also includes the scenic make-up that conveys the physical/mental state of the character (e.g. deep dark eye circles, a hollowed face, oily hair and an underweight body identify a character as a drug addict). This implies a series of behavioural features, including irresponsible actions, mood swings, and dependency on substances to face the pain, both physical and emotional.

Interlocutors

The interlocutor has a crucial role in determining the way a speaker selects the variety required in conversation. Not adapting one's communication to the interlocutor in a fictional context sends the

---

[37] "How Gangs are Identified," from the Official Site of the Los Angeles Police Department: http://www.lapdonline.org/get_informed/content_basic_view/23468. Accessed April 29, 2021.

audience-specific messages about the character. For example, a fictional *cholo* using a substandard variety with someone representing authority may be a challenge to the system (e.g. *Stand and Deliver*) or confirm the intellectual inferiority of the character (e.g. *Colors*). The main representatives of authority (very often but not always white) are police officers, jail wardens, legal authorities (e.g. parole officers, lawyers) and teachers.

Other possible interlocutors are the other gang members, who are expected to share the same cultural background, but not necessarily the status within the organization since gangs in the movies of this corpus are more or less rigidly hierarchical. In *Blood In Blood Out*, for example, the structure of the jail gang *La Onda* is explained in detail: the founders are called *capitanes*, and the *jefe* is their elected spokesperson. Under them are the *soldados*, who usually do the dirty jobs e.g. killing. Rival gang members are also common interlocutors. It could be other Chicano gangs or gangs of other ethnicities, especially white (which they call the polar bears) or African American (referred to as *mayates*).

One last option is non-gangster Chicanos, most often members of the family or — in the case of *Stand and Deliver* — other classmates. With family members, they usually have intense relationships, both in terms of affection and conflict. The oldest members of the family can be immigrants from Mexico with a (rather stereotypical) limited command of the English language. In *American Me*, there is also a girlfriend.

The scheme of intermodal relations

The modes of the audiovisual stereotype (setting, costumes and make-up, phenotype, interlocutors, music and behaviour) are turned into just as many categories in the scheme of analysis of the corpus. The subsequent step is to put these categories in relation to the ones from the textual dimension. To do so, I followed Pastra (2008) and Ramos Pinto & Mubaraki (2020), who simplified Pastra's categories to make the classification fit for translation work: "an extra category of confirmation" in order to account for the fact that "the choice of strategy or procedure is often mediated by the consideration of having the same meaning expressed in modes other than the speech mode" (Ramos Pinto & Mubaraki 2020, 21). This means that, when it is impossible to convey a certain meaning through speech in a given situation, the translator may conclude that other modes will efficiently convey the information.

In other words, when intersecting the linguistic categories with the other modes, there can be a relation of contradiction, when the two modes do not have anything to do with each other. Otherwise, the relation is of confirmation, and it is further divided between equivalence, when the two modes convey the same message, and complementarity when one mode completes the other (Figure 5).

Figure 5 Model of intermodal relations, drawn from Ramos Pinto and Mubaraki (2020).

These relations are applied to each intermodal category, which shows how each line is placed in relation to each non-textual element of the diegesis.

INTERMODAL RELATIONS																	
COSTUMES AND MAKE-UP			PHENOTYPE			BEHAVIOUR			INTERLOCUTORS			SETTING			MUSIC		
CONF EQUIV	CONF COMP	CONTRADICT	CONF EQUIV	CONF COMP	CONTRADICT	CONF EQUIV	CONF COMP	CONTRADICT	CONF EQUIV	CONF COMP	CONTRADICT	CONF EQUIV	CONF COMP	CONTRADICT	CONF EQUIV	CONF COMP	CONTRADICT

Figure 6 Intermodal relations in the scheme.

This part is integrated with the one concerning the linguistic dimension of the corpus, and repeated once for the source text and once for the target text. This shows how the intermodal relations are independently built; subsequently, it is possible to compare the two versions to see whether the relations have changed and to infer how this might potentially have changed or kept the overall message in the text.

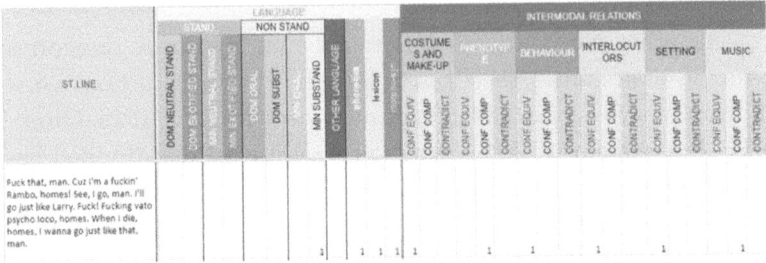

Figure 7 Tagged line uttered by Gato (*Colors*) with the intermodal relations in the scheme.

The logic of the scheme is to associate a certain variety with the surrounding non-textual elements to see how they are related. In this example, Gato is using a minority substandard language—vernacular CE. He is wearing the typical gangster outfit (checked shirt, bandana) and is holding his rifle. He has been drinking and smoking (presumably marijuana) with his fellow gang members after a revenge shootout where Larry, a respected member of the gang, was killed. This triggered Gato to have thoughts about the transient life of a gangster. As if he were an urban warrior (Rambo), he expresses the wish to die in battle, i.e. during a shootout. A gang member is playing a Mexican-like melody on his guitar, and they are on a deserted hill (part of their territory), filled with abandoned objects (a van can be seen on the right) on a night lit only by their bonfire and by the city lights of Los Angeles in the distance.

His minority substandard language (vernacular CE) can be considered equivalent to his gangster outfit, to his behaviour (smoking and drinking, holding a gun, and—seconds later—trying to stand up and falling to the ground), to his interlocutors (fellow gang members acting and talking just like him), and to the setting (as mentioned above, an abandoned hill is a typical place for gang meetings). It is complementary with the phenotype: indeed, the audience can expect the character to speak a minority variety due to his phenotypical traits, but the colour of his skin does not imply anything about his educational level, which is revealed only through his low-prestige speech. In fact, a fairly biased audience might well assume that Gato can only speak Spanish. A less biased audience might not be prejudicial and think that a Latino could well be educated. The skin alone does not provide definite information on the language, and it needs other elements to provide more specific coordinates. For similar reasons, the variety is complementary with music: while the music is traditional Mexican mariachi-style, the character is a modern-era Chicano. This means that the music accounts for the character's ethnic heritage, but not necessarily for his educational level or urban habitat. Does such a chain of relations change in the target version?

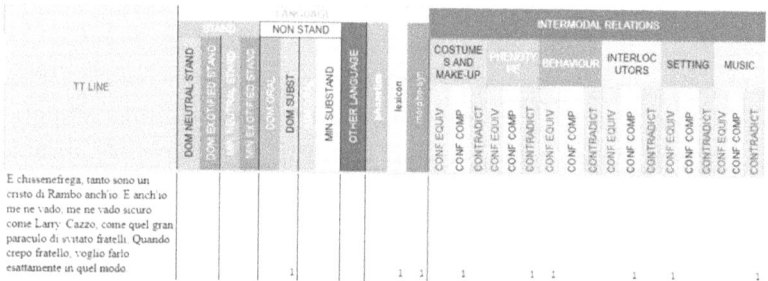

Figure 8 Gato's tagged line with intermodal relations in the target version.

As mentioned in the previous paragraph, the target line is still substandard, but the distinctive traits of Gato's belonging to a minority are not visible anymore, so it is a dominant substandard. The substandard speech is still equivalent to his behaviour and the setting: he acts like a thug and is in a typical thug meeting place. It contradicts his phenotypical traits and the music because he is talking like an uneducated white person is expected to talk. It is complementary with his clothing and interlocutors because he talks like a generic gangster, but his outfit and the fellow gang members surrounding him confirm that he belongs to a specific type of gang (a mostly Chicano gang that also accepts members from other ethnic groups).

Can this change of relations mean the translator has failed in passing the message? The purpose of this corpus is not to evaluate the work of the translator, but to describe what happens in the passage to the TT. And, in so doing, it is fundamental to make sure all elements are taken into consideration. First, this single line is part of a whole, and the impression about a character comes from the overall rendering and not just from a single line. Furthermore, the fact that the relations have changed does not imply that the audience doesn't have other ways to retrieve the intended meaning. This once again confirms the importance of having a corpus rather than a single case.

Certainly, I have tried to be as objective as possible in attributing certain values to the varieties and their intermodal relations with the rest of the film, and while objectivity is an impossible achievement, here the attempt was to consider more points of view before tagging. However, judgement can always be biased by culture or assumptions, which makes product-based studies difficult and stimulating at the same time. Undoubtedly, it would be even better to compare the observations coming from a young academic like myself, who has long studied linguistic variation and Chicano English, with the opinions of the supposed audience, who may or may not know the minorities portrayed in these movies. Indeed, a reception study would be the best outcome for the work carried out by this author, as will be explained in more detail at the end of this work.

For now, after having explained how the analysis was structured, the following step will be to show its hands-on application to the corpus.

Chapter 3
Broadened horizons: framework application and results

Having explained in detail how the categories for the analysis were designed, and having explored the ratio of tagging, the study now moves on to an analysis of the corpus itself. The lines in the ST and TT were not always the same: sometimes some ST lines were left untranslated, but most often TT lines were added. This especially functions to fill silences (a sort of *horror vacui*) or attribute a line to the wrong character in scenes where many people talk at the same time and/or the lips of the speakers cannot be seen clearly. That is why, in the following tables, the number of lines for the ST and TT of each character is reported separately.

There was a change of software between the tagging and the data elaboration. The former was carried out with Microsoft Office Excel™, whereas for the latter the software Mathcad™ was chosen. I had used Excel for the tagging as I had a certain familiarity with its basic functions but found its data elaboration quite rigid. After communicating with the postgraduate students of the Mechanical Engineering department of the Polytechnic University of Bari,[38] I decided to switch to Mathcad™ for data elaboration. Mathcad™ is primarily used in the field of engineering, and it is a powerful means to perform and analyse calculations: while its potential goes far beyond the needs of this research, it has non-negligible advantages compared to Excel™.

First, its interface simulates that of a notebook, in the sense that it has a fluid structure (while Excel has a rigid row/column organization), which makes it possible to alternate text lines, formulas and graphs. This makes sheet writing and reading simpler and more intuitive. Intuitiveness is also the key to another

---

[38] The elaboration of the data was only possible thanks to the patient help and support of this Department. This non-structured collaboration served as further proof of the unlimited potential of joining the forces of humanities and scientific departments.

advantage of Mathcad™: instead of having its own semiotics (like Excel™), it uses the standard universal mathematical language. As a consequence, it works with the very same formulas as the ones taken from any book of mathematics (e.g. means, percentages etc.). Furthermore, Mathcad™ allows the generating of graphs with personalized variables, and it can use data from Excel™ as a starting point.

Indeed, the first step was importing the tagged data from Excel™ and preparing it for Mathcad™ elaboration. Subsequently, formulas were designed to answer questions concerning the textual and the diegetic dimension:

- Which linguistic categories were used for each character in ST and TT? This requires hypothesising the overall strategies used by the translators and answering another question: which strategies might have been behind the change?
- What were the most common features for conveying a certain type of language? Did they change from ST to TT?
- How did these varieties build intermodal relationships with the other elements of the film? Did the relationships change from ST to TT, and to what extent?

3.1 Language variation in source and target films: the textual dimension

Stand and Deliver

As mentioned in the previous chapter, *Stand and Deliver* (1988) has two characters in the role of gangsters. One, Angel, is more moderate and leaves gang life to become a good student; the other, Chuco, is a typical *cholo*, but not a totally negative character: he respects Angel's choice and, in the end, fixes Professor Escalante's car with the help of his *vatos* (men, Polkinhorn et al. 2005, 63) and Angel himself.

In terms of linguistic categories, Angel's ST and TT were thus distributed:

Angel	Dominant neutral standard	Dominant exotified standard	Minority neutral standard	Minority exotified standard	Dominant oral	Dominant substandard	Minority oral	Minority substandard	Other language	Total
ST (64 lines)	0%	0%	3.1%	0%	0%	0%	32.8%	45.3%	18.8%	100%
TT (63 lines)	27.9%	0%	0%	0%	59%	1.6%	3.3%	0%	8.2%	100%

Table 1   Angel's ST and TT distribution in *Stand and Deliver* (1988).

The source text does not include any use of the dominant ethnic group language, which is to say California Anglo English in any of its possible subcategories. There is slight use of the minority neutral standard and significant use of Spanish (Other language), but the most used varieties are minority oral (32.8%) and minority substandard (45.3%) — the second of which is used in nearly half of the utterances by Angel. Indeed, even when he explains difficult concepts concerning science or mathematics, he does so with his usual *cholo* language like in the following example, when he explains what stars are to his non-educated friend Chuco:[39]

> The stars aren't really there, *ese*. What you're looking at is where they used to be, *man*. It takes the light ...1,000 years to reach the earth. *You know?* For all we know, they burned out a long time ago, <u>maaan</u>. God pulled the plug on us. He didn't <u>teeell</u> <u>nooobody</u>. (*Stand and Deliver* 1988, 1.06.34-1.06.57).

Conversely, his language shifts towards the dominant ethnic group in the TT, with most of his lines (59%) in the dominant oral category, and a relevant 27.9% in the most prestigious group: the dominant neutral standard. Although halved, not all Spanish has disappeared, scoring 8.2% in the TT.

---

[39] The lexical and morpho-syntactic features are visible in the example, and the phonetics, too, tend towards vernacular CE. Like in the previous chapter, the underlined words are pronounced with a circumflex intonation pattern (Matluck 1952, 119).

Chuco embodies more closely the stereotypes mentioned in the previous chapter, as he is a bully and drops out of school: he gives up on any hope of a different future before even trying.

Chuco	*Dominant neutral standard*	*Dominant exotified standard*	*Minority neutral standard*	*Minority exotified standard*	*Dominant oral*	*Dominant substandard*	*Minority oral*	*Minority substandard*	*Other language*	*Total*
ST (18 lines)	0%	0%	0%	0%	0%	0%	31.6%	63.2%	5.3%	100%
TT (17 lines)	5.6%	0%	5.6%	0%	61.1%	11.1%	0%	11.1%	5.6%	100%

Table 2 Chuco's ST and TT distribution in *Stand and Deliver* (1988).

His ST speech is clearly in the minority non-standard zone, with a significant 63.2% in the substandard followed, at a distance, by the minority oral (31.6%). He also uses some Spanish, but not to a particularly relevant extent. The linguistic profile changes quite significantly in the TT, where most of his speech is in the dominant oral category. Chuco's speech pattern, however, seems more scattered than in the ST, as the TT substandard of both dominant and minority groups have the same frequency—a rather low 11.1%. The other three categories have the same score of 5.6% and are quite different from each other: dominant neutral standard, minority neutral standard and Spanish.

The next question concerns the linguistic realization of the characters' profiles in both the ST and the TT. As mentioned in the previous chapter, in this case, more than one feature can be attributed to each line, since any utterance contains elements coming from lexicon, phonetics and morpho-syntax alike. This may also trigger the question: since almost all sentences of any language contain all the elements above, what is the point of this classification? In this case, the effort was to identify the features that the audience may perceive as marked, distinctive of a certain linguistic category.[40] As the numbers in the tables below show, the percentages associated with phonetics, lexicon and morpho-syntax are markers of the frequency of their presence in the realization of a specific category, not the extent to which one of these indexes contributes more or less than the others when more than one is present. This, in fact, cannot be evaluated objectively based on individual perception.

ANGEL	Phonetics ST	Lexicon ST	Morpho-syntax ST	Phonetics TT	Lexicon TT	Morpho-syntax TT
Dom. Neut. Stand.	0%	0%	0%	64.7%	70.6%	100%
Dom. Exot. Stand.	0%	0%	0%	0%	0%	0%
Min. Neut. Stand.	100%	100%	100%	0%	0%	0%
Min. Exot. Stand.	0%	0%	0%	0%	0%	0%
Dom. Oral	0%	0%	0%	0%	22.2%	91.7%
Dom. Subst.	0%	0%	0%	0%	100%	100%
Min. Oral	100%	28.6%	57%	0%	100%	100%
Min. Subst.	96.5%	79.3%	82.7%	0%	0%	0%
Other language	100%	100%	58.3%	100%	100%	40%
Weighted Average	**98.4%**	**67.2%**	**70.3%**	**25.4%**	**44.4%**	**88.9%**

Table 3 Angel's ST and TT realization in *Stand and Deliver* (1988).

The averages are weighted, in order to take into consideration the actual number of lines within each category: some linguistic

---

[40] By its nature, the identification of linguistic features depends on who is watching/listening/reading. The most important thing is to be aware of one's own biases and be ready to accept different views, especially when they come from a perception study. By analysing my own media language perception, I suggest that some features may be particularly influential in the process. One is age: I was born in 1989, which implies that I am somewhere in between old and new media, and that both have an influence on my perception of language. Another is education and training: with an education that specialised in media studies and subsequently in lingua-cultural mediation, foreign languages and translation (AVT in particular), I may perceive as important elements that might not make a difference for other types of audience. However, as mentioned in the previous chapter, I attempted to assume different points of view while tagging and analysing the data.

categories were only used a few times, and should not have the same weight as the most common ones.

CHUCO	Phonetics ST	Lexicon ST	Morpho-syntax ST	Phonetics TT	Lexicon TT	Morpho-syntax TT
Dom. Neut. Stand.	0%	0%	0%	100%	100%	100%
Dom. Exot. Stand.	0%	0%	0%	0%	0%	0%
Min. Neut. Stand.	0%	0%	0%	0%	0%	0%
Min. Exot. Stand.	0%	0%	0%	0%	0%	0%
Dom. Oral	0%	0%	0%	0%	54.5%	90.9%
Dom. Subst.	0%	0%	0%	0%	50%	100%
Min. Oral	100%	50%	66.7%	0%	0%	0%
Min. Subst.	100%	75%	75%	0%	0%	100%
Other language	100%	100%	100%	100%	100%	100%
Weighted Average	100%	68.4%	73.7%	16.7%	66.7%	94.4%

Table 4 Chuco's ST and TT realization in *Stand and Deliver* (1988).

What is striking in both tables is the different role each type of feature plays in ST and TT. One example is phonetics, which should not be too surprising, given that the rules of Italian *dubbese* tend to impose a standardized non-regional pronunciation: proper elocution that dubbing actors are specifically trained to achieve. Indeed, the only times phonetics had a role in both Angel's and Chuco's TT is in defining the dominant neutral standard and the use of Spanish — the Other language. The weighted average of Angel's TT phonetics is much lower than the one of the ST, where it is clearly a predominant feature, always scoring between 96.5% and 100% in the varieties that were used. The difference becomes even more evident in TT Chuco, who speaks very little standard and certainly less Spanish than his friend — a fact which makes his use of phonetics fall below 20%. Conversely, ST Chuco makes constant use of vernacular CE phonetics as his main linguistic marker.

Moving on to the other categories, they play an especially important role in the TT, which has to do without phonetics everywhere apart from the dominant neutral standard. The morpho-syntax seems particularly relevant in TT Angel, as it is present as a marked element in most cases, with a weighted average of 88.9%. The only place where morpho-syntax does not have a central role is in the category Other language, which is also the case in the ST. In these cases, the line in Spanish may not constitute a grammatical sentence. Morpho-syntax has an important role in the ST as well (weighted average 70.3%), although to a lesser extent than the TT. As for Chuco, morpho-syntax is the predominant feature in the ST and even more in the TT—further confirming its role in drawing speech away from the standard.

Finally, Angel's lexical features score differently from ST to TT, as they are slightly lower than morpho-syntax in the former, and below 50% in the latter. It is central to the realization of Spanish in both ST and TT. However, apart from that category, the lexicon is particularly important in the realization of minority substandard in the ST—the reason being the use of specific words signalling the belonging to a Chicano gang or code-switching of substandard words (e.g. *cabrón, chingón*). In Chuco's speech, the lexicon plays a similar role in both ST and TT, being slightly more present in the former (68.4% and 66.7% respectively).

Overall, both the translated characters seem to follow a similar pattern for what concerns the marking of linguistic variation: the TT counterbalances a lack of phonetic nonstandardness with an increased resort to morpho-syntax markers of orality and, to a lesser extent, to the lexicon.

To understand the strategies adopted in the translation, it is useful to visualize the way the concentration of linguistic varieties for the two characters changes from source to target text over the course of the film:

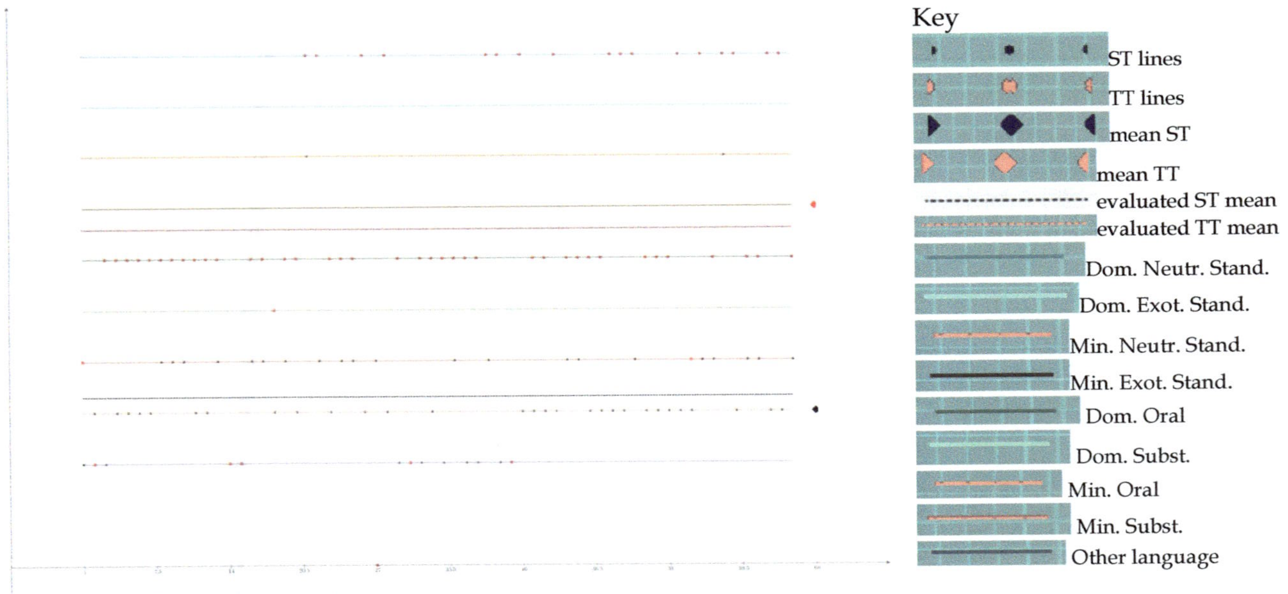

Figure 9 Angel's textual scatter plot.

In the graph above, each black dot represents an ST line, and each red dot a TT line, and the film proceeds chronologically from the left to the right (the red dot on the x-axis represents a line that was omitted in the target text, while black dots on the axis represent lines that were added in the TT). The ST shows a clear use of the minority substandard at the beginning when he is a bad boy and has another substantial increase before the end when he acts irresponsibly because of his disappointment. For the rest of the time, his lines are fairly balanced between oral and substandard. Only two lines are in the minority standard, both used ironically in dialogues with Professor Escalante. Spanish is instead concentrated in specific moments in which his Spanish-speaking grandmother is in the scene. This causes ST Angel's speech pattern to remain in the minority substandard category: the black dotted line shows where Angel's average lines actually are, while the large black dot shows the category that is closer to the average of his speech.

Overall, it can be inferred that ST Angel speaks a vernacular variety of CE, but he is bilingual, as he can switch to Spanish, and also occasionally elevate his language, although never concealing his Chicano background. When it comes to the target text, the speech follows a different and somewhat ambiguous trend. Quite consistently through the film, most lines are positioned in the dominant oral category. However, after the first scenes and increasingly more towards the end of the movie, coinciding with Angel's full transformation, there is a significant increase of the dominant neutral standard. The TT Spanish lines are in the same position as the ST ones but of a lower quantity. Overall, TT Angel tends to speak the oral language of the dominant group, associated with lesser prestige than the standard, but he gradually upgrades towards standard language during the movie. TT Angel very rarely shows linguistic signs of belonging to his ethnic group, but he is also able to speak some Spanish when required.

Looking at Chuco's trends, a substantial difference emerges between ST and TT. In the source text, Chuco's speech pattern is regular, and clearly shows his socio-cultural role and educational level, as well as his Chicano origin. In the target text, although most lines are concentrated in the dominant oral category, the constant fluctuation among lower-prestige categories generates an anomaly in the mathematical means, so that his speech pattern tends towards the dominant substandard category. This may give information concerning the strategy behind the work of the translators.

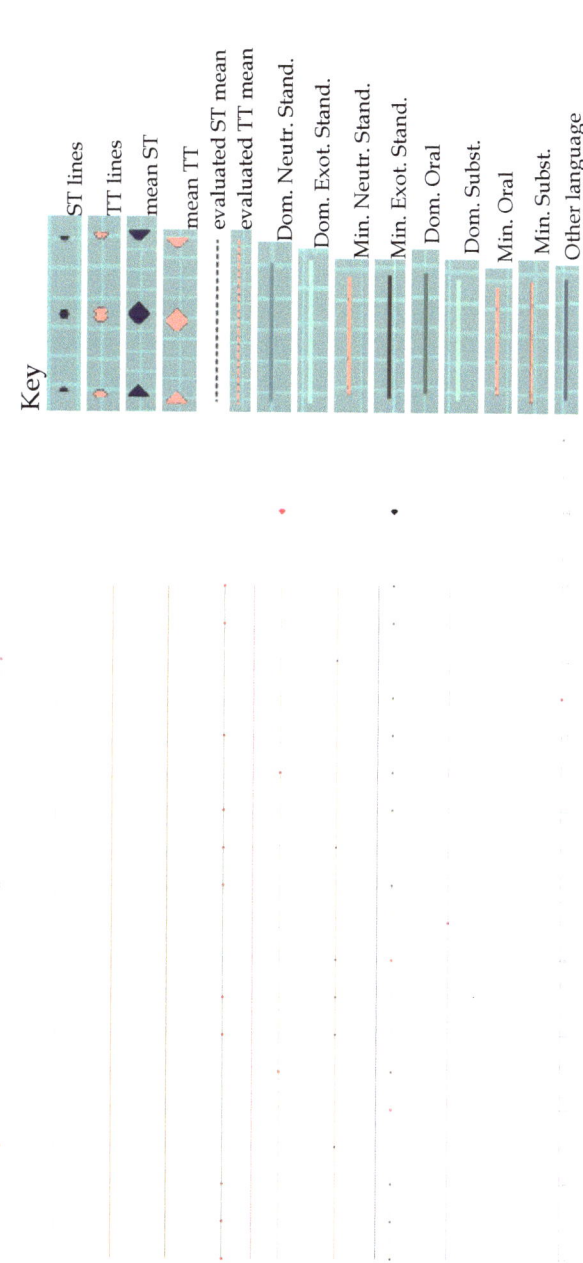

Figure 10 Chuco's textual scatter plot.

In fact, following Ramos Pinto (2017), it is possible to infer what type of strategies might have been adopted in translating the textual dimension of the film. Angel's translation shows instances of both centralization and discourse standardization. Centralization is what lies behind the shift from minority substandard/oral to dominant group oral, while discourse standardization was applied in the passage from minority substandard/oral to dominant neutral standard, the category furthest up the prestige scale. While his ST version mainly points at the linguistic authenticity of the ethnotype (portraying a *cholo* from East Los Angeles), the TT version seems to concentrate on the rendering of his life path and role in the plot: he symbolizes the liberation from ghetto life through education. Chuco was mainly translated through centralization: the overall impression is still that of a less educated person, especially when compared to his friend. His speech pattern includes inaccuracies aimed at showing his lack of education, e.g. when describing a starry sky, he says: "*certo che quelle stelle lassù non sono inquinate*" (surely those stars up there are not polluted), attributing the pollution to the stars rather than to the air. However, his language was not rendered completely, as his ethnic heritage only occasionally emerges, and mostly at the beginning (see the first red dots in Figure 10), when the character has just been introduced in the film.

Colors

With white police officers as protagonists, as well as a white director (Dennis Hopper) and screenwriter (Michael Schiffer), *Colors* is the film in the selection that dedicates the least space to looking into the Chicanos' psychology. The non-white characters are almost exclusively gangsters or immigrants.

The analysed characters are members of the '21 street gang,' the only gang whose members are on screen for any real period of time: the older leader Frog and the young and fiery Gato (whose name means 'cat' in Spanish). Both are drug addicts, with no intention of leaving gang life. In the following tables are the linguistic frequencies for each character:

Frog	Dominant neutral standard	Dominant exotified standard	Minority neutral standard	Minority exotified standard	Dominant oral	Dominant substandard	Minority oral	Minority substandard	Other language	Total
ST (50 lines)	0%	0%	0%	0%	0%	0%	24%	68%	9%	100%
TT (52 lines)	2%	2%	5.9%	2%	0%	0%	25.5%	47.1%	15.7%	100%

Table 5 Frog's ST and TT distribution in *Colors* (1988).

Gato	Dominant neutral standard	Dominant exotified standard	Minority neutral standard	Minority exotified standard	Dominant oral	Dominant substandard	Minority oral	Minority substandard	Other language	Total
ST (20 lines)	0%	0%	0%	0%	0%	0%	15%	85%	0%	100%
TT (21 lines)	9.5%	0%	0%	0%	28.6%	57.1%	0%	4.8%	0%	100%

Table 6 Gato's ST and TT distribution in *Colors* (1988).

In the ST, the two characters have fairly similar profiles. Both have no occurrence of standard language, and their speech patterns are constantly marked by their Chicano identity. Both ST Frog and ST Gato have most of their lines in the minority substandard category (68% and 85% respectively). However, the speech of ST Frog is slightly more diversified than ST Gato, with 24% of minority oral and some lines in Spanish (9%). ST Gato has only a small number of lines in the minority oral category and does not seem able to speak Spanish (0%).

The TT version of the characters has been handled in opposite ways from each other. TT Frog's lines are more or less in the same categories as his ST counterpart, with a slight use of minority standard (5.9% minority neutral and 2% minority exotified) and an increase of Spanish, whose use nearly doubled in the TT. TT Gato's use of minority substandard drops from 85% to less than 5%. Most of his lines are located in the dominant substandard category

(57.1%) and some in the dominant oral (28.6%), while nearly 10% of his lines are in the dominant neutral standard category.
How were those results obtained linguistically?

FROG	Phonetics ST	Lexicon ST	Morpho-syntax ST	Phonetics TT	Lexicon TT	Morpho-syntax TT
Dom. Neut. Stand.	0%	0%	0%	100%	100%	100%
Dom. Exot. Stand.	0%	0%	0%	100%	100%	0%
Min. Neut. Stand.	0%	0%	0%	100%	0%	0%
Min. Exot. Stand.	0%	0%	0%	100%	100%	100%
Dom. Oral	0%	0%	0%	0%	0%	0%
Dom. Subst.	0%	0%	0%	0%	0%	0%
Min. Oral	100%	58.3%	33.3%	100%	69.2%	76.9%
Min. Subst.	97%	94.1%	79.4%	95.8%	95.8%	70.8%
Other language	100%	100%	50%	100%	100%	100%
Weighted Average	98%	86%	66%	96.1%	82.4%	68.6%

Table 7   Frog's ST and TT realization in *Colors* (1988).

GATO	Phonetics ST	Lexicon ST	Morpho-syntax ST	Phonetics TT	Lexicon TT	Morpho-syntax TT
Dom. Neut. Stand.	0%	0%	0%	100%	100%	100%
Dom. Exot. Stand.	0%	0%	0%	0%	0%	0%
Min. Neut. Stand.	0%	0%	0%	0%	0%	0%
Min. Exot. Stand.	0%	0%	0%	0%	0%	0%
Dom. Oral	0%	0%	0%	0%	16.7%	100%
Dom. Subst.	0%	0%	0%	0%	100%	83.3%
Min. Oral	100%	0%	100%	0%	0%	0%
Min. Subst.	100%	100%	82.3%	0%	100%	100%
Other language	0%	0%	0%	0%	0%	0%
Weighted Average	100%	85%	85%	9.5%	76.2%	90.5%

Table 8   Gato's ST and TT realization in *Colors* (1988).

Something that immediately stands out while looking at Frog's use of linguistic features is the fact that both ST and TT show similar uses of lexical, morpho-syntactic and phonetic features. This use of phonetics in the TT is especially unusual: TT Frog is the only translated character of the whole corpus to keep phonetic features ascribable to his ethnic heritage in non-Spanish speech. It must be specified, however, that the TT phonetics that mark Frog as belonging to a minority are not those of Chicano English, but of Italian *dubbese*, spoken with a fictional Spanish accent.

In TT Gato, the role of phonetics has nearly disappeared (falling from 100% of ST to 9.5% in the TT), as they only identify the dominant standard category. Although less dramatically, the role of the lexicon also decreases. Vice versa, the role of morpho-syntax grows slightly from ST to TT, confirming the trend observed in *Stand and Deliver* (1988).

The graphs below visualize the linguistic trends for both characters:

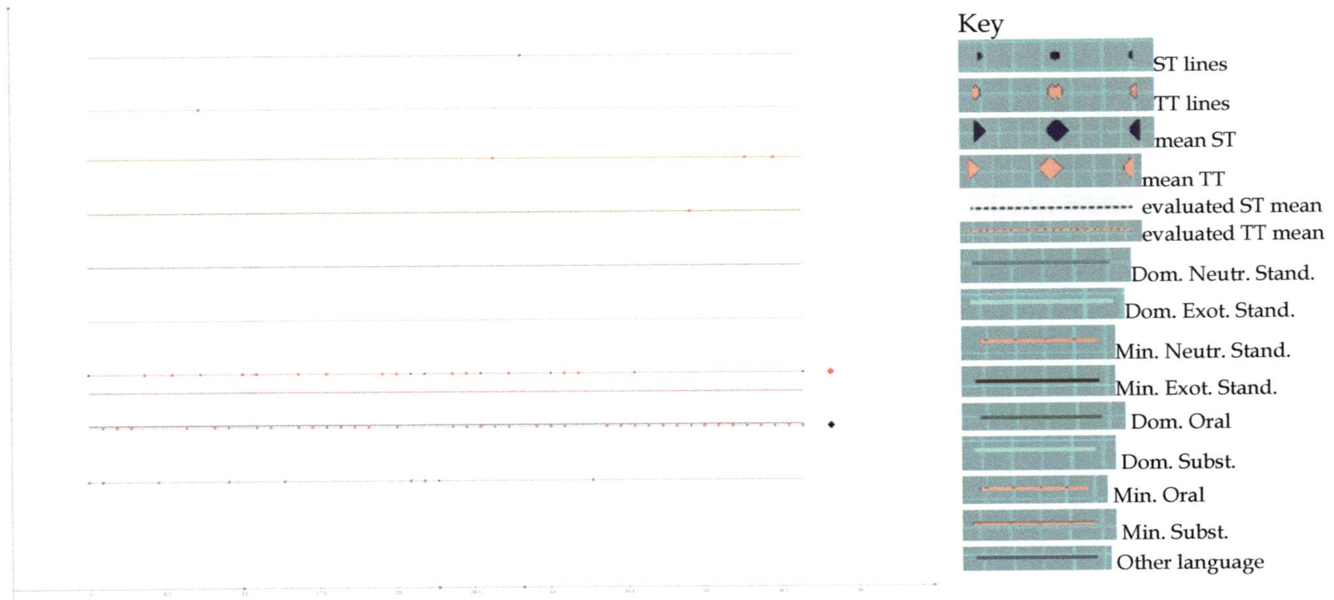

136 DORA RENNA

Figure 11 Frog's textual scatter plot.

LANGUAGE VARIATION AND MULTIMODALITY 137

Key

- ST lines
- TT lines
- mean ST
- mean TT
- evaluated ST mean
- evaluated TT mean
- Dom. Neutr. Stand.
- Dom. Exot. Stand.
- Min. Neutr. Stand.
- Min. Exot. Stand.
- Dom. Oral
- Dom. Subst.
- Min. Oral
- Min. Subst.
- Other language

Figure 12 Gato's textual scatter plot.

Frog's graph shows an increase of Spanish items in the TT (red dots), as well as the relative proximity of ST and TT items in general — although a few TT lines expand higher up towards more prestigious varieties. Gato's lines seem more scattered along different lines, with almost no occurrence in the non-standard language of the minority he belongs to. In the ST, the only difference between the two is that Gato does not seem able to switch to Spanish, while the ST audience may assume Frog has some degree of bilingual ability. In the TT, Frog's bilingualism is emphasised, while Gato's speech pattern drifts away from his Mexican heritage.

In the light of these results, it can be assumed that different strategies have been used for the two characters. TT Frog's speech patterns were clearly reconstructed using maintenance, but also a form of decentralization. Two elements hint at this strategy for TT Frog: the increase of Spanish items, and the use of a foreign accent instead of the vernacular CE one. TT Gato, on the other hand, was mainly translated through discourse standardization and centralization.

American Me

American Me aimed to show the dramatic life of East Los Angeles Chicanos, affected by discrimination, poverty and omnipresent crime and drugs. Gang life is presented as a sort of virus that, sooner or later, can be contracted by anyone (even those who seem far from or against it). Escaping it is shown to be a nearly impossible task, despite the tragic suffering it heralds for gang members and their loved ones.

The analysed characters are all members of *La Eme*, the Mexican mafia: the protagonist, Santana, his best friend JD (who eventually becomes his antagonist), their other friend Mundo and the two brothers Puppet and Lil' Puppet.

The main character is Santana, who shows a leader's attitude from the very beginning of the movie: he reacts to his non-idyllic family situation by setting up his own gang, which becomes much larger after he is convicted. In *La Eme*, he is the one everyone looks up to, the one who has the final say when it comes to important decisions, such as executions. That is until he realizes the damage gang life causes to Chicanos. It is relevant to specify that Santana is the narrating voice in the film. However, since the context from which he is telling his story remains undisclosed until the end (when the audience finds out it is his last love letter before being assassinated in jail), those lines were not considered in his statistics because they are isolated from a non-textual context, are not comparable with the lines uttered in the scene by the rest of the characters, and only become clear in their purpose at the very end of the film.

Santana	*Dominant neutral standard*	*Dominant exotified standard*	*Minority neutral standard*	*Minority exotified standard*	*Dominant oral*	*Dominant substandard*	*Minority oral*	*Minority substandard*	*Other language*	*Total*
ST (219 lines)	0%	0%	5.1%	0.5%	0%	0%	38.2%	47%	9.2%	100%
TT (221 lines)	20%	3.6%	0%	0%	52.7%	7.7%	4.5%	4.5%	6.8%	100%

Table 9 Santana's ST and TT distribution in *American Me* (1992).

ST Santana mainly speaks minority substandard, shortly followed by minority oral (47% vs 38.2%). Some of his lines are registered in the category of minority neutral standard and minority-exotified standard, and he also switches to Spanish on some occasions. Conversely, TT Santana's lines are mainly positioned in the dominant oral category, with a significant number of lines in the dominant neutral standard and some in Spanish—although fewer than ST Santana.

While Santana is certainly the main character, he is often seen side by side with his friend, the Anglo JD:

J.D.	Dominant neutral standard	Dominant exotified standard	Minority neutral standard	Minority exotified standard	Dominant oral	Dominant substandard	Minority oral	Minority substandard	Other language	Total
ST (61 lines)	0%	0%	8.3%	1.7%	0%	0%	10%	60%	20%	100%
TT (60 lines)	13.3%	3.3%	0%	0%	35%	18.3%	1.7%	13.3%	15%	100%

Table 10 JD's ST and TT distribution in *American Me* (1992).

The ST speech of JD tends even more clearly towards minority substandard, and there are a considerable number of Spanish switches in his lines (20%). Minority oral and minority neutral standards are also present on more occasions. JD's TT speech follows the already observed tendency to be scattered across different categories, the most recurrent being dominant oral, followed by dominant substandard and Spanish. Paradoxically, dominant neutral standard and minority substandard share the same frequency (13.3%), despite being at the opposite ends of the continuum.

The other characters have a smaller space (and several lines) in the film. Mundo has been Santana and JD's friend from their teenage years. Initially the weakest, he is often in charge of executions.

Mundo	Dominant neutral standard	Dominant exotified standard	Minority neutral standard	Minority exotified standard	Dominant oral	Dominant substandard	Minority oral	Minority substandard	Other language	Total
ST (34 lines)	0%	0%	0%	0%	0%	0%	12.1%	57.6%	30.3%	100%
TT (34 lines)	5.9%	0%	0%	0%	50%	14.7%	5.9%	11.8%	11.8%	100%

Table 11 Mundo's ST and TT distribution in *American Me* (1992).

ST Mundo has a low social positioning, with more than half of his lines in the minority substandard category. Another element of his ST speech should not be ignored: he speaks Spanish in more than

30% of his lines, making him the most bilingual character of the entire corpus. TT Mundo, however, seems to have been translated in a similar way to JD, with most of his lines in the dominant oral category (50%) and the rest scattered across different categories.

The other two characters are Puppet and Lil' Puppet, two Chicano brothers with a tragic destiny (the elder will be forced by the gang to kill his young sibling).

Puppet	Dominant neutral standard	Dominant exotified standard	Minority neutral standard	Minority exotified standard	Dominant oral	Dominant substandard	Minority oral	Minority substandard	Other language	Total
ST (22 lines)	0%	0%	0%	0%	0%	0%	31.8%	59.1%	9.1%	100%
TT (22 lines)	18.2%	4.5%	0%	0%	31.8%	9.1%	13.6%	13.6%	9.1%	100%

Table 12 Puppet's ST and TT distribution in *American Me* (1992).

Lil' Puppet	Dominant neutral standard	Dominant exotified standard	Minority neutral standard	Minority exotified standard	Dominant oral	Dominant substandard	Minority oral	Minority substandard	Other language	Total
ST (27 lines)	0%	0%	0%	0%	0%	0%	18.5%	66.7%	14.8%	100%
TT (27 lines)	3.7%	3.7%	0%	0%	33.3%	33.3%	11.1%	11.1%	3.7%	100%

Table 13 Lil' Puppet's ST and TT distribution in *American Me* (1992).

In both cases, the ST Puppet brothers' speech patterns fall prevalently into the minority substandard category (59.1% Puppet, 66.7% for Lil' Puppet). Puppet uses minority oral more often than his younger brother, who in turn switches to Spanish more often. None of the two uses any more prestigious varieties.

The two brothers take different paths in the TT. There, Puppet's lines are mainly in the dominant oral category, followed by the dominant neutral standard. His Spanish remains unchanged (a steady 9.1%). Most of TT Lil' Puppet's lines fall into either the dominant oral or dominant substandard category, followed at a distance by minority oral and minority substandard. The number of Spanish lines is significantly decreased, while some dominant standard (both neutral and exotified) appears.

SANTANA	Phonetics ST	Lexicon ST	Morphosyntax ST	Phonetics TT	Lexicon TT	Morphosyntax TT
Dom. Neut. Stand.	0%	0%	0%	100%	100%	100%
Dom. Exot. Stand.	0%	0%	0%	0%	87.5%	12.5%
Min. Neut. Stand.	100%	0%	8.3%	0%	0%	0%
Min. Exot. Stand.	0%	0%	0%	0%	0%	0%
Dom. Oral	0%	0%	0%	0%	29.3%	94.8%
Dom. Subst.	0%	0%	0%	0%	94.1%	88.2%
Min. Oral	100%	18.1%	100%	0%	100%	100%
Min. Subst.	100%	75.5%	92.2%	0%	100%	90%
Other language	95%	95%	50%	93.3%	100%	46.7%
Weighted Average	100%	51.2%	87.1%	26.4%	61.8%	89.5%

Table 14 Santana's ST and TT realization in *American Me* (1992).

JD	Phonetics ST	Lexicon ST	Morphosyntax ST	Phonetics TT	Lexicon TT	Morphosyntax TT
Dom. Neut. Stand.	0%	0%	0%	100%	100%	100%
Dom. Exot. Stand.	0%	0%	0%	0%	100%	0%
Min. Neut. Stand.	100%	0%	0%	0%	0%	0%
Min. Exot. Stand.	100%	100%	0%	0%	0%	0%
Dom. Oral	0%	0%	0%	0%	38.1%	100%
Dom. Subst.	0%	0%	0%	0%	90.9%	81.8%

LANGUAGE VARIATION AND MULTIMODALITY 143

Min. Oral	100%	16.7%	83.3%	0%	100%	100%
Min. Subst.	100%	88.9%	91.7%	0%	100%	87.5%
Other language	100%	100%	25%	100%	100%	44.4%
Weighted Average	100%	76.7%	68.3%	28.3%	76.7%	83.3%

Table 15 JD's ST and TT realization in *American Me* (1992).

As seen in the other ST texts analysed so far, ST Santana's language relies heavily on phonetics for its realization (100%), followed by morpho-syntax. Lexicon is only indicative of status in 51.2% of the lines. As usual, the phonetic features nearly disappear in the TT, as they only have a role in defining the dominant neutral standard and the Spanish lines. The most important feature in TT Santana's speech is morpho-syntax (89.5%), followed by the lexicon. JD follows a very similar pattern, with a dramatic decrease of phonetic items from ST to TT, compensated for by an even greater increase of marked morpho-syntactical items, while the importance of lexical features remains unvaried.

MUNDO	Phonetics ST	Lexicon ST	Morpho-syntax ST	Phonetics TT	Lexicon TT	Morpho-syntax TT
Dom. Neut. Stand.	0%	0%	0%	100%	100%	100%
Dom. Exot. Stand.	0%	0%	0%	0%	0%	0%
Min. Neut. Stand.	0%	0%	0%	0%	0%	0%
Min. Exot. Stand.	0%	0%	0%	0%	0%	0%
Dom. Oral	0%	0%	0%	0%	58.8%	94.1%
Dom. Subst.	0%	0%	0%	0%	100%	100%
Min. Oral	100%	25%	100%	0%	100%	50%
Min. Subst.	100%	89.5%	89.5%	0%	100%	100%
Other language	100%	100%	80%	100%	100%	25%
Weighted Average	100%	84.8%	87.9%	17.6%	79.4%	85.3%

Table 16 Mundo's ST and TT realization in *American Me* (1992).

LIL' PUPPET	Phonetics ST	Lexicon ST	Morpho-syntax ST	Phonetics TT	Lexicon TT	Morpho-syntax TT
Dom. Neut. Stand.	0%	0%	0%	100%	100%	100%
Dom. Exot. Stand.	0%	0%	0%	0%	100%	0%
Min. Neut. Stand.	0%	0%	0%	0%	0%	0%
Min. Exot. Stand.	0%	0%	0%	0%	0%	0%
Dom. Oral	0%	0%	0%	0%	33.3%	88.9%
Dom. Subst.	0%	0%	0%	0%	100%	100%
Min. Oral	100%	60%	100%	0%	100%	100%
Min. Subst.	100%	100%	100%	0%	100%	100%
Other language	100%	75%	75%	100%	100%	0%
Weighted Average	100%	88.9%	96.3%	7.4%	77.8%	88.9%

Table 17 Lil' Puppet's ST and TT realization in *American Me* (1992).

Mundo's ST realization is similar to that of his fellow gang members from the street gang *La Primera* (Santana and JD), although the importance of lexicon significantly increases in his speech pattern. However, the TT realization seems generally less marked, as the usual decrease in phonetics does not seem compensated for by the increase of other items. All the categories have a lower frequency (morpho-syntax being the most recurrent), which means that each line has fewer characterising elements compared to those of Mundo's fellows. In this sense, it is comparable to Lil' Puppet's TT rendering, where all the elements have a diminished frequency — especially evident for phonetics, but also present in the other two groups.

PUPPET	Phonetics ST	Lexicon ST	Morpho-syntax ST	Phonetics TT	Lexicon TT	Morpho-syntax TT
Dom. Neut. Stand.	0%	0%	0%	100%	100%	100%
Dom. Exot. Stand.	0%	0%	0%	0%	100%	0%
Min. Neut. Stand.	0%	0%	0%	0%	0%	0%
Min. Exot. Stand.	0%	0%	0%	0%	0%	0%
Dom. Oral	0%	0%	0%	0%	42.9%	100%
Dom. Subst.	0%	0%	0%	0%	100%	100%
Min. Oral	100%	0%	100%	0%	100%	66.7%

Min. Subst.	100%	92.3%	100%	0%	100%	100%	
Other language	100%	100%	0%	100%	100%	100%	
Weighted Average	100%	63.6%	90.9%	27.3%	81.8%	90.9%	

Table 18 Puppet's ST and TT realization in American Me (1992).

Puppet follows a pattern of his own, being the only one in the film whose TT rendering sees an increase of lexical items, while the importance of morpho-syntax remains unchanged.

The sharp decrease in the importance of phonetical items is a constant trait, only interrupted by *Colors*' TT Frog, while the increase in the use of morpho-syntax is widespread across the whole corpus. In fact, the only three characters without an augmented morpho-syntax are minor ones, and they all still have morpho-syntax far higher than 50%, which remains a higher value than TT phonetics. Lexicon fluctuates slightly, never going below 50%.

The next step is attempting to identify the possible strategies behind the characters.

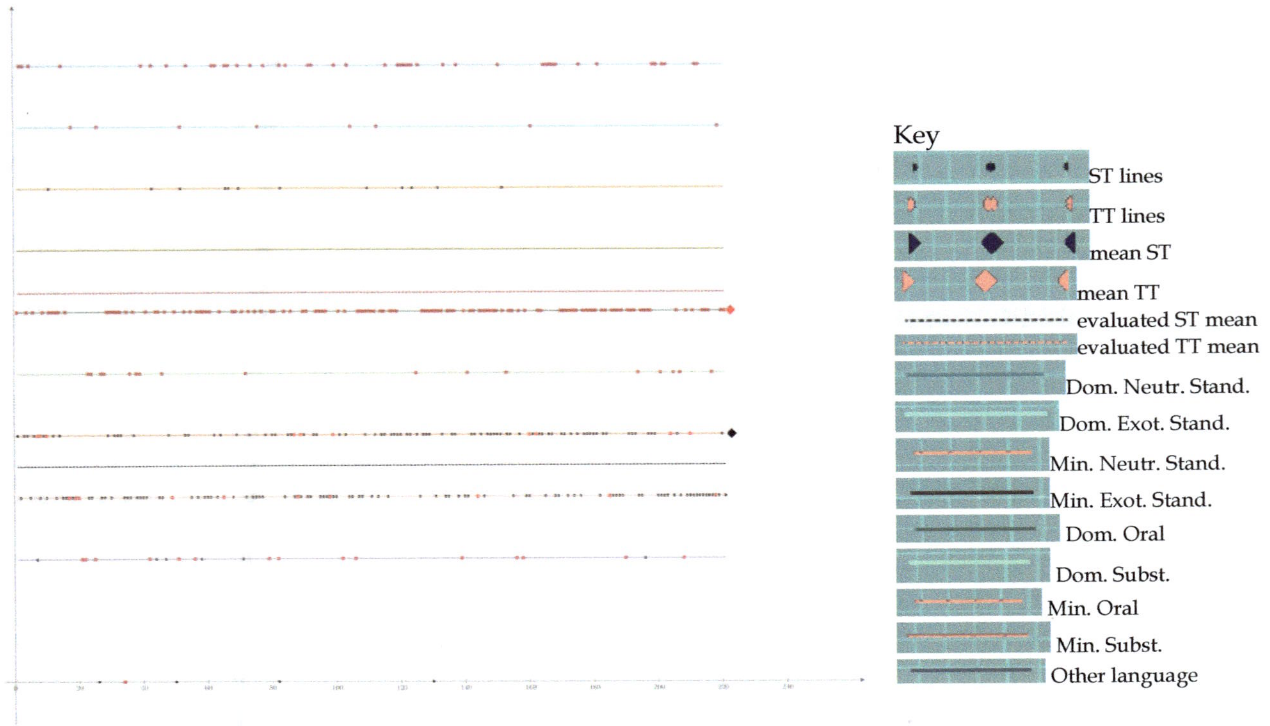

Figure 13 Santana's textual scatter plot.

ST Santana's speech pattern falls between minority oral and minority substandard, although his recurrent shift to a higher register (minority standard) pulls his speech towards a higher prestige level. In the film, he declares he has studied history and Chicano culture in jail, and at the beginning, he is seen reading a book by Leo Tolstoy. He is a charismatic leader, followed by the others for his wisdom and rationality (the same characteristics which lead him to change his opinion on gang membership and drug trafficking when he sees their effects on the *barrio*). ST Santana's minority neutral standard lines are mostly used after he has already grown up, and especially when he speaks to non-gangsters (e.g. his father or his girlfriend Julie), which testifies to his personal development.

Although some lines are scattered across the whole range, most of TT Santana's lines are placed in the dominant oral category, placing his speech somewhere in between TT Angel and TT Gato. Overall, it seems like the most used strategy for Santana was centralization and a certain amount of discourse standardization. In fact, his ST speech pattern is somewhere in between minority oral and minority substandard, with a slight preference for minority oral. The TT decreases the signs of his heritage, though not eradicating them completely, and it also shifts his speech to the dominant standard category.

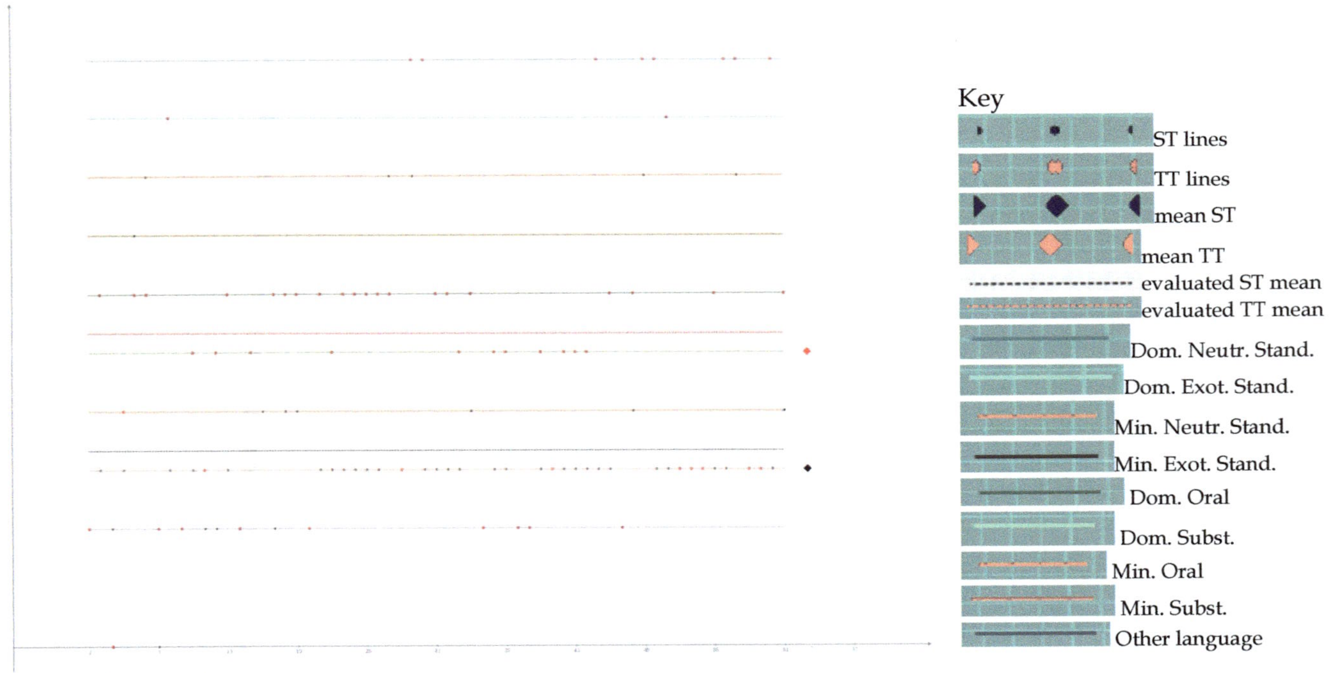

Figure 14 JD's textual scatter plot.

ST lines in JD's speech reflect his need to sound Chicano although he is not. In the film, it appears that it took him some time to become proficient in Spanish. The audience identifies him as a non-Chicano immediately because he is white and blond, but also because his very first line in the film (greeting Santana) is an awkward Spanish mistake, immediately self-corrected: "*Orale! Qué traes de huevos?* I mean *de nuevo*" (*qué traes de nuevo?* is a greeting comparable to 'what's up?' while *huevos* means 'eggs' but can also be a crude reference to male intimate parts). He does speak a fair amount of Spanish throughout the film, although less than Mundo, and emphasises his association with Chicanos through the use of a vernacular sub-variety of CE.

JD's lines in the TT follow the general tendency observed so far: they shift towards the non-standard language of the dominant group, although a fair number of lines are still in the minority substandard and most of his Spanish is maintained. This somewhat compensates for the loss of CE affiliation in his normal speech. Overall, JD has undergone some degree of centralization, while discourse standardization is only occasional, and never happens at the beginning, when the audience needs to recognise JD as a (white) member of a Chicano gang.

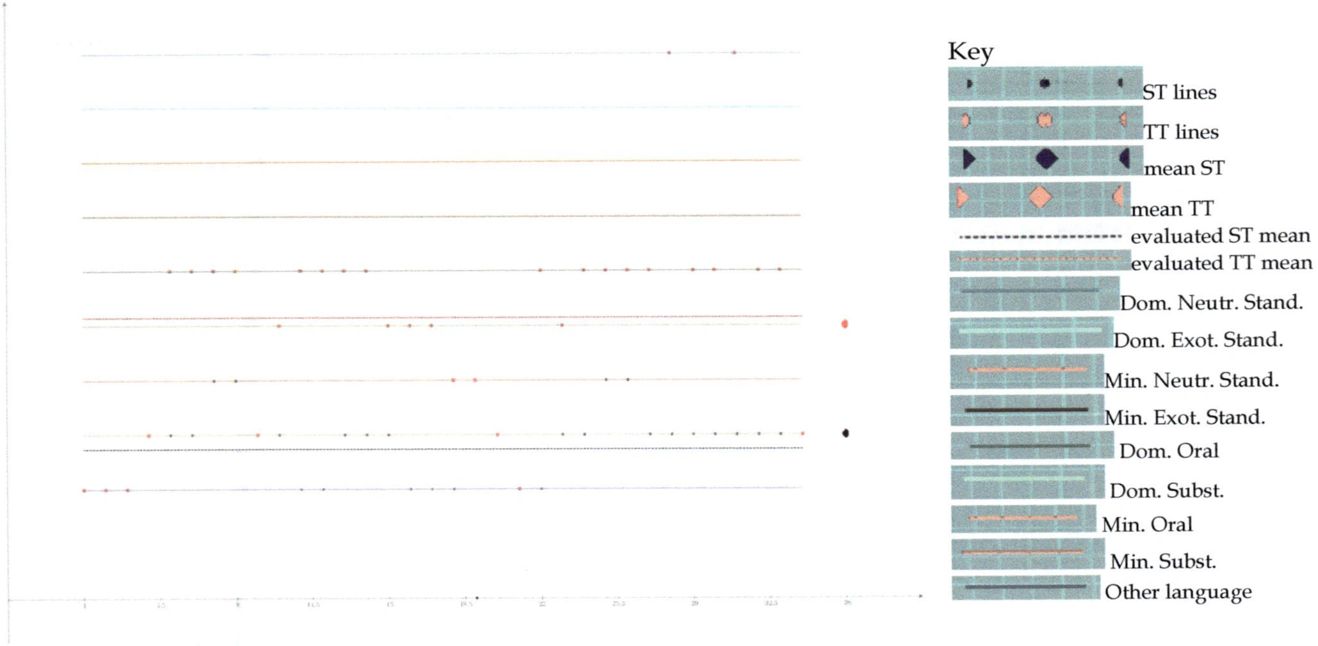

Figure 15 Mundo's textual scatter plot.

The categorization of Mundo's speech pattern is rather neat in both ST and TT. ST Mundo is clearly a minority substandard speaker, although his frequent use of Spanish draws his speech slightly lower, towards the Other language category. Indeed, ST Mundo often utters whole sentences in Spanish. In two scenes, he never says anything in English. Although he appears to be the most proficient bilingual in the film, his English does not hint at a high cultural level. TT Mundo loses most of these heritage markers, which somewhat distinguishes him from the rest of the group. That said, one of his full-Spanish scenes is kept in — one in which he utters shorter lines, but which is positioned right at the beginning, and serves to counterpoise the absence of Spanish switches in the rest of the film. Mundo is mainly dealt with through centralization: his speech remains substandard but loses the markers that make him sound like a Chicano.

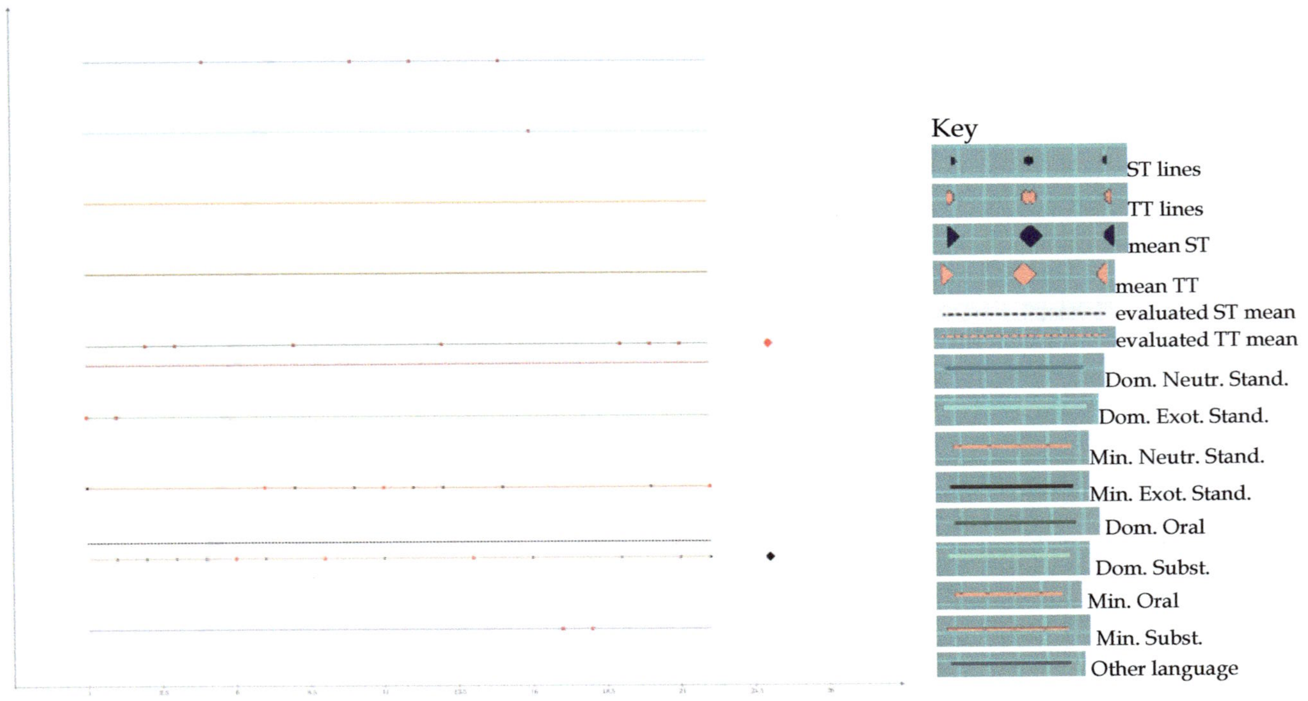

Figure 16 Puppet's textual scatter plot.

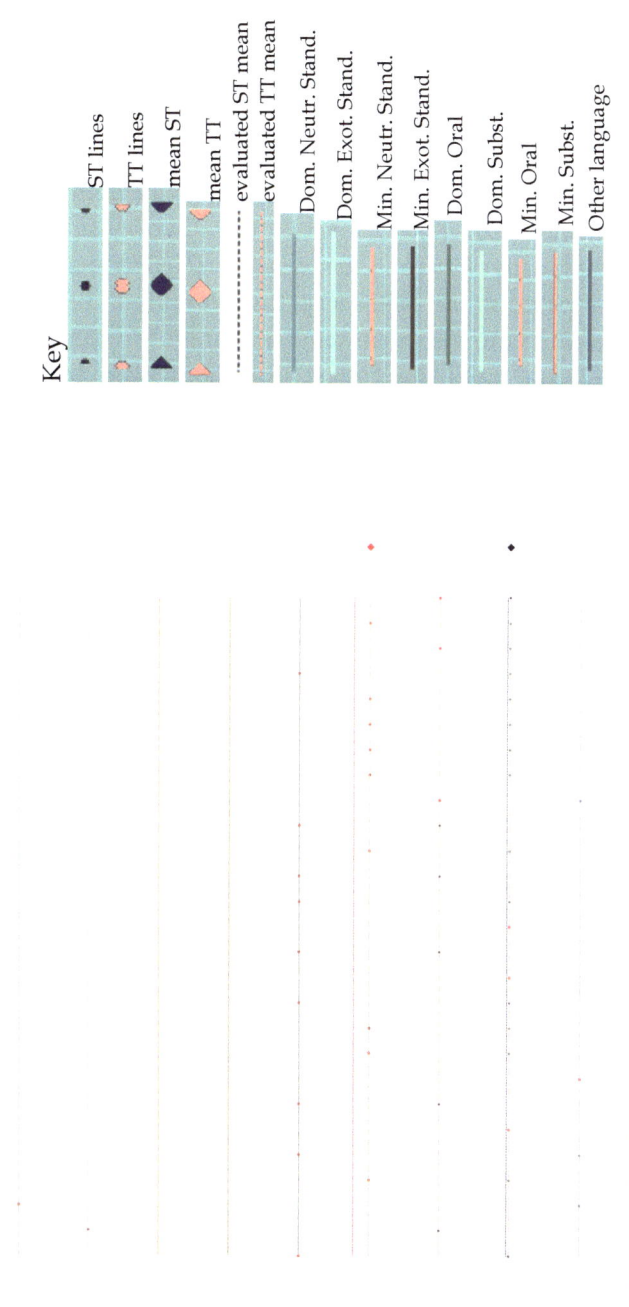

Figure 17 Lil' Puppet's textual scatter plot.

Although they have a similar profile in the ST, the Puppet Brothers are translated in a slightly different way. ST Puppet and Lil' Puppet appear to have a similar socio-cultural and educational background, the elder showing a slightly higher level of linguistic prestige. This difference is accentuated in the TT, where Puppet shifts to dominant oral, while Lil' Puppet passes on to the dominant substandard. Both, however, keep some of their minority substandard lines. The linguistic choices of the translators reflect the brothers' different functions in the plot. Puppet is centralized and, to some extent, also subject to discourse standardization. He seems to participate in *La Eme* mainly for protection, as he is aware that jail life can be very difficult without some kind of affiliation. That is also why he lets his younger brother into the gang, but then realizes his mistake: Lil' Puppet is not as cold-blooded as a gangster should be. Indeed, the little brother is uneducated and disingenuous, fundamentally a good kid who probably only meant to be a tattoo artist in the first place. The TT choice to simply centralize Lil' Puppet's speech without standardising it implies that he does not have the intellectual/rational means to decide for himself.

Blood In Blood Out

The last film analysed in this corpus displays numerous common points with *American Me*. Both are gangster films, centred on the gang life of Chicanos, and some of the characters between the two films have overlapping aspects. There are, however, some substantial differences. *Blood In Blood Out*, which centres on the half Chicano Miklo Velka, also follows the life stories of two former gang members who have chosen diverging paths. The result is a three-hour-long film that relies on several Latino/Chicano stereotypes and presents an ambivalent vision of gang life and of what it means to be a Chicano from a *barrio*, opening out to more possible answers.

The main characters are Miklo and his two cousins — the stepbrothers Cruz and Paco. When Miklo is convicted, he encounters gangsters from different ethnic backgrounds (including the white Aryan Vanguard) and, despite his white skin, wants to join the Chicano gang. Cruz, after being attacked and severely injured by a rival gang, suffers from constant back pain. He deals with it by becoming addicted to heroin, which costs him his opportunity to become a famous artist and the life of his younger brother Juanito. Paco prefers joining the army to being convicted, which will turn his former friends into enemies and generate identity issues for him. Montana is Miklo's mentor in jail (his character overlaps with Santana in many respects). When he realizes that crime is wrong, he will be betrayed and killed by the ones he trusted most. Popeye is a despicable and slimy gangster, only interested in personal profit, who develops a deep hatred for Miklo.

Miklo	Dominant neutral standard	Dominant exotified standard	Minority neutral standard	Minority exotified standard	Dominant oral	Dominant substandard	Minority oral	Minority substandard	Other language	Total
ST (293 lines)	0%	0%	6.6%	1%	3.4%	1.4%	28.3%	49%	10.3%	100%
TT (298 lines)	23%	2.4%	0%	0%	42.9%	16.2%	3.7%	9.5%	2.4%	100%

Table 19 Miklo's ST and TT distribution in *Blood In Blood Out* (1993).

Miklo has the looks of his white father, but he feels that the blood of his Chicana mother is what really determines his identity. That is why he desperately tries to be accepted by the *Vatos Locos*, the Chicano gang led by his cousin Paco, and later on, decides to join the powerful Chicano jail gang *La Onda* from San Quentin. The situation, however, seems to be much more difficult in jail. In fact, once his blood ties with other Chicanos and his gang-like clothing are taken away, no one is initially willing to recognise him as a Chicano. There are only two elements left to make him recognisable as part of the Chicano group: his Vatos Locos tattoo and his linguistic behaviour. That is why nearly 80% of ST Miklo's language is divided between minority oral and minority substandard (28.3% and 49% respectively). He also makes strategic use of Spanish code-switching whenever he is required to prove his loyalty to *La Onda* and his Chicano identity (Renna 2017). If 10% may not seem much, it is important to bear in mind that Miklo utters nearly 300 lines in total (making him the most prolific character of the corpus). His use of Spanish, not always fluid but as a means to create solidarity with other Chicanos, echoes the bilingual semi-speaker profile (Dorian 1981)[41]. He sometimes uses the more prestigious minority neutral or exotified standard, especially when he interacts with the authorities (e.g. his parole officers). Miklo is also the only ST character to use dominant speech, although to a minimum extent (dominant oral 3.4% and dominant substandard 1.4%). He does so exclusively when he needs to deceive a member of the Aryan Vanguard to obtain advantages for *La Onda*.

TT Miklo has less than 3% of Spanish utterances, and his speech patterns are shifted to dominant oral (42.9%), followed by dominant neutral standard (23%). Some of his lines remain in the minority area (nearly 15% between minority oral and minority substandard).

Paco	Dominant neutral standard	Dominant exotified standard	Minority neutral standard	Minority exotified standard	Dominant oral	Dominant substandard	Minority oral	Minority substandard	Other language	Total
ST (241 lines)	0%	0%	8.4%	1.7%	0%	0%	20.5%	61.9%	7.5%	100%
TT (248 lines)	24.2%	1.2%	0%	0%	40.7%	15.3%	2%	14.5%	2%	100%

Table 20 Paco's ST and TT distribution in *Blood In Blood Out* (1993).

---

[41] Dorian's classification (1981) of speakers of a language that is receding to let another one take over includes individual factors that might determine a certain level of competence, especially pertaining to the familial background, in the case of the "semi-speakers." These, although having an imperfect command of the language, still use it in some contexts. The reasons to use a language in which they are not fully proficient might lie in their family bonds to older members, especially grandparents, or in a natural tendency of the person to try accommodating the older speakers by using their preferred language. In other cases, the semi-speakers may be the youngest in a relatively large family, whose elder siblings are usually fluent bilinguals importing the dominant language from school. Another possibility is a temporary absence from the community (like Miklo), which serves to revive a sense of belonging in the speaker, who will feel the urge to express his/her identity through language — no matter how imperfect it may sound.

Despite becoming a detective and a respectable member of society by giving up on gang life, ST Paco still has over 80% of his lines falling into minority oral and minority substandard (20.5% and 61.9% respectively). He also adds some minority-standard (both neutral and exotified), which make up around 10% of his lines. He does switch to Spanish, although slightly less than his cousin. Linguistically speaking, the two cousins do not seem too far away from each other in the ST. Indeed, at the end of the film, Cruz will point out that Miklo has become the leader of a powerful jail gang in a desperate attempt to imitate Paco's younger age deeds (when he was the leader of the *Vatos Locos*). The situation does not change much in the TT, where the two protagonists seem even more similar to each other in terms of linguistic frequencies. Just like his cousin, TT Paco has his highest frequency in the dominant oral category, followed by the dominant neutral standard. He also keeps some degree of minority oral and substandard (around 15% altogether).

Cruz	Dominant neutral standard	Dominant exotified standard	Minority neutral standard	Minority exotified standard	Dominant oral	Dominant substandard	Minority oral	Minority substandard	Other language	Total
ST (201 lines)	0%	0%	4%	3%	0%	0%	22.1%	49.2%	21.6%	100%
TT (204 lines)	19.2%	2%	0%	0%	42.4%	11.8%	6.9%	15.8%	2%	100%

Table 21 Cruz's ST and TT distribution in *Blood In Blood Out* (1993).

ST Cruz's speech pattern is concentrated in the linguistic categories that show off his ethnic heritage. He feels himself to be a proud descendant of Quetzalcoatl, a legendary Aztec divinity (Portillo *et al.* 1982) and often makes references to the Mexican tradition. Most of his speech is in the minority substandard category (49.2%), but minority oral and Spanish register nearly the same frequency (22.1% and 21.6% respectively). TT Cruz follows a similar pattern to those of his TT stepbrother and cousin. Most of his lines are in the dominant oral category, followed by the dominant neutral standard, with a sharp fall in his Spanish competence (only 2%). The only notable difference is that more lines were left in the minority oral and substandard categories (slightly less than 25% altogether). Of the three protagonists, he is the one scoring highest in these categories.

Montana	Dominant neutral standard	Dominant exotified standard	Minority neutral standard	Minority exotified standard	Dominant oral	Dominant substandard	Minority oral	Minority substandard	Other language	Total
ST (79 lines)	0%	0%	24.4%	2.6%	0%	0%	26.9%	30.8%	15.4%	100%
TT (80 lines)	55.7%	5.1%	0%	0%	22.8%	3.8%	0%	10.1%	2.5%	100%

Table 22 Montana's ST and TT distribution in *Blood In Blood Out* (1993).

Popeye	Dominant neutral standard	Dominant exotified standard	Minority neutral standard	Minority exotified standard	Dominant oral	Dominant substandard	Minority oral	Minority substandard	Other language	Total
ST (79 lines)	0%	0%	0%	3.3%	0%	0%	8.3%	76.7%	11.7%	100%
TT (80 lines)	16.4%	1.6%	0%	1.6%	27.9%	6.6%	6.6%	32.8%	6.6%	100%

Table 23 Popeye's ST and TT distribution in *Blood In Blood Out* (1993).

Montana and Popeye are supporting characters with very different roles. Their differences are fully reflected in their ST line categorization. Montana, like *American Me*'s Santana, is a charismatic leader who has decided to study while in jail (in his very first appearance, Montana is also seen reading a book). Miklo finds out that he has written an essay about jail reform and is about to write a book about the difficult conditions of Chicanos. ST Montana speaks an even more prestigious language than Santana, as over 25% of his lines are in the minority standard categories, letting the ST audience presume he has some level of education. Nevertheless, he also has more than 50% of his lines in the minority non-standard categories (26.9% minority oral, 30.8% minority substandard). With 15.4% of lines in Spanish, it is also likely that Montana is bilingual, given that he is able to utter rather complex sentences, e.g. *"Quinientos años hemos sufrido la opresion de nuestra raza. Pero aqui, entre nosotros, vamos a parar ese desmadre. Porque esta tierra es de nosotros! Sangre por sangre!"* (For five hundred years we endured the oppression of our race. But now, here, among ourselves, we are going to mend this disaster. Because this land is ours! Blood in, blood out! 1:20:00-1:21:06).

Conversely, as anticipated in the previous chapter, Popeye represents the most odious example of a gangster stereotype. In line with the above-mentioned poetics of stereotyping, this means that ST Popeye's lines are almost entirely classifiable as minority substandard (76.7%). Around 10% is registered for both the minority oral and Spanish, while the rare instances of the minority-exotified standard are generally used ironically.

TT Montana is taken to a whole other level, with 55.7% of his lines in the dominant neutral standard category, followed by 22.8% in the dominant oral and 10.1% in the minority substandard. TT Popeye scores highest in the minority substandard category (32.8%), shortly followed by dominant oral (27.9%) and, albeit more distantly, by dominant neutral standard (16.4%).

How were those results obtained?

MIKLO	Phonetics ST	Lexicon ST	Morpho-syntax ST	Phonetics TT	Lexicon TT	Morpho-syntax TT
Dom. Neut. Stand.	0%	0%	0%	97.1%	98.5%	97.1%
Dom. Exot. Stand.	0%	0%	0%	0%	100%	0%
Min. Neut. Stand.	100%	5.3%	0%	0%	0%	0%
Min. Exot. Stand.	100%	100%	0%	0%	0%	0%
Dom. Oral	100%	10%	100%	0%	33.1%	89%
Dom. Subst.	100%	100%	25%	0%	93.8%	56.3%
Min. Oral	97.6%	30.5%	78%	0%	72.7%	54.5%

Min. Subst.	100%	78.2%	82.4%	0%	96.4%	82.1%
Other language	100%	100%	86.7%	85.7%	85.7%	85.7%
Weighted Average	100%	60.7%	75.9%	24.3%	68.2%	81.8%

Table 24 Miklo's ST and TT realization in *Blood In Blood Out* (1993).

Miklo follows the pattern already observed in other cases. Phonetics goes from the most recurrent marked feature of his speech to a minor one (from 100% to 24.3%). As compensation, both lexical and morpho-syntactic items increase their frequency, although acquiring less than 10%. Once again, the TT seems to rely on morpho-syntax to characterize distance from the standard.

PACO	Phonetics ST	Lexicon ST	Morpho-syntax ST	Phonetics TT	Lexicon TT	Morpho-syntax TT
Dom. Neut. Stand.	0%	0%	0%	81.7%	81.7%	81.7%
Dom. Exot. Stand.	0%	0%	0%	0%	100%	0%
Min. Neut. Stand.	100%	5%	10%	0%	0%	0%
Min. Exot. Stand.	100%	50%	0%	0%	0%	0%
Dom. Oral	0%	0%	0%	0%	27.7%	91.1%
Dom. Subst.	0%	0%	0%	0%	78.9%	55.3%
Min. Oral	98%	32.7%	87.8%	0%	100%	100%
Min. Subst.	100%	87.2%	89.9%	2.8%	91.7%	72.2%
Other language	83.3%	83.3%	72.2%	40%	60%	20%
Weighted Average	98.7%	68.6%	80.3%	21%	60.9%	78.2%

Table 25 Paco's ST and TT realization in *Blood In Blood Out* (1993).

CRUZ	Phonetics ST	Lexicon ST	Morpho-syntax ST	Phonetics TT	Lexicon TT	Morpho-syntax TT
Dom. Neut. Stand.	0%	0%	0%	100%	100%	100%
Dom. Exot. Stand.	0%	0%	0%	0%	100%	0%
Min. Neut. Stand.	100%	50%	50%	0%	0%	0%
Min. Exot. Stand.	100%	83.3%	50%	0%	0%	0%
Dom. Oral	0%	0%	0%	1.2%	34.9%	88.4%
Dom. Subst.	0%	0%	0%	0%	87.5%	58.3%
Min. Oral	95.5%	38.6%	88.6%	0%	100%	78.6%
Min. Subst.	100%	91.8%	95.9%	3.1%	93.8%	71.9%

LANGUAGE VARIATION AND MULTIMODALITY 161

Other language	97.7%	97.7%	83.7%	75%	75%	75%
Weighted Average	99%	79.9%	88.9%	21.7%	69.5%	81.8%

Table 26 Cruz's ST and TT realization in *Blood In Blood Out* (1993).

Paco, like *American Me*'s Mundo and Lil' Puppet, undergoes a general down-toning, as all his marked features lose some degree of importance: lexicon drops from nearly 100% to just above 20%. While Mundo's less marked translation may be a consequence of his secondary role, in Paco's case it might be an attempt to take his role change into account—from gangster to detective. However, a similar destiny is followed by TT Cruz, who is also toned down in translation. In both cases, the TT has the highest frequencies in the morpho-syntax.

MONTANA	Phonetics ST	Lexicon ST	Morpho-syntax ST	Phonetics TT	Lexicon TT	Morpho-syntax TT
Dom. Neut. Stand.	0%	0%	0%	100%	100%	100%
Dom. Exot. Stand.	0%	0%	0%	0%	75%	0%
Min. Neut. Stand.	78.9%	0%	0%	0%	0%	0%
Min. Exot. Stand.	100%	100%	0%	0%	0%	0%
Dom. Oral	0%	0%	0%	0%	22.2%	83.3%
Dom. Subst.	0%	0%	0%	0%	100%	33.3%
Min. Oral	100%	33.3%	85.7%	0%	0%	0%
Min. Subst.	100%	83.3%	66.7%	0%	100%	50%
Other language	75%	75%	66.7%	100%	100%	100%
Weighted Average	91%	48.7%	53.8%	58.2%	81%	83.5%

Table 27 Montana's ST and TT realization in *Blood In Blood Out* (1993).

POPEYE	Phonetics ST	Lexicon ST	Morpho-syntax ST	Phonetics TT	Lexicon TT	Morpho-syntax TT
Dom. Neut. Stand.	0%	0%	0%	100%	100%	100%
Dom. Exot. Stand.	0%	0%	0%	0%	100%	0%
Min. Neut. Stand.	0%	0%	0%	0%	0%	0%
Min. Exot. Stand.	100%	50%	0%	0%	100%	100%
Dom. Oral	0%	0%	0%	0%	29.4%	100%
Dom. Subst.	0%	0%	0%	0%	100%	75%

Min. Oral	100%	40%	80%	25%	100%	100%
Min. Subst.	100%	95.7%	95.7%	5%	95%	90%
Other language	100%	100%	85.7%	100%	100%	100%
Weighted Average	100%	90%	90%	26.2%	78.7%	93.4%

Table 28 Popeye's ST and TT realization in *Blood In Blood Out* (1993).

TT Montana seems to follow the general trend of compensating for the lack of phonetics with an increased morpho-syntax. However, given that most of his lines are in the dominant neutral standard, his phonetic value is decreased but not as dramatically as in other cases. Furthermore, both morphosyntactic and lexical elements have sensibly increased in the target version. TT Popeye has only a slight increase of TT morpho-syntax, a trend in contrast with phonetic and lexical items — both having a lower frequency in the TT.

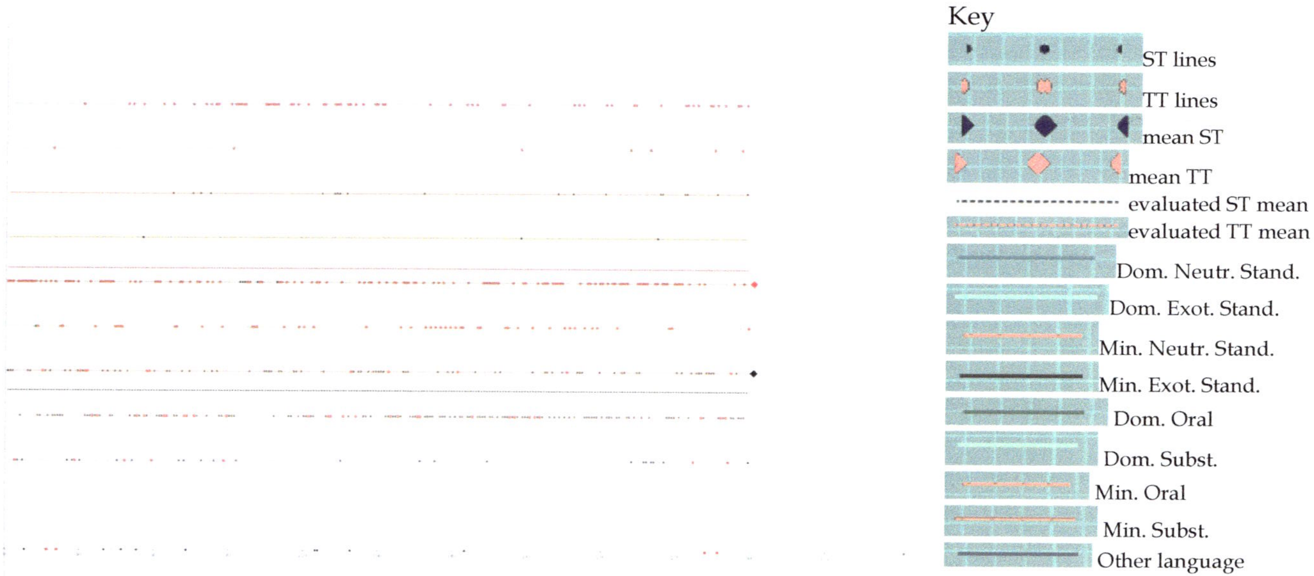

LANGUAGE VARIATION AND MULTIMODALITY 163

Key

ST lines
TT lines
mean ST
mean TT
evaluated ST mean
evaluated TT mean
Dom. Neutr. Stand.
Dom. Exot. Stand.
Min. Neutr. Stand.
Min. Exot. Stand.
Dom. Oral
Dom. Subst.
Min. Oral
Min. Subst.
Other language

Figure 18 Miklo's textual scatter plot.

ST Miklo's lines are generally split between minority substandard and minority oral, although his use of more prestigious categories pushes his average speech slightly closer to the minority oral. The positioning of the black dots on the graph above demonstrates how the other varieties are used in specific moments, thus underlining their diegetic function in the plot. Miklo uses minority neutral standard when trying to persuade the parole officer of his successful rehabilitation in jail, and Spanish when trying to enter *Vatos Locos* and then *La Onda*, and — towards the end — when affirming his leadership of *La Onda*. The few TT dominant lines correspond to his infiltration of the Aryan Vanguard to kill one of their most dangerous members. TT Miklo's lines (the red dots) are widespread, reaching almost every line in the graph — which means he used at least one of almost all the varieties included in the scheme. However, the highest concentration of lines is in the dominant oral category, as shown clearly by the position of his average values. The results suggest that Miklo might have been translated through centralization and, to a minor extent, discourse standardization, as proven by the evident increase in dominant neutral standard.

Figure 19 Paco's textual scatter plot.

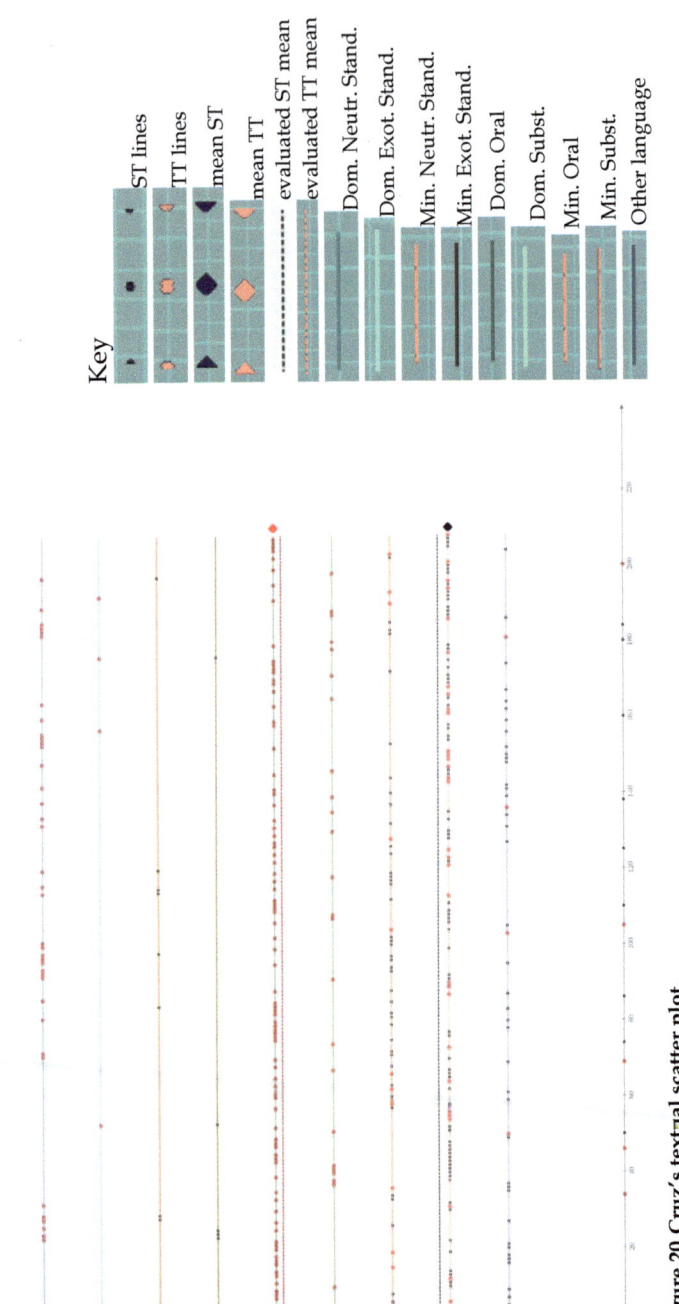

Figure 20 Cruz's textual scatter plot.

The two stepbrothers Paco and Cruz were translated similarly to the main character Miklo. Neither of the two, however, ever speaks a dominant variety in the ST. Paco, despite his change of status, does not significantly change his way of speaking. In the same way, he does not really change his attitude, but only directs it towards a more noble cause. The scatter plot visualizes the fact that, shortly after his conversion to honest citizenship, Paco stops using Spanish.

Cruz goes from *cholo* to promising painter from the *barrio*, then to heroin addict. Eventually, after obtaining his family's forgiveness, he manages to quit drugs and tries to inspire Paco to let go of his anger and sense of guilt. Indeed, both Miklo's imprisoning and disablement (Paco shoots Miklo's leg off during a theft carried out by the latter) and Cruz's spine damage and heroin addiction, are more or less directly caused by Paco's youthful rashness.

Both the stepbrothers have been translated, like Miklo, through centralization and — to a minor extent — through discourse standardization.

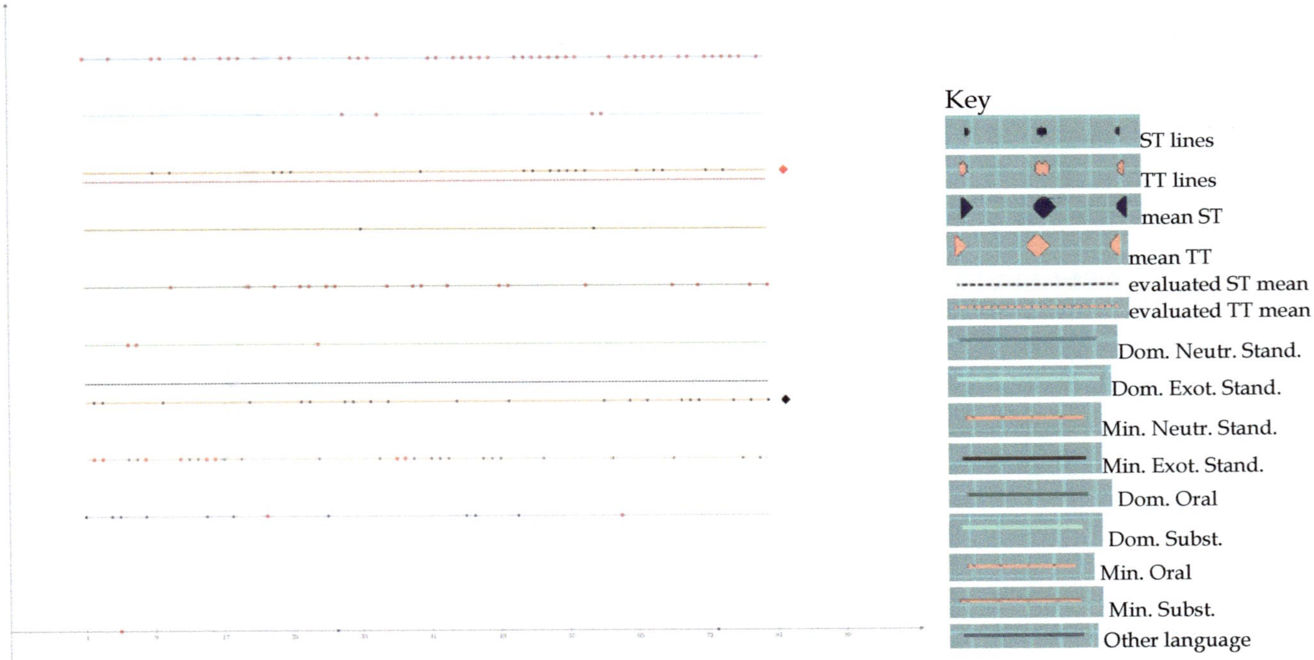

Figure 21 Montana's textual scatter plot.

LANGUAGE VARIATION AND MULTIMODALITY 169

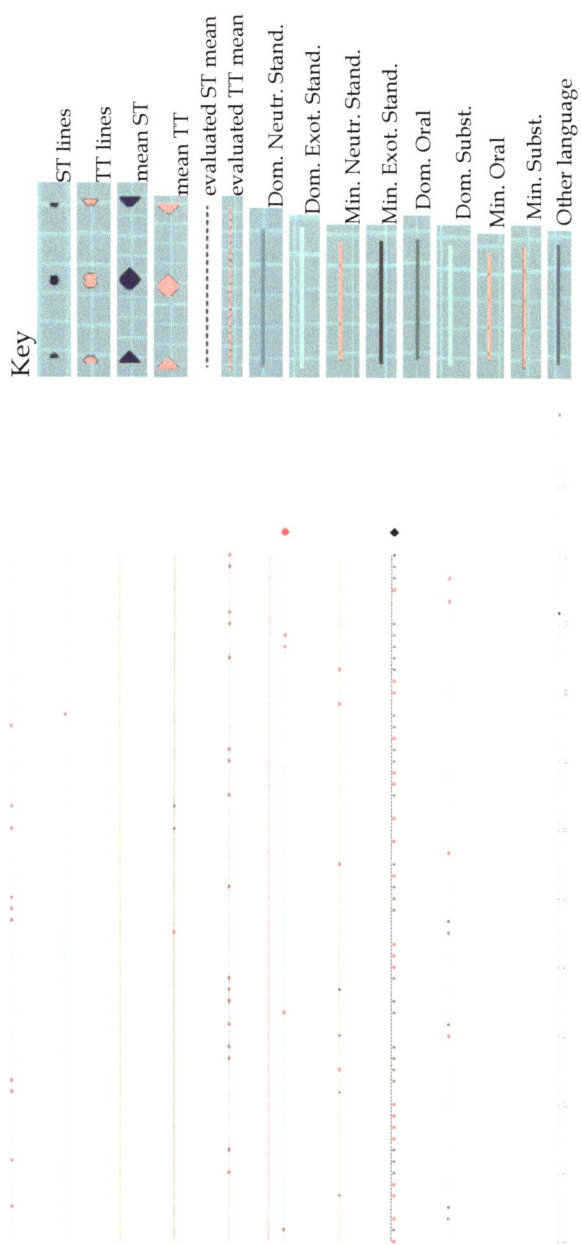

Figure 22 Popeye's textual scatter plot.

Montana is the character that has undergone the most dramatic transformation since most of his TT lines are in the dominant neutral standard category. However, many of his lines are positioned further down the prestige scale: this ensures that some traces of non-standardness are left in his TT speech pattern. Overall, the way his lines were translated is not consistent: the extreme fluctuation of his lines generates an anomaly in the calculation, which places his average TT speech in a position where no TT lines can actually be found in the scatter plot. This mathematical phenomenon (the graphs are generated automatically by Mathcad™) might trigger reflection concerning the way such a dichotomic translation is perceived by the target audience.

Popeye's translated version has a certain degree of fluctuation as well. However, the fact that many of his lines were left in the minority substandard category ensures that his average TT speech does not go any further than dominant substandard. This means that Popeye was translated with a not-so-strong centralization strategy, while Montana has mainly been dealt with through discourse standardization — albeit with some centralization involved, leaving traces of Montana's ST speech.

3.2 Language and multimodality: the diegetic dimension

Stand and Deliver

The next step consists in looking at the way linguistic category changes affected intermodal relations. In other words, were the relations of confirmation and contradiction kept, partially kept, or substantially altered?

LANGUAGE VARIATION AND MULTIMODALITY 171

Intermodal relations ST Angel

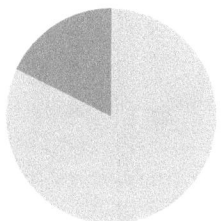

Confirmation ■ Contradiction

Figure 23 Intermodal relations ST Angel.

Intermodal relations TT Angel

Confirmation ■ Contradiction

Figure 24 Intermodal relations TT Angel.

Intermodal relations ST Chuco

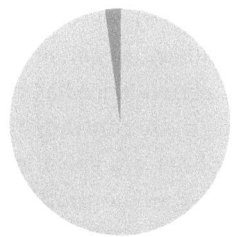

Confirmation ■ Contradiction

Figure 25 Intermodal relations ST Chuco.

Intermodal relations TT Chuco

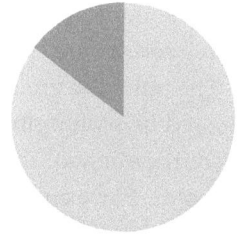

Confirmation ■ Contradiction

Figure 26 Intermodal relations TT Chuco.

The charts above show the overall proportion of confirmation and contradiction for the two characters in *Stand and Deliver*. TT Angel has a larger portion of contradiction compared to the source text: in the ST, confirmation between textual and non-textual is attained in 82.1% of the lines, while contradiction happens in 17.9% of the lines; in the TT, confirmation can be found in 71.5% of the cases versus 28.5% of contradiction. The same happens with Chuco – in the ST he nearly constantly speaks in confirmation with the other modes (costumes and make-up, phenotype, behaviour, setting, interlocutors and music). This proportion is less blatant in the TT, where the 98% vs 2% proportion becomes 85% vs 15%. The relation has changed but was not subverted.

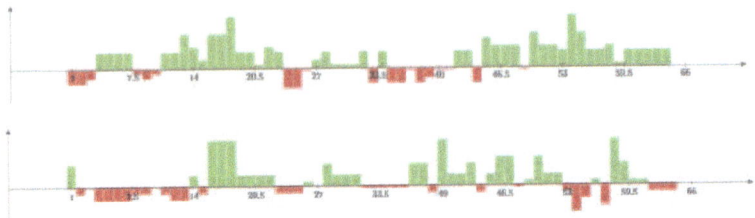

Figure 27 Angel's ST and TT alternation of intermodal confirmation and contradiction in the film.

The bar graph visualizes the way confirmation (both equivalent and complementary) and contradiction alternate during the film. The x-axis represents the film chronologically, beginning on the left and ending on the right, while each bar represents a line uttered by Angel. Confirmation equivalence was attributed a value +1, complementarity 0, and contradiction -1. For each line, the values of each non-textual mode (see the previous chapter) were added: overall positive results are expressed by green bars; negative ones by red bars. The taller the green bar, the more equivalence has been achieved; the red bars plunging below indicate more contradiction.

In the source version, the contradictory lines are specifically linked to the plot. For example, the initial lines are contradictory because he acts like a *cholo* in a context — the school — where students are not expected to act like thugs or disregard authority. Another ST moment of contradiction, right at the beginning of the second half, happens when Angel is at the clinic for his grandmother and speaks to the non-Latina nurse either in a too informal way or in Spanish.

The target version displays a more significant amount of contradiction right after the beginning when Angel is asking his professor to help him study while still pretending to be a tough anti-school gangster. In the TT, his formal language contrasts with his behaviour, although not completely, as it reflects his intentions. The contradictions in the second third of the graph reflect the ones of the ST, although to a lesser extent. Towards the end, a series of contradictions appear: his irresponsible behaviour after the exam invalidation and his pretend-*cholo* mockery with the investigators are not rendered with a gangster-like speech, which creates a contradiction with his appearance, but also with the context around him.

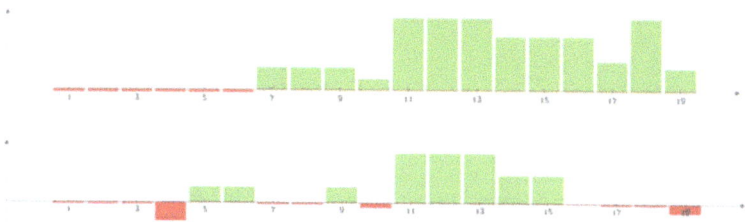

Figure 28 Chuco's ST and TT alternation of intermodal confirmation and contradiction in the film.

Chuco is less present throughout the film. His initial role is to disrupt the tranquillity of the class, acting like a bully with the professor and ignoring the rules — that is why his initial ST contradictions are deliberate. When he drops out of school, his stereotypical *cholo* language is in harmony with both his attitude and the surroundings. In the Italian version, the pattern is generally kept, although in a less evident way. The real increase in TT contradiction happens towards the end, in his last appearance on the screen: he has fixed Escalante's car with Angel and the other gang members, and his TT speech is too formal for his appearance, behaviour and context.

Colors

Since the two characters perform differently from a linguistic point of view, it would be likely for them to build different intermodal relations, too.

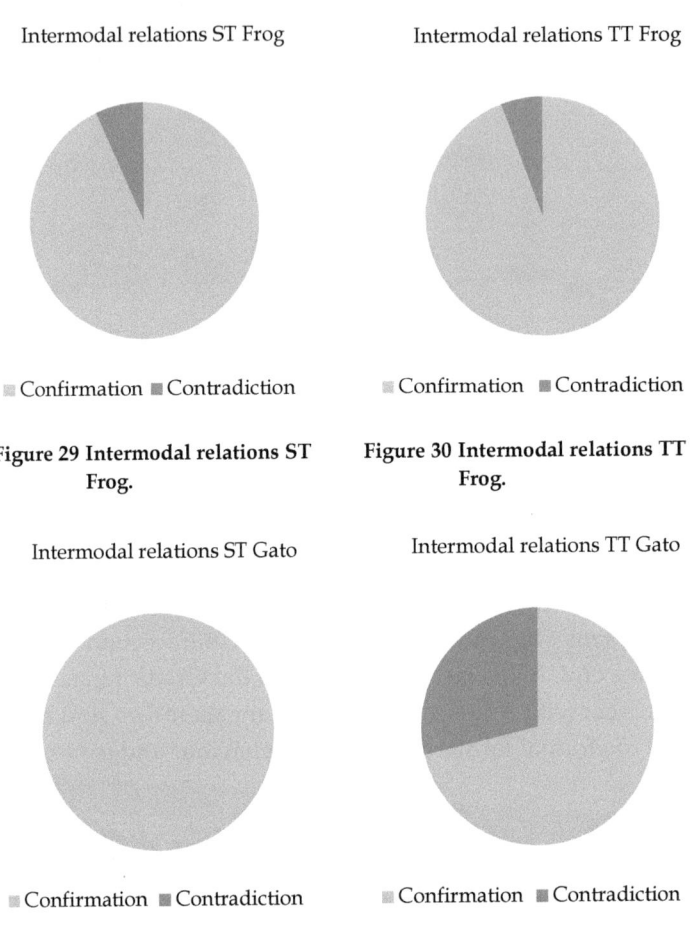

Figure 29 Intermodal relations ST Frog.

Figure 30 Intermodal relations TT Frog.

Figure 31 Intermodal relations ST Gato.

Figure 32 Intermodal relations TT Gato.

The graphs above confirm the differences between the two characters. Frog's intermodal relations are kept approximately unvaried, in contrast to the results of the characters in *Stand and Deliver*. The contradiction generated by the few more standardized lines is often counterbalanced by their resorting to Spanish as a form of compensation.

The ST contradiction in Frog's speech often derives from his non-adaptation to different interlocutors, which in some cases has a diegetic function in the plot. Frog has, for example, a friendly relation with Hodges, one of the two protagonist police officers, and talks to him without trying to adjust his register. In other situations — e.g. when he is arrested — he acts and speaks to the police officers as if they were his fellow gang members, e.g. calling them *homes*, which is short for *homeboy*, a way to address a friend/comrade, drawn from AAVE, (Cagliero & Spallino 2010, 369-370). This inability to adapt to the context around him seems partly due to his use of drugs, which often makes his speech sound drawled, a feature that is particularly marked in the source version.

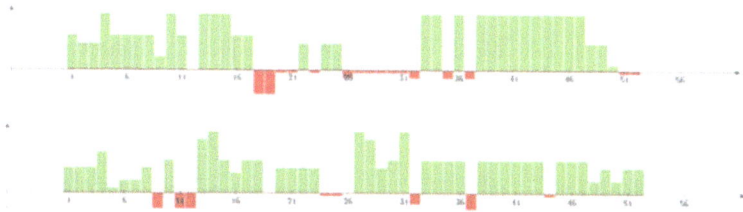

Figure 33 Frog's ST and TT alternation of intermodal confirmation and contradiction in the film.

On the other hand, Gato's contradiction increases significantly. None of his few lines seemed contradictory in the ST, but contradiction increases to 29% in the TT. That is because he barely ever uses any linguistic feature showing his background, and at times he uses dominant standard language. Both tendencies are especially in contrast with his costumes and make-up, which fully correspond to the ethnotype, but also with his main interlocutors — his fellow gang members.

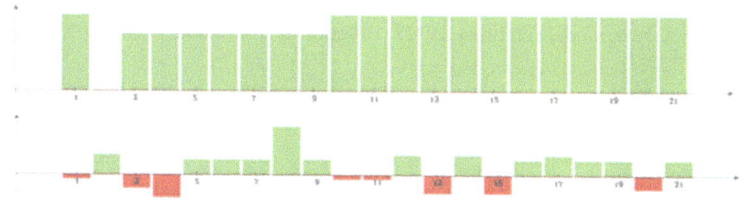

Figure 34 Gato's ST and TT alternation of intermodal confirmation and contradiction in the film.

American me

Here, too, there is likely to be an increase in contradiction in the TT. Indeed, all the characters follow a similar pattern:

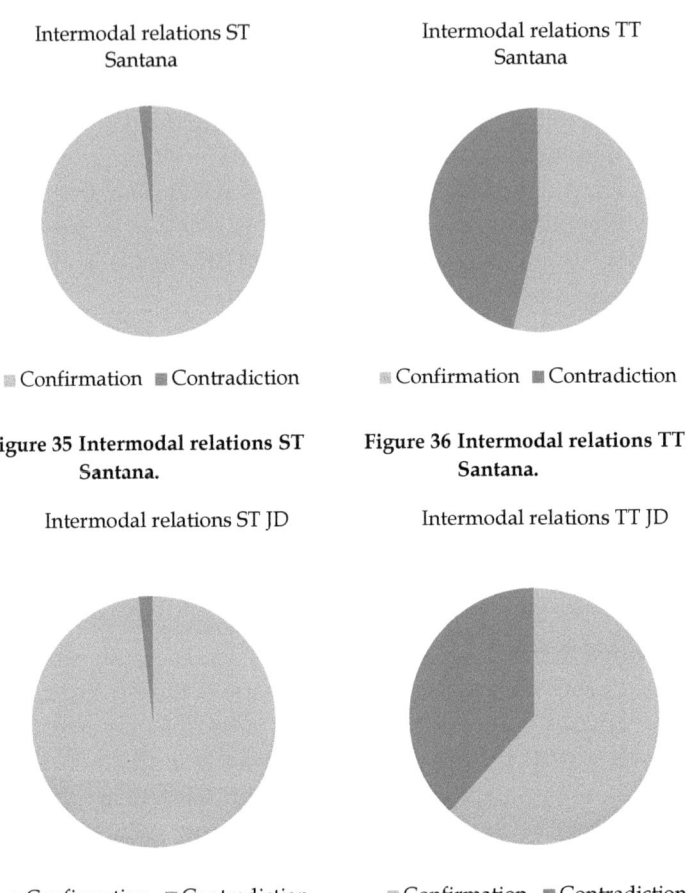

Figure 35 Intermodal relations ST Santana.

Figure 36 Intermodal relations TT Santana.

Figure 37 Intermodal relations ST JD

Figure 38 Intermodal relations TT JD

LANGUAGE VARIATION AND MULTIMODALITY 177

Intermodal relations ST
Mundo

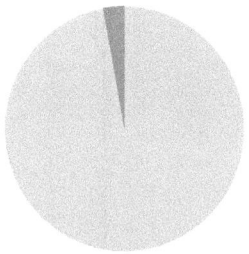

Confirmation ■ Contradiction

Figure 39 Intermodal relations ST Mundo.

Intermodal relations TT
Mundo

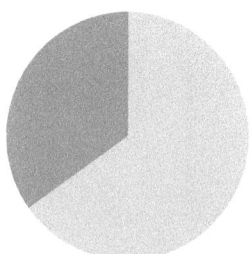

Confirmation ■ Contradiction

Figure 40 Intermodal relations TT Mundo.

Intermodal relations ST
Puppet

Confirmation ■ Contradiction

Figure 41 Intermodal relations ST Puppet.

Intermodal relations TT
Puppet

Confirmation ■ Contradiction

Figure 42 Intermodal relations TT Puppet.

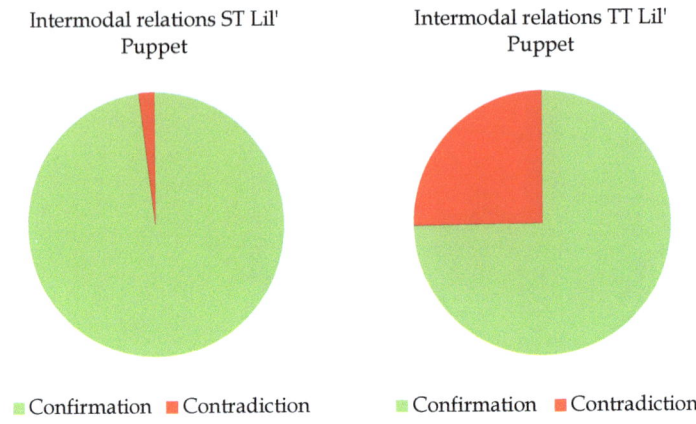

Figure 43 Intermodal relations ST Lil' Puppet.

Figure 44 Intermodal relations TT Lil' Puppet.

All the ST characters have a high confirmation frequency, in all cases scoring between 97.1% and 100%. As far as the TT is concerned, it seems that the more important the character, the more the contradiction increases, with Santana having 46.2% of lines in contradiction with the other modes and Lil' Puppet 25.3%.

Looking at the way the different proportions are distributed along the film sheds some light on this phenomenon.

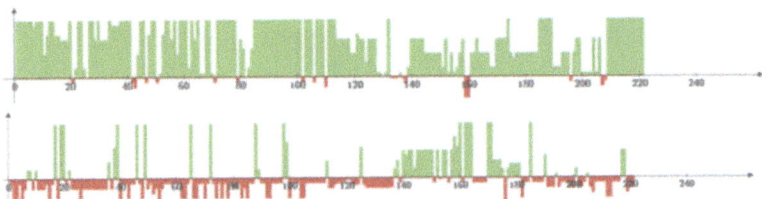

Figure 45 Santana's ST and TT alternation of intermodal confirmation and contradiction in the film.

As previously discussed, short red bars represent a line that is mainly contradictory with the rest of the modes, but with some degree of confirmation. From the density of the bars, it is easy to see that Santana is the character with most lines in the film, as well as more lines than most of the characters in the entire corpus. The only solid confirmation block in TT is obtained when Santana, out of jail, tones down his gangster looks and attitude to interact with family members and his beloved Julie—she does not like gang life, and by the end of the film the audience finds out that she used to be a homegirl herself.

The increase in TT intermodal contradiction derives from the fact that, especially while in jail, he acts like a gang member, dresses like a gang member, only interacts with thugs and drug addicts, but speaks a rather prestigious variety. Certainly, a criminal can have a high education—and that is why in many cases the contradiction levels are quite low—but TT Santana does not always seem in line with his interlocutors and his speech, at times, diverges from his behaviour. Furthermore, his TT speech pattern does not always have a relation to his phenotypical traits. Indeed, while the amount of contradiction has grown significantly, the balance between confirmation and contradiction has not been subverted. The intention was probably similar to the one behind the translational choices of *Stand and Deliver*. Rather than contextual adherence, the rendering of Santana seems to pursue a (stereotypical) correspondence with the plot: because he is wiser than the typical jail inmate, he speaks a more prestigious variety.

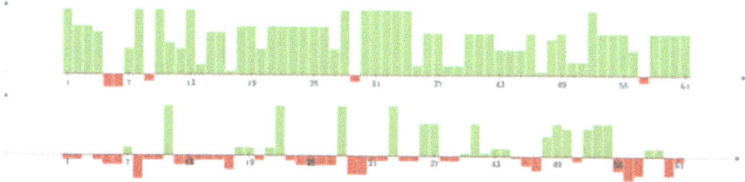

Figure 46 JD's ST and TT alternation of intermodal confirmation and contradiction in the film.

JD's increased TT contradiction is not as dramatic, a detail explained by the fact that speaking a dominant group variety establishes a relation of confirmation with his phenotypical traits. It is, however, still in contrast with his interlocutors, behaviour and settings. Conversely, in the ST, he manages to overcome the contrast between his language and his phenotype by acting like a Chicano gangster even more than the other gang members—eventually in fact proving far crueller than Santana.

Mundo and the Puppet brothers, having a smaller number of lines, experience similar changes in the intermodal relations, although to different extents:

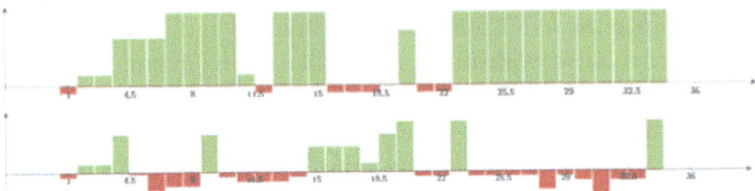

Figure 47 Mundo's ST and TT alternation of intermodal confirmation and contradiction in the film.

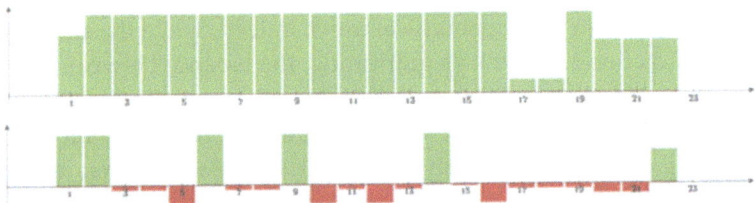

Figure 48 Puppet's ST and TT alternation of intermodal confirmation and contradiction in the film.

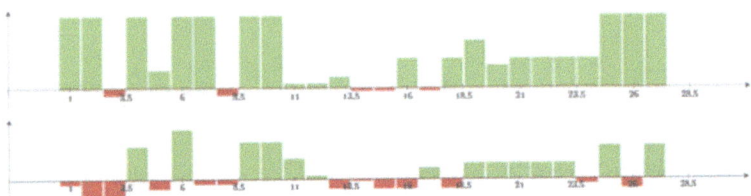

Figure 49 Lil' Puppet's ST and TT alternation of intermodal confirmation and contradiction in the film.

TT Mundo's longest sequence of lines that contradict the other modes occurs when he and the other gang members in jail are about to kill the son of Scagnelli, the Italian mafia boss. In the ST they create a very informal situation to deceive him and make him lower his guard. That is why they all act in a friendly, spontaneous manner, but also use many references to CE and Chicano culture to confuse him. In the TT, the contradiction is given by his formal language, which contrasts with the whole atmosphere.

ST Puppet nearly always acts according to the context. Only towards the end, the confirmation is slightly lower, because he acts unnaturally with his brother (just before killing him). This unnaturalness is dramatized in the TT.

Lil' Puppet's confirming attitude lowers from the middle of the film, starting with his wedding ceremony. He realizes he does not want to be a gangster anymore, gets (stereotypically enough) drunk and high, and acts in a way that is completely out of place, embarrassing his bride and fellow gang members alike. In the ST he does so while still using his vernacular CE, while in the TT he uses a formal language that is in complete contrast with his uncontrolled behaviour.

Blood in blood out

Being the longest film in the corpus and having one main character and two co-protagonists, *Blood In Blood Out* also offers a series of different communicative situations that may make the preserving of the intermodal relations more difficult for translators. At the same time, a three-hour feature might help the audience familiarize itself with the characters.

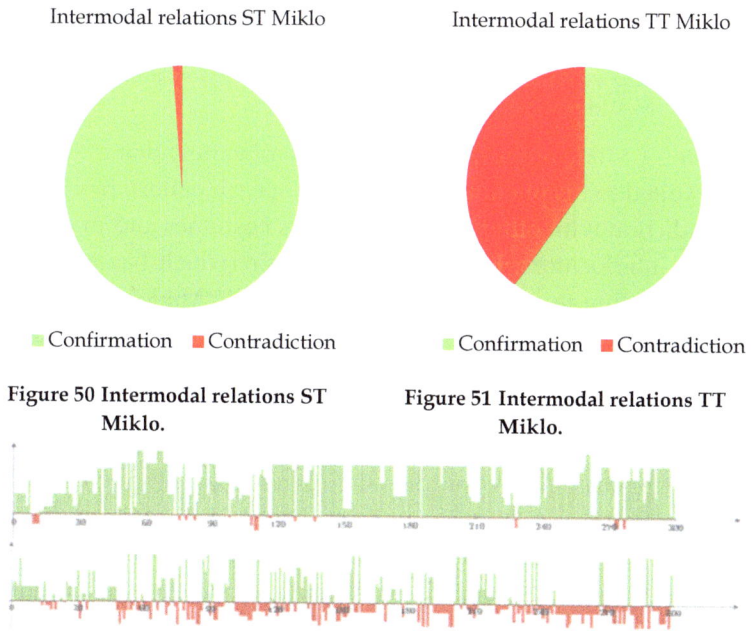

Figure 50 Intermodal relations ST Miklo.

Figure 51 Intermodal relations TT Miklo.

Figure 52 Miklo's ST and TT alternation of intermodal confirmation and contradiction in the film.

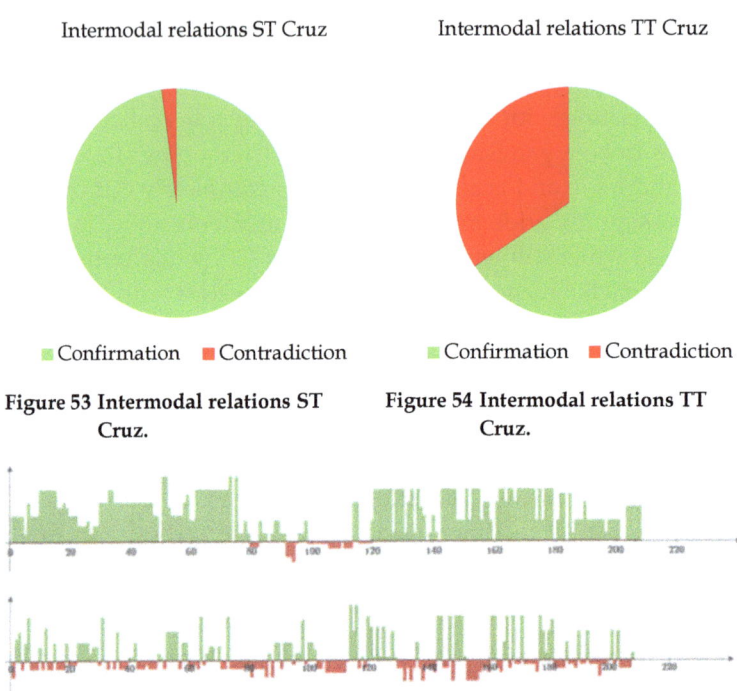

Figure 53 Intermodal relations ST Cruz.

Figure 54 Intermodal relations TT Cruz.

Figure 55 Cruz's ST and TT alternation of intermodal confirmation and contradiction in the film.

Despite TT Miklo often speaking a dominant variety that may seem more suited to his phenotypical trait, his speech pattern remains in contradiction with other elements such as costumes and make-up, setting, interlocutors, behaviour, and music (which has a greater role in this film than in the others). That is why Miklo's contradiction has shot up to 40% in the TT from the very low percentage of the ST (1.3%). Miklo spends the whole film behaving like a Chicano gangster, interacting with them, and sharing their spaces. Indeed, the phenotype is most often the only contrasting element in the ST, which explains the low contradiction frequency. Although at risk, however, the proportion has not been subverted. Looking at the alternation of confirmation and contradiction during the film, it is possible to observe that TT contradictions are almost always counterbalanced by high confirmation bars — although the perception of Miklo's TT confirmation might be somewhat influenced by his phenotypical traits. The only longer block of TT contradiction happens in the last quarter when Miklo argues with Montana and then persuades Magic to conspire against their leader, who has lost his strength (just like *American Me*'s Santana). In the ST Miklo alternates minority substandard and Spanish, while the TT lines are further up in the prestige scale.

Passing from 2.1% to 34.2%, Cruz's contradiction percentage changes in a similar way to Miklo's. The growth in contradictory relations is due to Cruz's full and constant visual immersion in the environment of East Los Angeles, as well as to his behaviour and usual attire. In ST Cruz, the only long moments of contradiction are part of the plot and happen when Cruz — who has nearly made it as a painter — launches his first exhibition. He interacts with white people in an elegant building and tries his best to be credible, but then his friends from the *barrio* visit him, hoping to be given some cash to buy drugs. The situation causes a series of contradictions, aimed at underlining the awkwardness of adapting to a different social environment. Just like TT Miklo, TT Cruz alternates between confirmation and contradiction throughout the film.

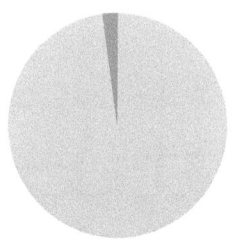

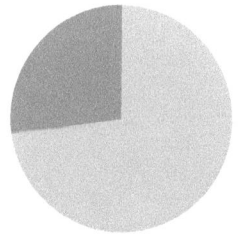

Figure 56 Intermodal relations ST Paco.

Figure 57 Intermodal relations TT Paco.

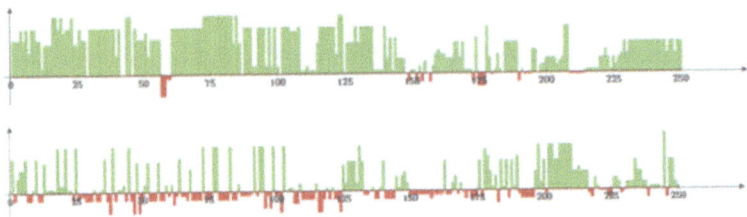

Figure 58 Paco's ST and TT alternation of intermodal confirmation and contradiction in the film.

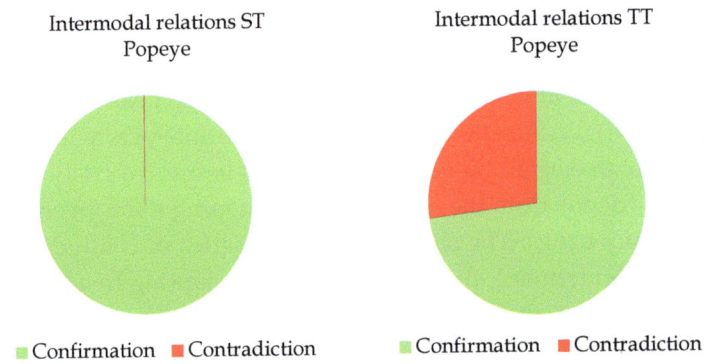

Figure 59 Intermodal relations ST Popeye.

Figure 60 Intermodal relations TT Popeye.

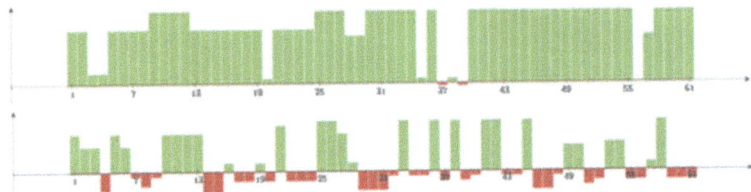

Figure 61 Popeye's ST and TT alternation of intermodal confirmation and contradiction in the film.

Paco and Popeye have scored similarly, although for different reasons. Despite his Anglo fashion attire after abandoning the gang, Paco's interlocutors and settings are, for the most part, still the same as they were when he led the *Vatos Locos*. He only seldom sits at his desk at the police department, and he is most often out on the streets. This ensures that his ST minority substandard average speech is in confirmation with his surroundings, as well as with his own behaviour. He still keeps his aggressive attitude and is often particularly rude to criminals—almost as if through mistreating them he was punishing himself for what he used to be. TT Paco's contradiction increases along with the decrease of his marked linguistic traits—the contradiction is more evident in the first part of the film when he is still the leader of the gang *Vatos Locos*.

ST Popeye is barely ever in contradiction with the other modes: he acts and speaks like a stereotypical Chicano thug, and he is either in jail, in a squalid pad (under the effect of drugs), or trying to act like a boss on the streets—when he does not really have many talents as a leader, and only manages to deceive his *carnales,* who trust him. The only time he uses a higher-prestige language he does so ironically, pretending to be innocent while being searched by Paco. TT Popeye, like the other characters of the film, constantly fluctuates between confirmation and contradiction. The growth of that contradiction is due to the TT recurrence of more prestigious variety—out of context as well as out of character for this two-dimensional depiction of an unredeemed criminal.

Lastly, Montana's case stands out for its uniqueness. In fact, La Onda's leader has a subverted confirmation-contradiction ratio in the TT. While confirmation is consistent in the ST (99,6%), in the target text it drops to 41%, leaving more space for contradiction. He has the looks of a Chicano and is the respected boss of a Chicano prison gang (he is only seen in prison), but the strong standardization that took place from a linguistic point of view deprived Montana of both the substandard speech and the marked CE features—leaving him with a *dubbese* that clashes especially with his phenotype and his comrades. This phenomenon can be partly justified given his minor role in the film, but may also reflect a prejudice according to which an enlightened leader speaks a variety that is much closer to the diegetic centre of prestige.

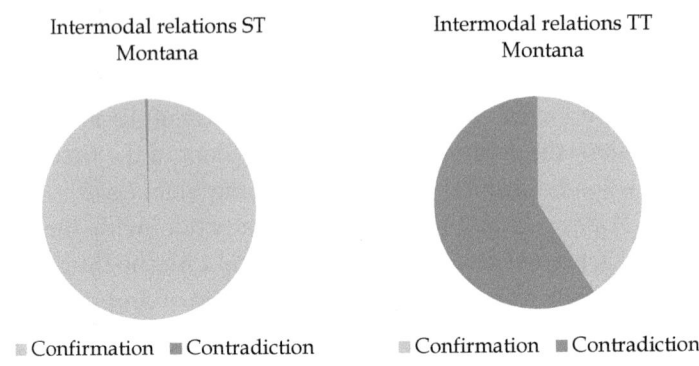

Figure 62 Intermodal relations ST Montana.

Figure 63 Intermodal relations TT Montana.

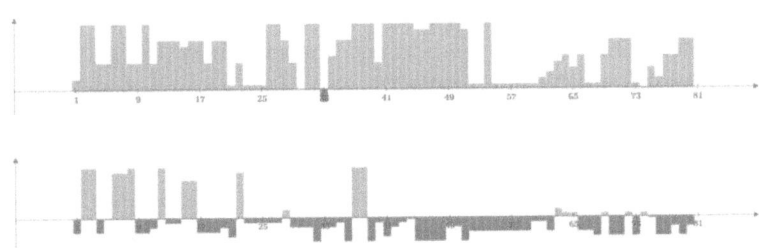

Figure 64 Montana's ST and TT alternation of intermodal confirmation and contradiction in the film.

3.3 An invitation to contextualization: the sociocultural dimension and some considerations on the overall results

Stand and Deliver

Overall, it does not seem like the heavy change in terms of linguistic varieties has made the characters completely unrecognisable, as just looking at the language might have suggested. Although contradiction was often present between the dominant group language used in the TT and Angel's phenotypical features and costumes, it is more coherent with other aspects, such as interlocutors and setting, and also at times compensated for by the complementary relations.

Rather than on coherence with the sociocultural context of East Los Angeles, the target text seems focused on conveying plot-related aspects such as Angel's good nature and behavioural evolution. Chuco's character is merely sketched in both versions, although in different ways. In the source text, he simply replicates the stereotypes presented in the previous chapter, although in a somewhat sugar-coated way: he is never seen committing serious crimes, and respects — and even supports — his friend's decision to become a good student. In the target text, his superficial rendering may be due to his minor role: the only section of the movie where his speech is more accurately translated is the beginning when he is on the scene to develop the plot by showing the difficulties of teaching in a rough area like East Los Angeles — but also to show that Escalante is not easily intimidated.

When it comes to the dimension in which the ST originated, it is worth noting that the 1980s witnessed the emergence of the English-only movement and its racism against people of Latino heritage, which long pervaded the debate on education (Citrin *et al.* 1990). The film appears to respond to the subtle discriminating insinuation that Latinos are somehow less intelligent than Anglos, by showing that — when given trust and high-quality teaching — Latinos can achieve amazing results. To do so, the film draws from a true story that took place about ten years before, which also inspired a book on the teacher Jaime Escalante (Mathews 1989). The commitment of the film to the topic of Latino and Chicano discrimination at school is confirmed by a small tribute to the L.A. walkouts of 1968 (García & Castro 2011): when unfairly accused of cheating, the character Javier (Patrick Baca) stands up and walks out of the class to show his indignation. His action inspires Angel to react against the investigators. From a cinematic point of view, there was a trend for the inspirational teacher movie genre in that period, as demonstrated by numerous films with similar plots released between the 1980s and 1990s.[42]

---

[42] Some inspirational teacher movie examples from the same period include: *Teachers* (1984), *Lean On Me* (1989), *Dead Poets Society* (1989), *Sister Act 2: Back In the Habit* (1993) and *Dangerous Minds* (1995). Certainly, however, the genre was not invented then, as there are other examples much earlier, e.g. *Goodbye, Mr. Chips*

The target audience cannot be assumed to know much about the specific historical references, especially since—as previously discussed—the film was released in a period that did not allow for the gathering of information on foreign events with the same ease as today. It must also be remembered that those in charge of creating the Italian dialogues are generally not trained as translators and do not see themselves as such (Pavesi & Perego 2006)—one of their main tasks being to make the script speakable and performable for the dubbing actors. That probably explains the choice to privilege plot rendering rather than the authenticity of ghetto linguistic features. Given the strict rules of *dubbese*, it might have seemed more important to convey and emphasise only the linguistic information that is functional to the plot. Indeed, the audience can probably see for themselves that the whole class belongs to a non-white (thus potentially discriminated against) ethnicity in a poor area, and the teacher Escalante explains that studying mathematics is a way to defy discrimination because it is a science that speaks for itself. Surely, the Italian audience needs a greater "suspension of disbelief" (Chiaro 2008) to be convinced that a *cholo* from the ghetto can have an elevated vocabulary or—even more than that—a perfectly standard accent. However, as just seen above, the whole product conveys a certain amount of information that should prevent the researcher from assuming that everything was simply lost in translation: the target audience of the time was most likely accustomed not to rely on phonetics to obtain certain types of information, given the omnipresence of *dubbese* across translated audiovisual products.

Colors

Colors aims at showing the difficult situations caused by the gang war in Los Angeles, as confirmed by the disclaimer aired before the film starts:

> The Los Angeles Police Department and the Los Angeles County Sheriff' each has a gang crime division. The Police Department's division is called

---

(1939), and some during the 1960s, such as *The Miracle Worker* (1962), *To Sir, with Love* (1967) and *Up the Down Staircase* (1967).

C.R.A.S.H. (Community Resources Against Street Hoodlums) and the Sheriff's division is called O.S.S. (Operation Safe Streets). The combined anti-gang force numbers 250 men and women.
In the greater Los Angeles area there are over 600 street gangs with almost 70,000 members.
Last year there were 387 gang-related killings. (*Colors*, 1988: 00.24-00.43)

The uneven distribution of forces and the number of killings reported in the disclaimer contribute to generating a sense of an impossible and dangerous task for the police officers even before the characters appear on the screen. Indeed, the movie follows the daily routines of the police officer protagonists, only occasionally showing a little more of the gangsters' lives. Without getting to know them, we are presented with Chicano characters that are part of a general, broad threat. In this sense, by creating such an intimidating atmosphere, the film seems perfectly in line with the generation of "public hysteria" activated by the media in periods of economic recession and social struggles (Bender 2002, 38). As previously discussed, increased migration is often involved in public debates about border security and domestic policing alike. With only one white gang member in the whole *barrio*, *Colors* seems to align itself with the idea that non-whites have some degree of criminality in their DNA or their culture while, if and when Anglo gangs are ever mentioned, their behaviour is not attributed to the whole ethnic group. The Anglo criminals "are dismissed as wayward youth, as disturbed adults" (Bender 2002, 39); the bad apples of an otherwise civilized society.

From this context, ST Frog and Gato emerge as two-dimensional, stereotyped drug-addicted gang members who are not willing to change their ways—Frog initially tries to keep his young brother Felipe out of real gang life, but eventually gives in and lets him become a member. No personal background is provided so that the audience does not know how these people decided to become gang members—the characters seem to believe the gang is their family, and they embrace the idea of being killed in a shootout.

The Italian audiences of the late 1980s and early 1990s could not really relate to such a situation, as second-generation immigrants were not a crucial issue and criminality hitting the headlines was often domestic, e.g. Italian organised crime, (Pasquini 2016). This lack of socio-political affinity between the US and Italy, however, can be compensated for by equating the stereotype of *Colors* with the *Bandido* from western movies. This could be the reason for making Frog sound like a first-generation immigrant (rather than a Chicano), but there is also another contextual element. Frog was dubbed by Francisco Javier Moriones, − AKA Saverio Moriones, an Italian-Spanish dubbing actor who has often voiced Latino actors and characters.[43] It must be remembered that dubbing actors have an important role in the Italian dubbing world, to the extent that they have their say in the way their characters will be interpreted (Antonini 2009, 99; Chiaro 2008, 145). In this case, it is impossible to say by just watching the dubbed film whether Moriones decided to emphasise the character's Latino phonetics or was hired because he could act with an accent.

Conversely, TT Gato's speech patterns do not seem to have been a primary preoccupation for the adapters, possibly because the character has a minor role in the movie (he only utters about twenty lines) and considering that limited time and resources may prevent him from accurately studying a character who is only sketched out in the ST to begin with (Zabalbeascoa 2009). In this sense, TT Frog seems to compensate for TT Gato, whose belonging to the gang is only evident because of his extremely stereotypical *cholo* attire. Taken together and within their context, the two translated characters still convey the ST racial stereotyping, albeit adapted for general purposes, so as to allow the fruition without focusing on the specific socio-cultural context that originated the ST.

American Me

American Me is a gangster movie, centred on gangster life — particularly its most dramatic aspects. Edward James Olmos, who portrays Santana and is also the director of the film, had already starred in *Stand and Deliver* and *Zoot Suits*. It is possible to hypothesize that

---

[43] https://www.antoniogenna.net/doppiaggio/voci/vocism.htm. Accessed April 29, 2021.

the intention was to show that joining a gang is a youth mistake, caused by the inevitability of encountering gang life in the *barrio* as probably the only form of socialization and peer cohesion. The protagonists state several times that gang membership is about gaining and maintaining respect and proving themselves to others. While of course, this is the perception they have during their youth, some of them change their minds growing up (Santana and, eventually, the Puppet brothers), but unfortunately organised crime is not easy to extricate oneself from, and they are all invested in a destiny they chose without understanding the consequences — an error that most young kids seem destined to repeat. The film, in fact, ends with the gang initiation rite of a child: he receives his *placa* (the gang tattoo on the palm of the hand), takes drugs and is privy to his first drive-by shooting. The whole film appears to be conceived to be a painfully realistic portrait of life in the *barrio* — although the lack of alternative life paths it considers is a testament to the way the movie indulges in stereotypes about Chicanos even as it attempts to explain their behaviour. This intention behind the film was probably what motivated the ST linguistic choices: most characters speak a vernacular CE variety, and the only one who can use a more prestigious variety is Santana, who declares that he spent his jail time reading and acquiring awareness on *la Raza* and Chicano history and identity. He tries to defend his criminal life by saying that it is a way to defend his people in jail, but eventually, he has to admit that Julie is right in saying he is nothing more than "a fucking dope dealer" (*American Me*, 1.35.52).

His main counterpart is JD, who does anything to be one of the Chicanos, overcoming the initial prejudice of the other Chicanos thanks to Santana's support — but this will not stop JD from eventually ordering his friend's killing. JD's desperate attempt to be part of the gang is reflected in his vernacular CE speech patterns and his exaggerated embodiment of an idea of machismo that eventually seems to reflect the distorted idea white people have of what it means to be a Chicano.

The other characters have little space in the film, are less characterized, and their minority substandard speech patterns in the ST echo and resonate with each other and reinforce the visual stereotypes presented in the films.

Gangs composed of ethnic minorities/domestic citizens are not the main concern of 1992's Italy, and Mexicans are not a notable ethnic group in Italy (see the previous chapter). Consequently, the ethnic aspects of the context might have seemed a minor concern to the translators. Of course, they could count on the fact that most Italians are likely to be familiar with narrations of organised crime with a familiar or local base, be they fictional or coming from the news. In the same year the film was released, the strenuous fight against the Italian mafia carried out by the brave magistrates Giovanni Falcone and Paolo Borsellino had culminated in the killing of both in tragic attacks (Pasquini 2016). In fiction, the successful TV series *La Piovra* (the octopus, referring to the numerous tentacles of the mafia) had been showing Italians the issue of organised crime's inhumanity. From the United States' cinematic tradition, Italian audiences could count on the image of the *Bandido* from the western movies as well as on successful films such as *The Godfather* (1972) and *Goodfellas* (1990), both focused on Italian American organised crime. At the same time, Italy had just started dealing with mass immigration, with the first arrivals of refugees from Albania in 1991 (King & Mai 2013).

From a more translational point of view, the standardising power of the Italian dubbing tradition cannot be underestimated. It was unlikely for the main character to repeatedly violate grammar rules in an audiovisual translated text because this would have affected the sense of responsibility towards viewers, and "especially young children" (Pavesi & Perego 2006, 106), strongly felt by Italian film translators. This probably explains the general tendency of elevating the linguistic prestige of the characters' speech patterns. Nevertheless, the translators of *American Me* have left some traces of the characters' otherness, keeping at least the proportion between multimodal confirmation and contradiction. Given the context, even a little non-standardness may be enough to grasp the communicative meaning and the diegetic functions of the characters.

Blood In Blood out

Blood In Blood Out was released just one year after *American Me*, and both share several themes and inspirations (see the previous chapter). The two films thus come from the same historical background and are immersed in the same target context.

However, *Blood In Blood Out* offers insight into more than one character, each embodying some stereotypes about Chicanos. Miklo is the white guy who wants to be Chicano: in his mind, to be a Chicano means to be a gangster, and he manages to become the best, the most powerful of them all. This shows that white people can be just as cruel and ruthless, while indirectly implying that white people are so superior that they can become the leaders of a Chicano gang (see previous chapter). Another possible interpretation is that Miklo embodies the white prejudice associating the Chicano lifestyle with gang membership, while his two Chicano cousins eventually move away from the stereotype. Popeye is the most stereotyped, close to that ruthless and de-humanized *Bandidos* from the western tradition, while also being comedic in his exaggerated behaviours, e.g. before attempting to rape[44] Miklo, he pushes him to the ground and exclaims: "All right, you white bitch. Gimme some *chon chon!*"[45] Cruz embodies the psychological weakness of Chicanos who, unable to take the pain of an injury, have to resort to drugs—often causing tragic events. Paco represents the aggressiveness and the machismo of Chicano males: even after becoming a police officer, rather than pursuing justice with a rational attitude (i.e. like a stereotypical white hero), he remains short-tempered, and at times bullies the gangsters. Montana—who has acquired a remarkable cultural level and tries to preach to Chicano liberation

---

[44] In *American Me*, there are three rape scenes, much more tragic than the one in *Blood In Blood Out*, where Popeye is interrupted by Montana before he can do anything to Miklo, and in general rapes in the film are only a threat, which never actually happens.

[45] Presumably from Spanish *cojones* (testicles), from which *chones* (underwear), it is a rude invitation to have a sexual intercourse (Cagliero & Spallino 2010, 154). This somewhat ridiculous line seems to have attracted the US audience's attention: when looking up the expression on the online *Urban Dictionary*, the first three entries all reference Popeye's line: https://www.urbandictionary.com/define.php?term=chon+chon. Accessed April 29, 2021.

from the chains of organised crime – is assassinated by those he was trying to save.

Blood In Blood Out seems less dramatic in its overall depiction of gang life. Two out of three protagonists find their way out of gang life, while the third deliberately decides to remain a gang member because he has found a new family in *La Onda*.

Given the different realities of the two audiences, the translated stereotype had to rely on new backgrounds. The original stereotype is strongly ethnolinguistic and culturally embedded. It is centred on the idea of *La Raza*: derived from the theory of *La Raza Cósmica* by Vasconcelos (1925; 1979), this term has come to represent people of Mexican descent, wherever they were born and live, and it also embodies the idea of solidarity among Mexican Americans. That is why Miklo – once discriminated against for the colour of his skin, then made leader of a Chicano gang – says to his cousin Paco that he thanks him for sending him to jail, because it is there that he found "the strength of *La Raza*." In a pilot study that is a qualitative/quantitative analysis of some aspects of Miklo's speech patterns, I discovered an abundant use of family-related terms in his TT version (Renna 2017, 262). This corroborates the hypothesis already proposed for *American Me*: associating the Chicano gangsters with more familiar Italian and Italian American organised crime may have had some role in the choice of centralizing the gangsters towards the dominant ethnic group while keeping their language below standard.

Overall Considerations

After analysing the films one by one, it is possible to draw some more general conclusions about the whole corpus. An important concept to underline is that in no way should the differences between ST and TT be considered a translation failure– at least, not before this has been proved by perception studies on all possible kinds of audience. Having analysed most of the movies featuring the Chicano gangster character in the 1988-1993 period, it is possible to suggest some generalizations about the whole corpus that can serve as a starting point rather than as a definitive conclusion.

From a textual point of view, the fourteen characters analysed across the four films behaved in similar ways across all the source versions. Most of their speech patterns are positioned in the minority substandard category in quite a clear-cut way, with only a few exceptions: Santana (*American Me*) and Montana (*Blood In Blood Out*) speak a more prestigious variety: Santana's average speech is somewhere in between dominant substandard and dominant oral, while Montana's average is positioned on the minority oral. Mundo from *American Me*, with his recurrent Spanish switches, tends slightly towards the "other language" category. All the others, despite their (more or less occasional) variation, remain in the minority substandard. This confirms Fought's (2002) view on films starring Chicanos: they often portray gangsters speaking the most vernacular subvarieties of CE possible.

The TT results are less regular. Two cases behave in completely different ways from the rest and each other: *Colors'* TT Frog is the only one steadily remaining in the minority non-standard area, with an average between oral and substandard. Conversely, *Blood In Blood Out* Montana's scores are much higher, as his average speech is in the standard spectrum. Another case of its own is Angel from *Stand and Deliver*, whose TT lines are in the dominant oral category, but also tend towards the standard area. All other TT characters are usually divided between dominant oral and dominant substandard. In particular, the main characters (Angel, Santana, Miklo, Paco and Cruz) are more or less evidently placed in the dominant oral category, while many among the secondary ones (e.g. JD, Mundo, Lil' Puppet and Popeye) are in the dominant substandard category. The only secondary characters in different categories are the above-mentioned Montana, Puppet — whose average is dominant oral — and Chuco, somewhere in between dominant oral and substandard.

The way these linguistic categories were linguistically rendered shows another regularity as well: the source texts rely on phonetics to represent the linguistic non-standardness of the characters, as the overall weighted average of the ST recurrence of phonetics is 98.9%. Considering that most of the characters speak far below standard, this indicates that phonetics is seen as an effective marker of low socio-cultural and educational level, confirming (at least in the fictional worlds created in these films) the critical linguistic theories identifying the perception of accent as a potential cause of discrimination against minorities (Lippi-Green 1997; Macedo *et al.* 2003). However, all the ST linguistic features are quite recurrent: the overall morpho-syntax weighted average use is 79.6%, while, with a score of 72.9%, the lexicon is just slightly lower.

The TT versions have their specificities. Firstly, the most recurrent variety is more prestigious than the one of the ST; secondly, *dubbese* phonetics hardly manages to represent any variety apart from its own standardized fictional non-localized self; lastly, *dubbese* imposes other linguistic boundaries (which will be discussed later in this paragraph). The study carried out here has shown that the linguistic feature most used to convey a certain TT fictional linguistic variety in this corpus is morpho-syntax, with an overall weighted average of 85.6%, in agreement with previous studies on the frequent use of morpho-syntactic features (especially dislocation) in Italian dubbing as a marker of orality (Pavesi & Perego, 2006). Lexical items, which do not seem to have significantly changed from those of the ST, follow with an overall weighted average of 71.8%. My pilot studies had already shown a tendency to keep the distinguishing lexicon of the Chicano gangster more or less unchanged (Renna 2017; Renna 2018a; Renna 2019). The most evident change is the one in the use of phonetics in the TT: given that *dubbese* has a rather strict set of non-written rules imposing non-localized elocution to the dubbing actors, it does not seem surprising that phonetics is only a marker of standardness (with the sole exception of Moriones dubbing Frog), thus scoring a rather low 29% overall weighted average.

In the light of these results, it is possible to hypothesize that most characters were translated with two strategies in mind. The first is centralization: as previously discussed, it is a preservation strategy that diminishes the number of non-standard linguistic features of the character, while still leaving some traces of his lower sociocultural positioning. The only evident exception is Frog, translated alternating maintenance and even decentralization: the dubbed character, rather than a Chicano, may sound like a stereotyped immigrant of Hispanic origin.

Centralization is the main strategy for eleven characters out of fourteen. The second most recurrent strategy was discourse standardization, but its use is not omnipresent. Thus, it would be wrong to assume that these characters speak like highly educated professionals from a dominant ethnic group: several traces of non-standardness, and even some traces of their ethnic belonging, were left for the audience to create a link with the rest of the audiovisual product.

The connection between the language and the other modes was also taken into consideration. The ST has an overwhelming majority of lines in confirmation with costumes and make-up, phenotype, behaviour, setting, interlocutors and music. Confirmation in the ST scored 97% against a mere 3% of contradiction. This does not mean that there are no contradictions whatsoever. While the contradictory elements may exist, they are almost always counterbalanced by others that confirm or complement the use of a certain linguistic variety. For example, when the white Miklo or J.D talk like Chicanos, this is in constant contradiction with their phenotypical traits. However, all the other elements confirm and validate their use of vernacular CE as the most adequate variety for situations like a Chicano gang meeting in an East Los Angeles *barrio*. ST contradiction is usually required by the plot: for instance, when Angel and Chuco enter Escalante's class late, acting and talking like thugs, their contradictory relationship with the surroundings has a specific communicative meaning, as it expresses the incompatibility between gang members' attitudes and successful education.

Growing contradiction in the TT, however, might imply some degree of danger. An excess of contradiction may disrupt textual and diegetic dimensions, breaking the non-written agreement between translators and the audience. Where is the threshold? Is it really possible to draw a line beyond which a translated text is nonsense? Probably the answer depends on what genre, product, and audience are taken into consideration.

In the films analysed here, there is undoubtedly a growth in contradiction. Nonetheless, apart from Montana's case, the ratio is kept with an overall average of 68% confirmation versus 32% of contradiction. Certainly, contradiction happens around ten times more often in the TT, but confirmation is still achieved in most cases. There is room to suggest that the translation has conveyed at least part of the communicative meaning of the source.

In order to understand translation choices, however, it is important to look at the broader socio-cultural context that has generated a certain translation. Ramos Pinto (2017) suggests considering some aspects, and they are all relevant to this study.

The first one is the *ideological context* that generated the translation, which may or may not "be supportive of creative uses of discourse" (Ramos Pinto 2017, 30). Research so far carried out on the Italian dubbing culture has shown that, at least in the period considered here, it strongly hinged upon a non-written set of rules and conventions limiting the liberties in TT implementation (Antonini 2008; Bucaria 2008; Chaume 2004). Another important factor to consider is the status granted to dubbing translators: "where the translator is assumed to be a creative agent, s/he will feel more comfortable to recreate non-standard discourse in the TT than in contexts where the translator fears that the deviation encountered in the TT will be interpreted as a bad translation" (Ramos Pinto 2017, 30). This factor often works together with the translators' working condition in creating a more or less favourable environment for innovation. As explained by Chiaro, while "the first translation is usually word for word [...] it is the adaptor or 'dubbing translator' who subsequently adjusts the rough translation to make it sound like natural target language dialogue" (Chiaro 2008, 145). Although these two processes may be carried out by the same person, they are still part of a sort of industrial project directed by a manager, who has to negotiate concrete aspects such as schedule and costs; s/he also is in charge of casting for dubbing actors. Moreover, the dubbing actors usually have the freedom to make their own changes to the screenplay they are given, and the dubbing directors can always intervene with their opinion about the text. Thus, it can be hard to attribute the dubbed film to a specific person, as it is the product of a complex apparatus, where each part acts according to different purposes. Often, those purposes tend to drift very far away from textual accuracy or quality and penalize the translators with fairly harsh working conditions, including tight deadlines and low wages (Antonini 2008, 99).[46] "Legibility and intelligibility challenges" (Ramos Pinto 2017, 30) are also crucial: as anticipated in the previous paragraph, the main objective in creating a script for dubbing is speakability and performability for the dubbing actors, which is crucial to saving time and money in the dubbing phase (Pavesi & Perego 2006, 106). In this sense, elements like a comfortable lip-sync may be more urgent than linguistic accuracy in representing a linguistic minority.

Other elements expand even beyond the dubbing industry itself. One example is the difference between source and target cultures (Hatim and Mason 1990; Ramos Pinto 2017). As previously discussed, the average Italian audience of the 1980s and 1990s had little or no knowledge of the Chicanos, as well as a relatively new experience of immigration. They therefore cannot be assumed to have been particularly familiar with contact varieties developing among local peoples of foreign descent. Moreover, as seen in the previous chapter, Italy has a different migration history where Mexicans play a minor role (Calvanese 2011, 34; Reyneri 2011, 99–100).

Other important factors concern the target audience's profile (Rosa 2004) and the expected function of the target product (Ramos Pinto 2010), whose specificities for this corpus can only be hypothesized, and deserve specific historical/sociocultural research to be answered properly. Profiling the target audience is a complex process of paramount importance for the translator. If the people behind the translation of the movies in this corpus expected the audience not to be too concerned with linguistic authenticity, this might further justify opting for leaving just enough traces for the audience

---

[46] Although the issue of the working conditions of audiovisual translation workers deserves a study of its own, it is possible to mention one example of how their expertise and work are overlooked: the Italian collective national contract for dubbing workers does not foresee the existence of the professional figure of the translator, as it only mentions those of dubbing actor, dubbing director, dubbing assistant and dialogue adapter: http://www.saislc.cgil.it/index.php?option=com_content&view=category&layout=blog&id=41&Itemid=97. Accessed April 29, 2021.

to understand that some kind of low sociocultural level minority group was involved. This is especially true if the imagined function of the product is first of all entertainment, as is easy to assume with action or crime films, or even a film like *Stand and Deliver*, which follows an established and stereotyped genre tradition.

Overall, the understanding of an audiovisual product is a composite process, which means that a whole product can be more than a mere sum of its parts or, as Ramos Pinto (2017, 27) puts it: "Despite the lack of empirical evidence on how viewers would interpret this scene […], our experience as viewers tells us that there is room for the intended interpretation of both the communicative meanings and associated functions to be accomplished."

Conclusion

The design of a stereotyped character in an audiovisual product is a complex and multi-layered process, which passes through both textual and non-textual modes. Its translation for a new context requires strategies that consider all the modes.

This book has aimed to implement a framework able to provide information on character (re)design from source to target multimodal text, taking the stereotype of the Chicano gangster as a case study. The sociocultural context generating the source text is not the same as the one in which the target text will be presented. Similarly, each language has its own ways to display varying degrees of prestige, and each fictional language has its rules and conventions. The analysis of the communicative meaning carried out here has shown that this fact has influenced the way the Chicano gangster stereotype was presented in the American and the Italian context, but not to the extent that it is completely misrepresented in the target version.

This study took several aspects into account in order to avoid simplistic judgements based on partial elements, in compliance with the guidelines offered by descriptive translation studies and corpus linguistics. It was necessary to consider both textual and non-textual aspects of the audiovisual product at the same time. This required the selection of a corpus through precise criteria, the transcription of both the source and target versions, and the implementation of a tagging system that put the different modes of the films in relation. This allowed for the answering of the initial questions, at least regarding the Chicano gangster stereotype between 1988 and 1993.

The first question concerned the variety used in the source and target text. The analysis carried out here showed that the source text tends to create a fictional Chicano English that is accurate, but partial: in most cases, the gangsters spoke a low-prestige variety, whose communicative function was to show their educational and sociocultural positioning at the margin of American society — a Hallidayan "anti-society" (1978), embodying the antithesis to Anglo

American values. The target text version was not as consistently marginalized as the source text. Indeed, the Italian-Chicano gangsters' speech tends to fluctuate from the most standardized and prestigious varieties to the least prestigious ones, resulting in a fictional orality that, although often deprived of many of its ST markers, still preserves some traces of its speakers' heritage.

The second question concerned the strategies used by the translators to import the Chicano gangsters into a different sociocultural context. The data analysed here showed that most often the strategies created tension between neutralization, in the form of discourse standardization, and preservation, in the form of centralization. Centralization proved to be the most used strategy, retaining non-standard elements of the source text, but in smaller quantities or reducing their impact.

The answer to the first two questions, however, required the answering of another question concerning the type of features that marked a certain line as belonging to a specific variety. The source text showed a strong reliance on phonetics, omnipresent testifiers of Chicanos as speakers of "English with an accent" (Lippi-Green 1997), but the other features were also recurrent. The target text, certainly because of the influence of the *dubbese* tradition, rarely relied on phonetics, revealing a strong preference for morpho-syntax as the marker of non-standardness, followed by the lexicon. Lexicon, on the contrary, did not change much in frequency from source to target text.

These questions concerned the textual dimension, and the next stage of the work consisted of putting text in relation to the other modes of the film. The relations between different modes in both source and target text constituted the diegetic dimension. The relations considered were contradiction and confirmation, with the latter further divided between equivalence and complementarity.

The data showed that the source versions most often put textual and non-textual in confirmation with each other: the characters — talking, looking and acting like the stereotype they embodied — were mainly situated in stereotypical environments, surrounded by stereotypical interlocutors and stereotypical music. This high frequency of confirmation partly changed in the target text, where the contradictory relations sensibly increased in most characters. However, rarely was the ratio between confirmation and contradiction completely subverted: the textual tension between centralization and standardization resulted in a less extreme Chicano gangster stereotype, which still managed not to detach from its diegetic context. Once again, it is crucial to underline here that this work did not aim to analyse the real language of Chicanos — which has been done through on-field research by other authors, for example, Fought (2003) — but rather, to explore the communicative meaning of a fictional version of Chicano English in a fictional context, and its recreation into a fictional Italian. The real-life language is a starting point, a term of comparison for understanding how the language was deployed in the cinematic context here analysed.

According to Ramos Pinto (2017) and Ramos Pinto & Mubaraki (2020), the analysis would be completed by another dimension: the sociocultural dimension, focusing on the extratextual elements that influence the translators in their work. Since this book was mainly aimed at constructing a framework for product-based analysis, however, the sociocultural dimension was only hinted at here, based on what is already known in terms of the history of the source and target cultures and of dubbing tradition and conventions in Italy. Certainly, this study would benefit from a thorough investigation on this dimension, e.g. talking to the professionals who worked on these films or similar and/or contemporary projects (between the late 1980s and early 1990s). A sociocultural context, however, does not only consist of translators/dubbing actors, as the audience is also key to understand whether the results obtained here correspond to the viewers' perception. In this sense, a perception study would be invaluable for this research.

Another way of proceeding in this study would be to work on the framework to further improve it. Indeed, as this is among the first attempts in this direction, there are several ways to make the framework more functional — for example, by working with software developers to automatize, at least partially, the tagging procedure. This could enable the taking of a broader corpus into consideration, thus obtaining more general — and possibly more reliable—results. Other developments could work on the textual and diegetic dimensions, expanding them in other directions. For example, the same stereotype can be analysed within an expanded time frame, or by considering another type of product (e.g. a TV series). To broaden the scope of the study it would also be useful to experiment with using the same framework on other linguistic minorities or other stereotyped groups (e.g. people from a certain region or social class, or even from discriminated social groups based on religion, gender, sexual orientation/identity or profession).

Some of these developments are currently being pursued in my new research project at the Ca' Foscari University of Venice, financed by the Italian Ministry of University and Research (MIUR) within the Department of Excellence initiative. More specifically, the aims are 1) experimenting with new software to improve scalability and multimodality in corpus consultation; 2) testing the framework categories on a different ethnotype with different linguistic features (i.e. the Chinese diaspora in the US); 3) if possible, given the current restrictions on social gatherings,[47] organising focus groups to test perception with the audience. These goals were set because they seemed the most urgent to pursue in order to further test and improve the framework on three of its crucial aspects—namely its corpus-friendliness and tagging usability, its applicability on other case studies and the differences between researcher and audience perception.

The work is still ongoing, and the results presented here point the way towards crucial directions for the development of the discipline. Overall, this book works towards an AVT studies turn, so as not to turn a blind eye to multimodality, embracing it as a central feature of the audiovisual text, and finding ways to include it into the analysis. This is particularly important in today's society, where the widespread use of technological devices opens the door to infinite possibilities concerning multimodal entertainment.

Secondly, this work has shown once more that descriptive approaches are crucial in understanding translation, letting go of judgements about the success of a translator's work and not

---

[47] The work is being completed in early 2021.

assuming that the communicative meaning of an audiovisual product is necessarily lost in translation. Indeed, this work has proved that the text is just a part of the entire audiovisual message, which is conveyed through a variety of communicative layers that may function as an obstacle, but also as a complement to the target audience's comprehension.

Certainly, I do not presume to have provided definitive answers nor absolute truths: rather, the intention was to offer a spark to build upon by confirming, confuting and improving these findings in the continual pursuit of knowledge — a pursuit that research should never cease to embody.

References

National Film Registry *More Than a Box of Chocolates, Forrest Gump, Bambi, Stand and* Deliver Among Registry Picks. 2011. Accessed April 29, 2021. <https://www.loc.gov/item/prn-11-240/>.

Acuña, Rodolfo. 1996. *Anything But Mexican: Chicanos in Contemporary Los Angeles*. New York: Verso.

—— *Occupied America: A History of Chicanos*. 2011. Fourth Edition. Boston: Longman.

Allport, Gordon W. 1954. *The Nature of Prejudice*. Cambridge, US: Addison-Wesley.

Allwood, Jens. 2008. "Multimodal corpora." In Lüdeling, Anke and Merja Kytö (eds): *Corpus Linguistics: An International Handbook*. Berlin: Mouton de Gruyter. 207-224.

American Me. 1992. Dir. Edward James Olmos. Universal City: Universal Pictures.

Antihero definition. n.d. Accessed April 29, 2021. <https://www.britannica.com/art/antihero>.

Antonini, Rachele. 2008. "The perception of Dubbese: an Italian Study." In Chiaro, Delia, Heiss, Christine and Bucaria, Chiara (eds): Between text and image: updating research in screen translation. Amsterdam: John Benjamins Publishing Company. 135-148.

——, and Delia Chiaro. 2009. "The Perception of Dubbing by Italian Audiences." In Díaz Cintas, Jorge and Anderman, Gunilla (eds): *Audiovisual Translation. Language Transfer on Screen*. New York: Palgrave Macmillan. 97-114.

Aristophanes. "Lysistrata." Circa 411 BC. n.d. Accessed April 29, 2021. <http://www.perseus.tufts.edu/hopper/text.jsp?doc=Perseus:text:1999.01.0035>.

Assis Rosa, Alexandra. 2015. "Translating Orality, Recreating Otherness." *Orality in Translation. Special Issue of Translation Studies* 8 (2): 209-225.

—— 2012. "Translating Place: Linguistic Variation in Translation." *Word and Text, A Journal of Literary Studies and Linguistics* 2 (2): 75-97.

Baker, Mona. 1993. "Corpus Linguistics and Translation Studies. Implications and Applications." In Baker, Mona, Gill, Francis and Tognini-Bonelli, Elena (eds): *Text and Technology: In honour of John Sinclair*. Amsterdam: John Benjamins Publishing Company. 233-250.

– 1996. "Corpus-based Translation Studies: The Challenges that Lie Ahead." In Somers, Harold (ed): *Terminology, LSP and Translation: Studies in Language Engineering in Honour of Juan C. Sager*. Amsterdam: John Benjamins Publishing Company. 175-186.

Bandia, Paul. 2011. "Orality and Translation." In Gambier, Yves and van Doorslaer, Luc (eds): *Handbook of Translation Studies (2)*. Amsterdam: John Benjamins Publishers. 108-112

Barrett, Rusty. 1999. "Indexing polyphonous identity in the speech of African American drag queens." Bucholtz, Mary, Liang, A. C. and Sutton, A. Laurel (eds): *Reinventing Identities: The Gendered Self in Discourse*. New York: Oxford University Press. 313-331.

Barth, Fredrik. 1969. *Ethnic Groups and Boundaries: The Social Organization of Culture Difference*. Boston: Little, Brown.

Bateman, John A. 2014. *Text and Image: A Critical Introduction to the Visual/Verbal Divide*. London: Routledge.

—, Wildfeuer, Janina and Tuomo Hiippala. 2017. *Multimodality. Foundations, Research and Analysis. A Problem-Orientated Introduction*. Berlin: De Gruyter.

Baugh, John. 1983. *Black Street Speech. Its History, Structure, and Survival*. Austin: University of Texas Press.

Bender, Steven. 2003. *Greasers and Gringos: Latinos, Law, and the American Imagination*. New York: New York University Press.

Berumen, Frank Javier Garcia. 1995. *The Chicano/Hispanic Image in American Film*. New York: Vantage Press.

Biber, Douglas. 1993. "Representativeness in Corpus Design." *Literary and Linguistic Computing* 8 (4): 243-257.

Blake, Norman. 1981. *Non-Standard Language in English literature*. London: André Deutsch Limited.

– 2004. *Shakespeare's Non-Standard English: A Dictionary of his Informal Language*. London, New York: Continuum.

Blood in Blood Out (Bound by Honor). 1993. Dir. Taylor Hackford. Burbank: Buena Vista Pictures Distribution.

Bordwell, David. 1985. "Space in the Classical Film." Bordwell, David, Thompson, Kristin and Staiger, Janet (eds). *The Classical Hollywood Cinema: Film Style and Mode of Production to 1960*. New York: Columbia University Press. 50-60.

Boulevard Nights. 1979. Dir. Michael Pressman. Burbank: Warner Bros.

Brisset, Annie. 1996. "The Search for a Native Language: Translation and Cultural Identity." In Venuti, Lawrence (ed): *The Translation Studies Reader*. London: Routledge. 162-194.

Brodovich, Olga I. 1997. "Translation theory and non-standard speech in fiction." *Perspectives: Studies on Translatology* 5 (1): 25-31.

Brother. 2004. Dir. Takeshi Kitano. Tōkyō: Shochiku Co., Ltd.

Bustamante, Jorge A., and Clark Winton Reynolds. 1992. *US-Mexico Relationships: Labor Market Interdependence*. Stanford: Stanford University Press.

Cagliero, Roberto and Chiara Spallino. 2010. *Dizionario universale. Slang americano. Slang americano-italiano*. Milano: Mondadori.

Camilli, Annalisa. 2017. Ius soli, ius sanguinis, ius culturae: tutto sulla riforma della cittadinanza. n.d. Accessed April 29, 2021. <https://www.internazionale.it/notizie/annalisa-camilli/2017/10/20/riforma-cittadinanza-da-sapere>.

Carrasco, Carlos. Actor Profile Page. n.d. Accessed April 29, 2021. <https://www.imdb.com/name/nm0140033/?ref_=tt_cl_t8>.

Carysta, David. 2004. *The Stories of English*. New York: Peter Mayer Publishers.

— 2012. *English As a Global Language*. Second Edition. Cambridge: Cambridge University Press.

Chalabi, Mona. 2018. "Terror attacks by Muslims receive 357% more press attention, study finds. Research by the University of Alabama shows attacks by Muslims receive an average of 105 headlines, others just 15." Accessed April 29, 2021. <https://www.theguardian.com/us-news/2018/jul/20/muslim-terror-attacks-press-coverage-study>.

Chapman, Raymond. 1994. *Form of Speech in Victorian Fiction*. London: Longman,

Chappel, Ben. 2012. *Lowrider Space: Aesthetics and Politics of Mexican American Custom Cars*. Austin: University of Texas Press.

Chaume, Frederic. 2002. "Models of Research in Audiovisual Translation." *Babel* 48 (1) : 1-13.

— 2004. "Film Studies and Translation Studies. Two disciplines at stake in audiovisual translation." *Meta* 49 (1): 12-24.

Chesterman, Andrew. 1997. *Memes of Translation*. Amsterdam, Philadelphia: John Benjamins.

Chiaro, Delia. 2008. "Issues in Audiovisual Translation." In Munday, Jeremy (ed): *The Routledge Companion to Translation Studies*. London: Routledge. 141-165.

Chon Chon Definition. n.d. Accessed April 29, 2021. <https://www.urbandictionary.com/define.php?term=chon+chon>.

Chun, Elaine. 2001. "The construction of White, Black, and Korean American identities through African American Vernacular English." *Journal of Linguistic Anthropology* 11 (1): 52-64.

Citrin, Jack, et al. 1990. "The 'Official English' Movement and the Symbolic Politics of Language in the United States." *The Western Political Quarterly* 43 (3): 535-559.

Clyne, Michael. 2000. "Lingua Franca and Ethnolects." *Sociolinguistica* 14 (1): 83-89.

Cohen, Ronald. 1978. "Ethnicity: problem and focus in anthropology." *Annual Review of Anthropology* 7 (1): 379-403.

Colors. Dir. Dennis Hopper. Beverly Hills: Orion Pictures. 1988.

Con Air. Dir. Simon West. Touchstone Pictures, Jerry Bruckheimer Films. 1997.

Contratto Collettivo Nazionale di Lavoro del Doppiaggio. n.d. Accessed April 29, 2021. <http://www.saislc.cgil.it/>.

Corbin, Caroline Mala. 2017. "Terrorists Are Always Muslim but Never White: At the Intersection of Critical Race Theory and Propaganda." *Fordham Law Review*, 86 (2): 455-485.

Damian Chapa, Actor Profile Page. n.d. Accessed April 29, 2021. <https://www.imdb.com/name/nm0152082/?ref_=nv_sr_1>.

Dangerous Minds. Dir. John N. Smith. Burbank: Hollywood Pictures. 1995.

Dead Poets Society. Dir. Peter Weir. Burbank: Buena Vista Pictures Distribution. 1989.

"Detailed Languages Spoken at Home and Ability to Speak English for the Population 5 Years and Over: 2009-2013." 2009. Accessed April 29, 2021. *US Census Bureau.* <https://www.census.gov/data/tables/2013/demo/2009-2013-lang-tables.html>.

Díaz-Cintas, Jorge. 2008. *The Didactics of Audiovisual Translation.* Amsterdam: John Benjamins Publishing.

—, Anna Matamala Ripoll, and Joselia Neves. 2010. *New insights into audiovisual translation and media accessibility: media for all* (2). Amsterdam, New York: Rodopi.

Dicerto, Sara. 2018. *Multimodal Pragmatics. Building a New Model for Source Text Analysis.* London: Palgrave Macmillan.

— *Multimodal Pragmatics: Building a New Model for Source Text Analysis.* 2014. University College London: PhD Thesis.

Dorian, Nancy C. 1981. *Language Death: The Life Cycle of a Scottish Gaelic Dialect.* Philadelphia: University of Pennsylvania Press.

Durrell, Martin. 2004. "Soziolect/Soziolekt." Ammon, Ulrich. *Sociolinguistics/Soziolinguistik* (1) Berlin: Walter de Gruyter, n.p.

Eckert, Penelope. 2008. "Where do ethnolects stop?" *International Journal of Bilingualism* 12 (1/2): 25-42.

Edward James Olmos, Actor Profile Page. n.d. Accessed November 14 2018. <https://www.imdb.com/name/nm0001579/>.

End of Watch. Dir. David Ayer. Paris: StudioCanal. 2012.

Even-Zohar, Itamar. "Polysystem Theory." 1979. Poetics Today, Special Issue: Literature, Interpretation, Communication 1 (1/2): 287-310.

— 1990. *Polysystem Studies*. Tel Aviv: Porter Institute of Poetics and Semiotics.

Fairclough, Norman. 1989. *Language and power*. Harlow: Longman.

Falling Down. 1993. Dir. Joel Schumacker. Burbank: Warner Bros. 1993.

Ferguson, Susan. 1998. "Drawing Fictional Lines: Dialect and Narrative in the Victorian Novel." *Style* 32 (1): 1-17.

Films about September 11 Tragedy. n.d. Accessed April 29, 2021. <https://www.imdb.com/list/ls056745046/>.

Fishman, Joshua A. 1972. "Domains and the Relationships between Micro- and Macrosociolinguistics." In Gumperz, John and Hyme, Dell (eds): *Directions in Sociolinguistics: The Ethnography of Communication*. New York: Basil Blackwell. 435-453.

Fluck, Winfried. 2003. "Film and Memory." In Hebel, Udo J (ed): *Sites of Memory in American Literatures and Cultures*. Heidelberg Universitätsverlag: 213-229.

Foucault, Michel. 1991. *Discipline and Punish: the birth of a prison*. London: Penguin.

Fought, Carmen. 1999. "A Majority Sound Change in a Minority Community: /u/-fronting in Chicano English." *Journal of Sociolinguistics* 3 (1): 5-23.

— 2003. *Chicano English In Context*. New York: Palgrave Macmillan.

— 2006. *Language and ethnicity*. Cambridge: Cambridge University Press.

Franceschi, Valeria. 2014. *ELF Users as Creative Writers: Plurilingual Practices in Fanfiction*. University of Verona: PhD Thesis.

Frazer, Timothy C. 1996. "Chicano English and Spanish Interference in the Midwestern United States." *American Speech* 71 (1): 72-85.

Freddi, Maria. 2013. "Constructing a corpus of translated films: a corpus view of dubbing." *Perspectives,* 21 (4): 491-503.

Gal, Susan. 1979. *Language Shift: Social Determinants of Linguistic Change in Bilingual Austria*. New York: Academic Press.

Gambier, Yves. 2006. "Multimodality and Subtitling." In Carroll, Mary, Gerzymisch-Arbogast, Heidrun and Nauert, Sandra (eds): *Proceedings of the Marie Curie Euroconferences MuTra: Audiovisual Translation Scenarios, 1-5 May 2006*, Copenhagen.

García, Alma M. 2002. *The Mexican Americans.* Westport, London: Greenwood Publishing Group.

García, Eugene E. 1983. "Becoming Bilingual during Early Childhood." *International Journal of Behavioral Development,* 6 (4): 375-404.

— 2005. *Teaching and Learning in Two Languages: Bilingualism and Schooling in the United States.* New York: Teachers College Press.

Genna, Antonio. La pagina di Saverio Moriones. n.d. Accessed April 29, 2021. <https://www.antoniogenna.net/doppiaggio/voci/vocism.htm>.

Giles, Howard. 1973. "Accent mobility: A model and some data." *Anthropological Linguistics,* 15 (2): 87-105.

—, and P.F. Powesland. 1975. *Speech Style and Social Evaluation.* London: Academic Press in association with the European Association of Experimental Social Psychology.

—, Justine Coupland, and Nikolas Coupland. 1991. *The Contexts of Accommodation: Developments in Applied Sociolinguistics.* Cambridge: Cambridge University Press.

González, Gustavo. 1984. "The range of Chicano English." In Ornstein-Galicia, Jacob (ed): *Form and Function in Chicano English.* Rowley: Newbury House Publishers: 32-41.

Goodbye, Mr. Chips. Dir. Sam Wood. Beverly Hills: Metro-Goldwyn-Mayer. 1939.

Goodfellas. Dir. Martin Scorsese. Burbank: Warner Bros. 1993.

Green, Lisa J. 2002. *African American English: a Linguistic Introduction.* Cambridge: Cambridge University Press.

Gumperz, John J. 1982. *Discourse strategies.* Cambridge: Cambridge University Press.

Gurskis, Dan. 2006. *The Short Screenplay: Your Short Film from Concept to Production.* Boston: Thomson Course Technology.

Halliday, Michael Alexander Kirkwood. 1978. *Language as Social Semiotic: the Social Interpretation of Language and Meaning.* London: Edward Arnold.

Halverson, Sandra. 1998. "Translation Studies and Representative Corpora: Establishing Links between Translation Corpora, Theoretical/Descriptive Categories and a Conception of the Object of Study." *Meta* 43(4): 494-514.

Hatim, Basil, and Ian Mason. 1990. *Discourse and the Translator.* London: Routledge,

Hermans, Theo. 1999. *Translation in Systems.* Manchester: St. Jerome.

Hill, Jane H. 1993. "Hasta La Vista, Baby: Anglo Spanish in the American Southwest." *Critique of Anthropology* 13 (2): 145-176.

Holmes, James S. 1988. "The Name and Nature of Translation Studies." In Holmes, James S (ed): *Translated! Papers on Literary Translation and Translation Studies*. Amsterdam: Rodopi. 66-80.

How Gangs Are Identified. n.d. Accessed April 29, 2021. <http://www.lapdonline.org/get_informed/content_basic_view/23468>.

Iedema, Rick. 2003. "Multimodality, resemiotization: Extending the analysis of discourse as multi-semiotic practice." *Visual Communication* 2 (1): 29-57.

Jenkins, Jennifer. 2000. *The Phonology of English As an International Language*. Oxford: Oxford University Press.

Jesse Borrego, Actor Profile Page on IMDb, n.d. Accessed April 29, 2021. <https://www.imdb.com/name/nm0001963/>.

Jiménez, Hurtado Catalina, and Claudia Seibel. 2012. "Multisemiotic and Multimodal Corpus Analysis in Audio Description: TRACCE." In Jiménez Hurtado, Catalina and Seibel, Claudia (eds): *Audiovisual Translation and Media Accessibility at the Crossroads, Media for All* (3), Leiden: Rodopi. 409-425.

—, and Silvia Soler Gallego. 2013. "Multimodality, translation and accessibility: a corpus-based study of audio description." *Perspectives* 21 (4): 577-594.

Karamitroglou, Fotios. 2000. *Towards a Methodology for the Investigation of Norms in Audiovisual Translation*. Amsterdam, Atlanta: Rodopi.

Katz, Jesse. 1993. "Reputed Mexican Mafia Leader Dies in Prison at 64." *LA Times*, November 10. Accessed April 29, 2021. <http://articles.latimes.com/1993-11-10/local/me-55229_1_mexican-mafia>.

Kid, Frost. "La Raza." 1990. Accessed April 29, 2021. <https://www.youtube.com/watch?v=SmcIRTtqj6U>.

— 1992. "Ain't no sunshine." Accessed April 29, 2021. <https://www.youtube.com/watch?v=2Q3R7kvhnhE>.

"K'in Sventa Ch'ul Me'tik Kwadalupe." n.d. Accessed April 29, 2021. <https://www.youtube.com/watch?v=oospWucgxac>.

King, Russell, and Mai Nicola. 2013. *Out Of Albania: From Crisis Migration to Social Inclusion in Italy*. New York, Oxford: Berghahn Books.

Kochman, Thomas. 1972. *Rappin' and Stylin' Out: Communication in Urban Black America*. Urbana, Chicago: University of Illinois Press.

Kress, Gunther, and Theo van Leeuwen. 1990. *Reading Images Sociocultural Aspects of Language and Education*. Geelong: Deakin University.

—, Carey, Jewitt, Jon, Ogborn, and Tsatsarelis, Charalampos. 2001. *Multimodal Teaching and Learning: the Rhetorics of the Science Classroom*. London: Bloomsbury Academic.

La Piovra. Dir. Damiano Damiani, Florestano Vancini, Luigi Perelli and Giacomo Battiato. Rome: RAI, 1984-2001.

Labov, William. 1966. *The Social Stratification of English in New York City*. Washington: Center for Applied Linguistics.

— 1972. *Sociolinguistic Patterns*. Philadelphia: University of Pennsylvania Press.

— 1997. "The Social Stratification of (r) in New York City Department Stores." In Coupland, Nikolas and Jaworski, Adam (eds): *Sociolinguistics. Modern Linguistics Series*. London: Palgrave. 168-178.

Landry, Rodrigue, and Richard Y Bourhis. 1997. "Linguistic landscape and ethnolinguistic vitality: an empirical study." *Journal of Language and Social Psychology*. 16 (1): 23-49.

"Latinopia Cinema 'Danny De La Paz In American Me.' (Video interview)." n.d. Accessed April 29, 2021. <https://vimeo.com/32768140>.

Laviosa, Sara. 2002. *Corpus-based Translation Studies. Theories, Findings, Applications*. Amsterdam, New York: Rodopi.

Le Page, Robert, and Andree Tabouret-Keller. 1985. *Acts of Identity: Creole-Based Approaches to Language and Ethnicity*. Cambridge: Cambridge University Press.

Lean on Me. Dir. John G. Avildsen. Burbank: Warner Bros, 1989.

Leerssen, Joep. 2007. "Imagology: History and Method." In Beller, Manfred and Leerssen, Joep (eds): *Imagology. The Cultural Construction and Literary Representation of National Characters*. Amsterdam; New York: Rodopi. 17-32.

Lemke, Jay. 1998. "Multiply meaning: Visual and verbal semiotics in scientific text." In Martin, J. R. and Veel, Robert (eds): *Reading science: critical and functional perspectives on discourses of science*. London: Routledge. 87-113.

Lippi-Green, Rosina. 1997. *English with an Accent: Language, Ideology, and Discrimination in the United States*. London, New York: Routledge.

Lodge, David. 1966. *The Language of Fiction: Essays in Criticism and Verbal Analysis of the English Novel*. London: Routledge.

Los Lobos. 1987. "One Time, One Night." Accessed April 29, 2021. <https://www.youtube.com/watch?v=qmgfLI1NBe8>.

— "Shotgun." 1993. <https://www.youtube.com/watch?v=GW_Ogn2zHW0>.

Lou Diamond Phillips, Actor Profile Page. n.d. Accessed April 29, 2021. <https://www.imdb.com/name/nm0001617/?ref_=ttfc_fc_cl_t19>.

Macedo, Donaldo P., Bessie Dendrinos, and Panayota Gounari. 2003. *The Hegemony of English*. Boulder: Paradigm Publishers.

Marchi, Regina. 2006. "El Dia de los Muertos in the USA: Cultural Ritual as Political Communication." In Santino, Jack (ed): *Spontaneous Shrines and the Public Memorialization of Death.* New York: Palgrave Macmillan.

Martinec, Radan, and Andrew Salway. 2005. "A System for Image-text Relations in New (and Old) Media." *Visual Communication* 4 (3): 337-371.

Mateo, Marta. 2012. "Music and Translation." In Gambier, Yves and van Doorslaer, Luc (eds): *Handbook of Translation Studies 3.* Amsterdam: John Benjamins Publishing. 115-121.

Mathews, Jay. 1988. *Escalante: The Best Teacher in America.* New York: Henry Holt & Co.

Matluck, Joseph H. 1952. "La pronunciación del español en el Valle de Mexico." *Nueva revista de filologia española* 6 (2): 109-120.

Matras, Yaron. 2009. *Language Contact.* Cambridge: Cambridge University Press.

McEnery, Tony, Richard Xiao, and Tono Yukio. 2006. *Corpus-based Language Studies: An Advanced Resource Book.* London, New York: Routledge.

Mendoza-Denton, Norma. 2008. *Homegirls: language and cultural practice among Latina youth gangs.* Malden: Blackwell Publishing.

Mesthrie, Rajend. 2000. "Clearing the Ground: Basic Issues, Concepts and approaches." In Mesthrie, Rajend et al. (eds): *Introducing Sociolinguistics.* Edinburgh: Edinburgh University Press. 1-43.

Metcalf, Allan. 1979. "The study of California Chicano English." *International Journal of the Sociology of Language* 1974 (2): 53-58.

Mi Vida Loca (My Crazy Life). Dir. Allison Anders. NYC: Sony Pictures Classics. 1993.

Milroy, James. 2002. "The consequences of standardisation in Descriptive Linguistics." In Bex, Tony and Watts, Richard J (eds): *Standard English: The Widening Debate.* London; New York: Routledge. 16-39.

Milroy, Lesley, and James Milroy. 1992. "Social Network and Social Class: Toward an Integrated Sociolinguistic Model." *Language in Society* 21 (1): 1-26.

Motta, Daria. n.d. 'Non ci posso credere...' *L'italiano del doppiaggio televisivo.* Accessed April 29, 2021. <http://www.treccani.it/magazine/lingua _italiana/speciali/fiction/motta.html>.

Mr. Mister. 1988. "Stand and Deliver." Accessed April 29, 2021. <https://www.youtube.com/watch?v=VpJtPXfMAwA>.

Munday, Jeremy. 2008. *Introducing Translation Studies: Theories and applications. Second Edition.* London, New York: Routledge.

Myers-Scotton, Carol. 1993. *Duelling Languages: Grammatical Structure in Codeswitching.* Oxford: Clarendon Press.

Noel Guglielmi, Actor Profile Page. n.d. Accessed April 29, 2021. <https://www.imdb.com/name/nm0346595/?ref_=nv_sr_1>.

Nolan, Francis. 2009. "The Pairwise Variability Index and Coexisting Rhythms in Language." *Phonetica* 66 (1-2): 64-77.

Nunberg, Geoffrey. 1983. "The Decline of Grammar. (Originally Published in The Atlantic Monthly)." Accessed April 29, 2021. <http://www.ling.upenn.edu/courses/ling001/Nunberg.html>.

Page, Norman. 1988. *Speech in the English Novel. Second Edition.* Basingstoke, London: Palgrave Macmillan.

Paolinelli, Mario, and Eleonora Di Fortunato. 2005. *Tradurre per il doppiaggio: la trasposizione linguistica dell'audiovisivo: teoria e pratica di un'arte imperfetta.* Milano: Hoepli Editore.

Pasquini, Mauro. 2016. *Falcone e Borsellino. Due vite per la giustizia.* Bologna: Area51 Publishing.

Pastra, Katerina. 2008. "COSMOROE: a Cross-Media Relations Framework for Modelling Multimedia Dialectics." *Multimedia Systems* 14: 299-323.

Pavesi, Maria, and Elisa Perego. 2006. "Profiling Film Translators in Italy: A Preliminary Analysis." *The Journal of Specialised Translation* 6: 99-114.

Penfield, Joyce, and Jacob Ornstein-Galicia. 1985. *Chicano English: An Ethnic Contact Dialect. Varieties of English Around the World* 7. Amsterdam: John Benjamins Publishing.

Pepe Serna, Actor Profile Page. n.d. Accessed April 29, 2021. <https://www.imdb.com/name/nm0346595/?ref_=nv_sr_1>.

Polkinhorn, Harry, *et al.* 2005. *El Libro de Caló: The Dictionary of Chicano Slang. Revised Edition.* Moorpark: Floricanto Press.

Poplack, Shana. 1980. "Sometimes I start a sentence in Spanish Y TERMINO EN ESPAÑOL: toward a typology of code-switching." *Linguistics* 18 (7): 581-618.

Portillo, José López, Demetrio M. Sodi, and Fernando Díaz Infante. 1982. *Quetzalcoatl, in Myth, Archeology, and Art.* New York: Continuum.

Pym, Anthony. 2008. "On Toury's Laws on How Translators Translate." In Pym, Anthony, Shlesinger, Mirian and Simeoni Daniel (eds): *Beyond Descriptive Translation Studies: Investigations in Homage to Gideon Toury*, Amsterdam; Philadelphia: John Benjamins Publishing. 311-329.

Rafael, Tony. 2007. *The Mexican Mafia.* New York, London: Encounter Books.

Ramírez Berg, Charles. 2002. *Latino Images in Film: Stereotypes, Subversion, and Resistance.* Austin: University of Texas Press.

Ramos Pinto, Sara. 2009. "How important is the way you say it? A Discussion on the Translation of Linguistic Varieties in Different Media." *Target* 21 (2): 289-307.

— 2010. *Tradução no vazio: As traducoes portuguesas de Pygmalion de Bernard Shaw e My Fair Lady de Alan Jay Lerner*. University of Lisbon: PhD Thesis.

— 2016. "Ya care how me speaks, do ya? The translation of linguistic varieties and their reception." In *inTRAlinea Special Issue: The Translation of Dialects in Multimedia III*: 2-18.

— 2018. "Film, dialects and subtitles: an analytical framework for the study of non-standard varieties in subtitling." The Translator 24 (1): 17-34.

—, and Aishah Mubaraki. 2020. "Multimodal Corpus Analysis of Subtitling: The Case of Non-standard Varieties." *Target: International Journal of Translation Studies* 32 (3): 389-419.

Reaser, Jeffrey. 2004. "A quantitative sociolinguistic analysis of Bahamian copula absence: Morphosyntactic evidence from Abaco Island, the Bahamas." *Journal of Pidgin and Creole Languages* 19 (1): 1-40.

Renna, Dora. 2016. "The route to identity: Italian translation and African American language(s) in Spike Lee's Get on the Bus." Iperstoria. Testi Letterature Linguaggi: 64/74.

— 2017. "Gangster voices in translation. Chicano English and Italian dubbing in the movie Blood In Blood Out (1993)." mTm — translation journal 9: 242-268.

— 2018. "Re-shaping Languages and Stereotypes in Dubbing. David Ayer's End of Watch (2013) from Chicano English to Italian." In Barschdorf, Stefanie and Renna, Dora (eds): *Translating Boundaries. Constraints, Limits, Opportunities. Foreword by Jeremy Munday*. Hannover: ibidem Verlag. 233-260.

— 2018. "Bandidos e gangster Chicanos: evoluzione di uno stereotipo linguistico nel cinema americano e nel doppiaggio italiano." In Rosso, Stefano and Dossena, Marina (eds): *Mondi e modi della Traduzione. Letteratura, cinema, teatro, televisione, editoria*. Verona: ombre corte. 93-115.

— 2019. "Lenguas Criminales: Languages in contact and dubbing of the Chicano villains in the movie Training Day (2001)." In Betti, Silvia and De Beni, Matteo (eds): *Conversaciones sobre el español de Estados Unidos*. Axiara Editions. 75-101.

Rothman, Jason and Amy Beth Rell. 2005. "A linguistic analysis of Spanglish: relating language to identity." *Linguistics and the Human Sciences* 1 (3): 515-536.

Santa Ana, Otto. 1993 "Chicano English and the nature of the Chicano language setting." *Hispanic Journal of Behavioral Sciences* 15 (1): 3-35.

— 1991. *Phonetic simplification processes in the English of the barrio: A cross-generational sociolinguistic study of the Chicanos of Los Angeles.* University of Pennsylvania: PhD Thesis.

— 1996. "Sonority and syllable structure in Chicano English." *Language Variation and Change* 8 (1): 63-89.

Santana, Carlos. 1969. "Jin-Go-Lo-Ba." Accessed April 29, 2021. <https://www.youtube.com/watch?v=qmuFqY8Gg-U>.

— 1970. "Oye Como Va." Accessed April 29, 2021. <https://www.youtube.com/watch?v=J7ATTjg7tpE>.

Saraceni, Mario. 2015. *World Englishes: a Critical Analysis.* London: Bloomsbury Publishing Company.

Schiffrin, Deborah. 1994. *Approaches to discourse.* Oxford: Blackwell.

Schumann, John. 1978. "The acculturation model for second-language acquisition." In Gingras, Rosario C (ed): *Second language acquisition and foreign language learning.* Arlington: Center for Applied Linguistics. 27-50.

Sinclair, John. 1992. "Lexicographers' needs." *Pisa Workshop on Text Corpora, January 1992.* Pisa, Italy.

— 1996. "Preliminary recommendations on Text Typology." *EAGLES (Expert Advisory Group on Language Engineering Standards).* <http://www.ilc.cnr.it/EAGLES96/corpustyp/corpustyp.html>.

Sister Act 2: Back in the Habit. Dir. Bill Duke. Burbank: Touchstone Pictures, 1993.

Smelser, Neil J., Julius William Wilson, and Faith Mitchell. 2001. *America Becoming: Racial Trends and Their Consequences* I. Washington: The National Academies Press.

Soliz, Jordan, and Howard Giles. 1987. "Relational and Identity Processes in Communication: A Contextual and Meta-Analytical Review of Communication Accommodation Theory." *Communication Yearbook, January 1987*: 1-62.

Stand and Deliver. Dir. Ramón Menéndez. Burbank: Warner Bros. 1988.

Stephan, Walter G., and David Rosenfield. 1982. "Racial and Ethnic Stereotypes." In Miller, Arthur (ed): *Eye of the Beholder.* New York: Praeger. 110.

Stubbs, Michael. 1993. "British traditions in text analysis: from Firth to Sinclair." In Baker, Mona, Francis, Gill and Tognini-Bonelli, Elena (eds): *Text and Technology: In Honour of John Sinclair.* Amsterdam: John Benjamins Publishing Company. 1-33.

— 1996. *Text and Corpus Analysis*. Oxford: Blackwell.

Swann, Joan. 2000. "Language Choice and Code-Switching." In Mesthrie, Rajend, et al (eds): *Introducing Sociolinguistics*. Edinburgh: Edinburgh University Press. 148-183.

Taylor, Christopher. 1999. "Look Who's Talking. An Analysis of Film Dialogue as a Variety of Spoken Discourse." In Lombardo, Linda et al (Eds): *Massed Medias. Linguistic Tools for Interpreting Media Discourse*. Milan: Led. 247-278.

Teachers. Dir. Arthur Hiller. Beverly Hills: Metro-Goldwyn-Mayer. 1984.

"The Constitution of the United States." 1776. Accessed April 29, 2021. <http://constitutionus.com/>.

The Fast and the Furious. Dir. Rob Cohen. Universal City: Universal Pictures. 2001.

The Godfather. Dir. Francis Ford Coppola. Hollywood: Paramount Pictures. 1972.

The Miracle Worker. Dir. Arthur Penn. Hollywood: United Artists Corporation. 1962.

Thomas, Erik R. 2007. "Phonological and Phonetic Characteristics of African American Vernacular English." *Language and Linguistics Compass* 1 (5): 450-475.

To Sir, with Love. Dir. James Clavell. Culver City: Columbia Pictures. 1967.

Toury, Gideon. 1995. *Descriptive Translation Studies – and Beyond*. Amsterdam, Philadelphia: John Benjamins

Training Day. Dir. Antoine Fuqua. Burbank: Warner Bros. 2001.

Trent'anni di Internet, la timeline. n.d. Accessed April 29, 2021. <https://www.repubblica.it/tecnologia/2016/04/29/news/30_anni_di_internet_la_timeline-138625953/>.

Trudgill, Peter. 1974. *The Social Differentiation of English in Norwich*. Cambridge: Cambridge University Press.

Up the Down Staircase. Dir. Robert Mulligan. Burbank: Warner Bros. 1967.

US Census Bureau Press Release. 2015. "Census Bureau Reports at Least 350 Languages Spoken in US Homes." n.d. Accessed April 29, 2021. <https://www.census.gov/newsroom/press-releases/2015/cb15-185.html>.

Valentini, Cristina. 2008. "Forlixt 1-The Forlì Corpus of Screen Translation." In Chiaro, Delia, Heiss, Christine and Bucaria, Chiara (eds): *Between text and image: updating research in screen translation*. Amsterdam: John Benjamins Publishing. 37-50.

van den Bulck, Jan. 2004. "Research Note: The Relationship between Television Fiction and Fear of Crime. An Empirical Comparison of Three Causal Explanations." *European Journal of Communication* 19 (2): 239-248.

van Doorslaer, Luc, Petr Flynn, and Joep Leerssen. 2015. *Interconnecting Translation Studies and Imagology*. Amsterdam: John Benjamins Publishing.

van Leeuwen, Theo and Carey Jewitt. 2000. *The handbook of visual analysis*. London: SAGE.

Vanderauwera, Ria. 1985. *Dutch novels translated into English: the transformation of a "Minority" literature*. Amsterdam: Rodopi.

Vasconcelos, José. 1979. *La Raza Cósmica/The Cosmic Race*. *(Original Spanish Essay published in 1925 Herederos de José Vasconcelos)*. Los Angeles: California University Press.

Walk Proud. Dir. Robert L. Collins. Universal City: Universal Pictures. 1979.

Walker, James A., and Miriam Meyerhoff. 2006. "Zero copula in the Eastern Caribbean: Evidence from Bequia." *American Speech* 81 (2): 146-163.

War. "Low Rider." 1975. Accessed April 29, 2021. <https://www.youtube.com/watch?v=WeKw6c9aTJ0>.

— "Slippin' into Darkness." 1971. Accessed April 29, 2021. <https://www.youtube.com/watch?v=RFSWW4O6QNM>.

Wasow, Thomas. 2001. "Generative Grammar." In Aronoff, Mark and Rees-Miller, Janie (eds): *The Handbook of Linguistics*. Oxford: Blackwell. 295-318.

Wendell, Eric. 2018. *Experiencing Herbie Hancock: A Listener's Companion*. Lanham: Rowman & Littlefield.

Winford, Donald. 2003. *An Introduction to Contact Linguistics*. Malden: Blackwell.

Yu, Jing. 2017. "Translating 'others' as 'us' in Huckleberry Finn: dialect, register and the heterogeneity of standard language." *Language and Literature 2017*, 26 (1): 54-65.

Zabalbeascoa, Patrick. 2009. "Priorities and Restrictions in Translation." In Vandaele, Jeroen (ed): *Translation and the (Re)Location of Meaning*. Leuven: CETRA Papers. 159-167.

Zelinsky, Wilbur. 2001. *The Enigma of Ethnicity: Another American dilemma*. Iowa City: University of Iowa Press.

Zong, Jie, and Jeanne Batalova. 2018. "Mexican Immigrants in the United States." *Migration Policy*, Accessed April 29, 2021. <https://www.migrationpolicy.org/article/mexican-immigrants-united-states>.

Zoot Suit. Dir. Luis Valdez. Universal City: Universal Pictures, 1981

ibidem.eu